Aged by Culture

Aged by Culture

Margaret Morganroth Gullette

THE UNIVERSITY OF CHICAGO PRESS ———— *Chicago & London*

MARGARET MORGANROTH GULLETTE is the author of *Declining to Decline: Cultural Combat and the Politics of Midlife,* which won a national award as the best feminist book on American Popular Culture. She is a resident scholar in the Women's Studies Research Center at Brandeis University.

The University of Chicago Press, Chicago 60637
The University of Chicago Press, Ltd., London
© 2004 by Margaret Morganroth Gullette
All rights reserved. Published 2004
Printed in the United States of America
13 12 11 10 09 08 07 06 05 04   5 4 3 2

ISBN (cloth): 0-226-31061-2
ISBN (paper): 0-226-31062-0

Library of Congress Cataloging-in-Publication Data

Gullette, Margaret Morganroth.
     Aged by culture / Margaret Morganroth Gullette.
          p.   cm.
     Includes bibliographical references and index.
     ISBN 0-226-31061-2 (cloth : alk. paper)—ISBN 0-226-31062-0 (pbk : alk. paper)
     1. Aging—Social aspects. 2. Ageism. 3. Identity (Psychology) 4. Autobiography—
Social aspects. 5. Aged—Social conditions—Study and teaching. 6. Old age—Study
and teaching. I. Title.
     HQ1061 .G863   2004
     305.26—dc21

                                                         2003012640

♾ The paper used in this publication meets the minimum requirements of the American
National Standard for Information Sciences—Permanence of Paper for Printed Library Materials,
ANSI Z39.48-1992.

TO MY AGE STUDIES POSSE:

Alix, Kathy, Ruth, Anne, Teresa, Susan, Glenda,
Mike, Tom, Steve, Harry, Rick;
to the other age critics I admire;
for those to come

Age is a nice new devil.

—WINSTON LANGLEY

Contents

Part One

Cultural Urgencies

Trapped in the
New Time Machines

IN THE SCIENCE MUSEUM

At the Boston Museum of Science, one exhibit in particular attracted long lines of children: "Face Aging." Access to the open booth was forbidden to people over fifteen, so I watched from just outside. After standing for long periods with remarkable patience, the youngsters sat down inside under bright illumination, faced forward trustingly—"frontality also implies in the most vivid way the subject's cooperation"—and had their portrait taken by an automatic camera.[1] After another wait, their digitized bust appeared on a TV monitor. Then, tapping a button like a VCR remote, each child could rapidly call up simulations of what she or he would look like at one-year intervals up to age sixty-nine. Flipped as fast as a Victorian zoetrope, the stills became a "movie." In seconds the computer added grotesque pouches, reddish skin, and blotches to their familiar features; the faces became elongated and then wider and then saggy; lines became more heavily rutted. Boys lost hair. Hair turned gray. The heads of both boys and girls grew and then shrank.

The children were almost uniformly shaken. One eight-year-old girl in the hearing of a *Boston Globe* reporter moaned, "I don't want to get old!"[2] While viewing the show, gerontologist Richard Griffin heard a boy "looking as if he had tasted something bad" say about another child's facial changes, "He's disgusting at forty-two." The teenagers, most of them white, were solitary or in small groups made up of age peers; they were on their own. But having a mother nearby didn't always cushion the shock. One woman with daughters told a son, "The girls say you're getting ugly." To another son who used the button to ride the years backward she said, "That's when you look the best—as a little boy."[3]

Nobody stayed in the booth long. Anyone could have stopped punching the button altogether at any age or lingered longer at a particular age (or gone backward): two girls I saw stopped at fifty-five and sixty-two. But most swept through the changes of their putative face-course to the bitter end. They came out preoccupied, distracted; some giggling recklessly, most edging away fast, not wanting to talk about the experience, not knowing what had happened to them in there. Afterward they fled.

This was the booth in the "Secrets of Aging" show that enticed the kids during the spring, summer, and fall of 2000. Everything promised them scientific "truth"—their location in a "Museum of Science" and the prestigious array of complex and nonhuman technologies involved: the robot eye with no human behind it, the computer-driven graphics, the "interactive" button that produced the same aging effect forward or backward, invariably. And children are deeply curious about their life course, that mystery where your particularity scrunches up against unknown laws. As Virginia Woolf says, "If you are young, the future lies upon the present, like a piece of glass, making it tremble and quiver."[4] Invariability was implied in the title of the exhibit too: "This is the way all faces age." When I interviewed the children exiting, I asked, "What did you learn?" The answer, in short, was, "I don't want to get old." They had nothing to add.

"Do you think that's really the way you will look?" I continued. The question seemed to astonish them. Hadn't that *mirror* just shown them how they would really look? Its thick glass gave them what they believed was information. As children, they had no sense of how to discount visual "evidence." Unlike them, I was old enough to associate the paraphernalia of booths with bureaucracy, know that "passport photo" is a byword for ugliness, and possess a Department of Motor Vehicles' distortion of my physiognomy. Only one boy, already fairly tall and with some width of chest (he might have snuck in) said, smirking, "I got bigger." Of all those interviewed, only he seemed satisfied. Disgust was otherwise unisex. But gender played out as perceptive resistance. "Well, it made *all* of us really red," one skeptical white girl of maybe twelve observed to me. Only she expressed the tiniest suspicion about the crystal ball's veracity.

← ⟶

I am neither a journalist nor a gerontologist but a writer and cultural critic who studies age issues—call me an age critic. Reading about the exhibit had made me naively curious about my own "truth": I had really wanted to go in and see myself age. I was disappointed at being excluded. Then it slyly occurred to me that if I sent the programmers a photo of me at eight or ten, they could use their procedures to depict a "me" at my age, which was fifty-nine. I could compare their semblance with photos of the real me, taken recently, in available light, in different moods, by different people. Although I say "the real me," I scarcely look the same in any two. (As the theorist and photographer Jo Spence points out, "Two cameras standing side by side could take totally different pictures of the same moment.")[5] Would the "I" of their simulation be recognizably the same as the person portrayed in any of my other photos? That was my motive for the first call I made, to Core Digital Pictures in Toronto.

I was also skeptical about the predictive power of the software they had used in the exhibit. Because I know beautiful people in their sixties, I had been surprised that no one on the monitor looked good, aging, to my willing eyes. No one looked *better* as they reached midlife, although youngsters can improve considerably with age, acquiring more harmoniously related features. The bogus faces had none of the qualities one might expect: drama, humor, intelligence, character. (These observations should have been a dead giveaway of what my sleuthing was about to discover.)

Ron Estey is the project manager at Core Digital responsible for the program. Estey's answer to my request was that they could not use my childhood photograph as their starting point. A subject has to be well lit, without expression, posed frontally against a black background, and young. The software has to recognize the chin, brow, ears, and so on, in order to operate. The increasing facial redness as the children aged was just an accident: it had to do with the original colorization of the Kodak film they used. The blotches were also unintentional: they developed from marks the kids already had on their faces: freckles, moles, pimples. Core Digital had added the wrinkles, swags, and grayness.

When I asked Estey how Core Digital had conceptualized "aging," he wouldn't say exactly. The software was proprietary. They had started with a photo of an eight-year-old girl; the algorithm was intended to create a "believable" image of her at sixty-something. When they constructed the oldest image, they asked their staff if it was credible. The responses made them add more "age effects." These required arbitrary decisions: at what age did they start sagging the line under the chin? By what age do ears droop? As someone who worked on designing the booth observed, "The age is an estimate. Their sixty-five looks like seventy-five or eighty to me." Only one component was scientific: they had worked with a cranial surgeon to identify the actual age-related growth in bones that produces longer noses and head shapes. For other potential clients—the FBI and forensic experts seeking people who have disappeared—they were adding some scientific components so that eventually they might be able to work from snapshots or group photos. But at present, Estey said, they could make no claim to be scientific or "rigorous." There were too many other circumstances the program did not account for, he added: gaining weight, having children, smoking, getting a disease. "It was only an entertainment," he explained. Core Digital does TV animation. This technology is typically deployed for cartoons and wizard ghoulishness in films, doctoring fashion photos so models look yet more emaciated, and falsifying historical documents. "We streamed together six or seven different ideas. We're a special effects studio."

←——→

The cyber-fi booth has been carted around the country, carried along in the "Secrets of Aging" show from one pedagogical site to another, like the smallpox germs secreted in blankets that colonists gave to Native Americans. After Boston, the exhibit went to L.A., and the cutoff age dropped to ten. But what exactly is going wrong in there, aside from the fact that Core Digital's secret is "morphing" and not "aging," or that the gizmo automatically uglifies and passes off its squint as truth? The software engineers hadn't asked, "What's the algorithm for making people look more beautiful, expressive, or individual as they grow up?" because they worked from our culture's preexisting notions of decline—skin, hair, outline. Caricature ruled. Decline overrode even the quirkinesses that never change: the shape of your eyebrows, the bow of your mouth.

Do an experiment with two of your own photos, taken as far apart in time as possible: Try to look for likeness. Not just the genetic but the life-historical kinds: that uplifted look of adoring inquiry you acquired at four, the bravado adopted at fourteen, the resolute jaw of thirty. Our faces and bodies—as I argue in chapter 9—are historical repositories. If your mind balks at detecting resemblances thirty-five years apart, start with a modest ten-year spread. This is a cultural test. If you have difficulties passing it, you have been successfully trained—taught to notice only the bad differences between yourself younger and now, not the similarities, or the improvements. If we mean by ideology a system that socializes us into certain beliefs and ways of speaking about what it means to be "human," while suppressing alternatives, it is useful to call this training "age ideology."

At the time I didn't know precisely what worries I felt for those children in the museum. It was also hard at first to specify what their experience had to do with the vast shadowy context of American age culture. Was the problem "ageism"? The term has many meanings.[6] In the narrow sense of stimulating blind prejudice against old people (Dr. Robert Butler's original definition) among the impressionable, the effect was probably not that. The title of the exhibit invited kids to "face *aging*" not "face *the elderly*." The experience might in fact lead them to think, in contrast to what they'd just seen, "Grandpa doesn't look nearly that purplish" and "Aunt Flo is as handsome as everyone says." Nor, thankfully, did this exhibit reinforce the medieval memento mori, "Remember you must die," deployed to clients by the fitness and pharmaceuticals industries in every allusion to longevity. (While they were utilizing digital animation, Core Digital could have shown the kids what they'd allegedly look like at 140, the span telomerists promise us, and really have produced a *frisson*.)

But there's another ageism, that "old age is a problem": this has become so intransigent a formulation even among alleged anti-ageists that children exposed to dominant cultures in the West probably overhear quite a lot of it.[7] Depending upon their age, their exposure to the media, their family's subculture, and their parents' relation to their own parents, many children no doubt came into the museum holding some preexisting negative views about old age. These the exhibit reinforced.

But the real trouble with the booth is not that it reinforces society's negative associations with old people. It is important to underscore that the grotesque big red face on the monitor is allegedly me myself. Forget others; in the United States aging is about me and me alone. "The future" is privatized. The first photo each child saw established the monitor as a mirror—and belief in cultural mirrors has devastating consequences in our hypervisual culture. Susan Sontag once observed, "The camera has ended by effecting a tremendous promotion of the value of appearances."[8] Appearance and selfhood, increasingly, are stickily twined, so that your appearance (minus your expressions) *is* your self. The crude algorithm of the exhibit was modeled on a dominant cultural assumption: that the body declines as if with no cultural intervention. (Everyone forgot that Core Digital intervened.) This "fact" overwhelms the thousand other qualities or practices that are also *you*, even as young as fifteen—your SAT score, your concern for Afghani kids, your passion for Narnia or *Jane Eyre*— which together over time trace an individual life. Tapping a button, the kids pressed ahead through the counterfeits as fast as if they were playing Nintendo and the goal were to knock off the ages. Speed-up. (Sontag warned us in 1974 about "faster and faster seeing.")[9] There was only one "special effect" to get, and they rushed to discover it. Aging equals decline, a devastating formula.

One person, the man who built the booth, had been concerned about making aging artificially fearful for his audience. Gary Renaud, the manager of Exhibitors, Inc., had been cautioned by the maker of another face-focused technique about potential harm to young viewers.[10] As a result, he said, he installed a monitor outside, where the children lined up. It showed photos of other kids as they were undergoing the special-effects distortions. His idea was that if a child found the preview too scary, she or he would drop out of the queue.

Unlikely. Face-aging wasn't about *them* until they got inside, and then suddenly it was. Moreover, children as consumers of movies are taught to toughen themselves. Where the box office is concerned, they learn early on that avoidance of unpleasantness looks "wimpy" or "girlish." The entire R-17 system teaches that as you get older, you should be able to bear increasingly dreadful visual horrors. The outside monitor thus served less as a warning than a taunt. The very pun in "Face Aging!" dares you to go in the booth.

There the computer screen tells you an authoritative story. In a few seconds postmodern techno-fragmentation click-clicks you through your years. If you paid a quarter for this in an arcade, the whole thing might be less troubling. But this is no game; it's "a copying machine"[11] certified by the Science Museum Exhibit Collaborative. The spectacle offers a prophecy about your own appearance that makes human aging entirely bodily, predictable, and inescapably awful. For its concepts of decline, Core Digital drew on the "before" photos of cosmetic-surgery candidates familiar to all of us, as well as on other North American caricatures of the midlife. The children have no reason not to believe what they were shown. The exhibit performed an experiment on them, cognitively and emotionally. They were led to personalize—"internalize" is the term used by psychology and cultural studies—the wordless message "Aging is terrible." This will become for them one of those "group-defining stories that go underground as cognition where they serve as mental equipment for the interpretation of events."[12] It is a powerful psy-fi operation. Most of us have undergone it, but few so young.

←——————→

When I described the Museum of Science exhibit to photographer Vaughn Sills, she said she had seen something like it in the Musée d'Art Moderne de la Ville de Paris. Hans-Peter Feldmann's show, also in 2000, started with the photograph of an eight-week-old named Felina; next to it was a picture of a one-year-old, with its name and age, and then an image of a baby of two, and so on. The photos continued around the gallery; there were a full one hundred. The walk around "A Century" ("Un Siècle" was the name of the show) was slowed down because the photographs represented a hundred *different* faces, men as well as women, of various ethnicities, mostly but not all white, in distinctive settings. Individuals, they were differentially attractive or vibrant or strong or personable at various ages. As Sills came toward her own current age, she was aware of becoming more involved. She was able to pick and choose people who more closely matched her imagined future: "This is what I might be like." By the end of that meditative walk, Sills said, she had gained an impressive sense of change (and obviously the people represented at the end appeared older than the sixty-nine, or eighty, of "Face Aging"). Un Siècle wasn't depressing; it wasn't upsetting. Sills was utterly engrossed and imaginatively stimulated.

Aging through a particular century, the twentieth. The figures inhabited backgrounds filled with furniture, photos, or other personal items, some of which carried period and historic associations, of events witnessed or memories accumulated over time. Such densely textured impressions might be complicated by other ideas—longevity, certainly; perhaps the striking and oddly reassuring impression that so much of life is now spent being what the cult of youth calls "old." To Sills the series was not even predictably chronological. From the artist's array, a woman at, say, eighty-three might look younger than another person at sixty-six. Indeed, Sills said, this happened quite often, at many of the ages shown. At any given age, "What next?" was not a foregone conclusion.

"The dominant fiction of chronological aging . . . plots our lives in continually increasing numbers," critic Mary Russo notes.[13] On the calm surface, chronology is a bureaucratic convenience and a motive for annual potlatches of celebration. But the media increasingly exploit these automatic sequences for their associated story of decline. In *Esquire* in 2001 a man published head shots of his wife from age thirty-one to fifty-five for an issue on "Women and Aging," a spread that was unlikely to raise the median age of the trophy wife.[14] The net effect of such sequences is to confuse the autobiography of anyone's unique mind-body with a universal arithmetic series supposedly etched on the body.

In Paris, Hans-Peter Feldmann, putting his photos side by side in numerical order, nevertheless avoided the traps. Using chronology, he disrupted linearity. The show avoided telling a simple decline story about the external signs of aging, which—as age critic Mike Hepworth points out—do not usually cause physical discomfort nor seriously affect bodily functions.[15] Feldmann probably did not know that the literary doctors of the nineteenth-century used to declare, in effect, "In no one thing do people differ more than in their aging." Yet wordlessly he had produced that idea. "The world is full of diversity and non-comparability and age is another fascinating difference" might be another lesson to carry away from these hundred images. Probably the same children who scattered in fright in Boston could have promenaded through the Paris show at their own self-directed and responsive pace, changed into curious agents by its lack of reference to themselves, its dense reference to other worlds, its invitation to imaginative identification with others at any age.

Photographs are thought to need text in order to channel meaning through the maelstrom of possible interpretations. The Boston and Paris exhibits suggest otherwise: that even without text, visual sequences always have life narratives secretively embedded in them. Such narratives declare the *meaning* of the passing of life time, not day by day but on a big scale. Since they help us tell our own stories, about the value of our own lives, the burning question is, what genre of story about aging gets wrapped in the narrative?

Jo Spence, an English pioneer in "phototherapy" using family albums, offers yet another way of constructing a life narrative—by yourself, autobiographically. "Get together all the pictures of yourself which you can find," she instructed her college-age students. "Now sort out one single picture for each year of your life and then lay them out in a line on the floor, starting with the earliest year. Play about with them until you are *satisfied that you have the ones which mean the most to you.*" [16] Spence suggested writing about the meaningful ones rather than a silent inward telling. This is life review for people as young as eighteen, or even younger. It is cued by images but not limited to the physical self that others see, which some theorists call the "specular body." It's important to get beyond face and "figure"—which are so vulnerable to our culture's hypercritical age gaze. The story you tell is your artifact, private and memory based, your truth.

Only you can decide which states of mind or age-selves have been significant to you, which events or people linger in your mind. (In chapter 7 I describe further how people do this saving kind of life storytelling, and in chapter 8 I propose an even more resistant telling that I call "age autobiography.") Your latest self might have changed its opinion of an earlier self: You might have hated the way you looked at twelve but now see how touching you were. Not all ages will matter equally. You might skip several years, not because you looked crummy then but because that period lacked narrative particularity. Although Spence's project too starts out as a linear effort, the addition of your inner storytelling breaks the strictly metronomic sequence. The nonvisual memories add rich text. The closer you get to your current age, the fuller your memories may be. Aging becomes maturation, change, history—more complex than a simple minus or a plus. At last.

←——→

What these three ways of representing age visually have in common is that they are all narratives of aging. But the stories they offer are quite different—

in technique, in affect, in ethical and psychological effects. At their best, as Spence's phototherapy suggests, narratives of aging are retrospective and produced by the owner of the life in question, can be told at any age, minimize mere appearance, and encourage the teller to include ever thicker layers of what it has meant to be an embodied psyche, in culture, over time. At their worst, as in "Face Aging," the narratives are fatally flat: prospective and phony, solipsistic, body-obsessed, pseudo-universal and context denying, cognitively inhibiting, and anxiety producing.

The meanings of age and aging are conveyed in large part through the moral and psychological implications of the narrative ideas we have been inserting into our heads, starting when we were very young indeed. Artistic and technological products, like the stories we ordinarily tell ourselves and one another, are permeated by the preexisting inventions of culture. It matters whether a given society—the United States, in this book—permits dense, interesting, encouraging narratives about aging, and for how long in the life course, and whether those ideas are dominant or merely subordinate or resistant. Our age narratives become our virtual realities. Certainly, whichever accounts you and I find ourselves living with and seeing the world through make a fundamental difference to the quality of our lives, starting with our willingness or reluctance, at any age, to grow older.

Decline is a metaphor as hard to contain as dye. Once it has tinged our expectations of the future (sensations, rewards, status, power, voice) with peril, it tends to stain our experiences, our views of others, our explanatory systems, and then our retrospective judgments. Once I feel I am at risk, the collective future can shrink to the fantasized autobiography of the Aging *Me*. It is decline ideology above all, I would argue, that makes each life span "a distinctive and enclosed trajectory, picked out from other surrounding events," as sociologist Anthony Giddens brilliantly describes it.[17] One of decline's saddest egocentripetal effects is to obscure anything suffered by those adjacent to us, in the polity and across the globe. The only history that matters is that of our times. Decline then squeezes the life span further, into an inflexible, biological, individual arc.

The three versions of aging outlined above provide alternatives but barely begin to explore all the imaginative possibilities there could be if we in the audience explicitly critiqued age ideology and demanded more care—and a bigger share—in representation. Despite the impression given by the freaky time machine, "aging" even at the merely visual level cannot have a single, invariable, universal, and ahistorical meaning. "We understand meaning not as a natural but as an arbitrary act—the intervention of ideology into language," Stuart Hall succinctly suggests.[18] If you have been waiting—perhaps impatiently—for me to argue against the belief that decline is *the* truth of aging, that is just what, by starting with my three narratives of aging, I am doing.

I don't like to trade in "secrets," a blatant marketing technique, but the basic se-cret of age was revealed decades ago by the very first works that could be called "age studies": Human beings are aged by culture.[19] It's a simple anthropologi-cal idea, but it ramifies marvelously. The process takes various forms in differ-ent subcultures, as those know who have envied, say, Chinese-born Americans or Jews because "they revere old age." Now the life-enhancing age ideologies of our subcultures are themselves under siege. What matters to those exposed to dominant American age ideology—whether in the United States or abroad, among the cosmopolitan elites that receive it "along with Cable News Network, Coca Cola and Visa credit cards"[20]—is that underneath its boastful surface it is surreptitiously telling much more dire and muddled stories.

American children live unavoidably in relation to our culture's constructs of "age" or "aging," which rocket around them even if they never enter a science museum. The audiences for "Secrets of Aging," young as they were, had had earlier encounters with items of age lore and the aging narratives implicit in them. The first time might have been when they heard, "Happy birthday to *you!*" or "She must be almost *three* now!" or "You're not old enough for that yet!" (Interesting how emphatically age lore gets presented: does it typically have exclamation marks attached? Only when children are its objects?) How the young get socialized into a particular age culture is a fascinating, necessary sub-ject for the field I call age studies.[21]

Age socialization must be bewildering. As with other social learning, children have to put together "uncoordinated pieces of information," in the words of two faculty members of the intriguingly named Department of Psychological Devel-opment and Socialization at the University of Padua.[22] Neuropsychologist Mer-lin Donald warns, "to a human child, adult culture must be revealed only grad-ually, layer upon layer, with extensive mentoring."[23] We know more about how children learn gender. The gender they acquire is usually like that of one parent, and so a parental "we" includes them. "Aging" too could be seen as a continuum along which they glide, to eventually join the adult "we." Having an "age," when separated off by itself, is more puzzling, because subjectively children feel stuck so long at one lowly state quite distinct from the adult: their age changes but their stage of life seems static. Children collect contradictory age-tinged language and revelations about older ages and about getting older in general, often without guidance, from peers, from overhearing adults, from ill-informed educators, haphazard reading, or, more and more, via the mass media. "You go from tree to tree: there is as yet no forest," as a John Berger character says.[24]

In all cultures, literate or illiterate, linguists tell us, children are exposed, early and unconsciously, to "the accepted story-structural forms," and learning them—being taught them—is an important activity.[25] These stories, whatever else they do, tell the meaning of time passing. Decline narrative—whether found in a science museum or *Esquire*—is one of these explanations: a road through the forest. This book might inspire readers to go hunting for other story forms of aging—other time machines. They are everywhere. We need to think soberly through all the implications of these new facts about being aged by culture. At the millennium, "Face Aging" signals that decline's flawed and injurious ideology is no longer surreptitious, that decline is an authoritative narrative, and that the already early age of the target audience is dropping: the age considered appropriate for acquiring information about decline and internalizing it is now under ten.

◄———►

"Since the audience is so young," I inquired of Estey, "why not have stopped the computer program at twenty or twenty-five or thirty?" Indeed, one mother I watched, who had a child of about six or seven on her lap, intuitively stopped the button at age fifteen. "You look so much like your father," she said approvingly. That was a span long enough to give her son an idea of bodily change, she must have thought, and one that he might regard as positive. (In fact, he squirmed away.)

But no one organizing the exhibit had thought of stopping the projection of "aging" that young. The client—the Boston Museum of Science—wanted the simulation for an *aging* show, in a world where "aging" means old age and a bodily fate, not a choice of narratives about time that children must make sense of. Other sections of "Secrets of Aging" represented the ages neutrally (the "universal design" and Tai Chi booths) and positively, or suggested multiple (bodily) narratives. But presenting decline (in the most alluring exhibit) as *the* truth had the effect of overriding any counterpossibility that age/aging is constructed by culture and could therefore be critiqued and reconstructed. (Even a science museum can inhibit age consciousness.) Although the project manager at the museum, Jan Crocker, had gathered a panel of gerontologists to assist with the concepts and a panel of evaluators, none of them stopped to consider whether this youngster-attracting gimmick might convey a shocking and unwanted message. I'm not saying that they themselves believe decline should be the acceptable life-course narrative for the young. My analysis even so far suggests, if anything, that the ways of conveying meaning about age are not easy to understand or to deal with, given our existing tools. But age ideology has forced on us a question that would formerly have been unthinkable: "*Should decline now be acceptable as a life-course narrative taught to the young?*"

Instead of simply saying no, I want to turn to the question of how children might be harmed by certain kinds of age narrative. For children younger than fifteen, a decade might be about as much personal physical change as they can comfortably assimilate. Studies on their psychological responses to broader kinds of changes suggest that confronting even a decade might be too much. One inference I draw from this research is that the experiment in the booth undermined the children's precious sense of "self-continuity." According to cross-cultural developmentalists, the conservation of self despite change is a "condition of any coherent conception of selfhood and consequently, of any collective moral order." Adolescents who cannot find a warrant for believing they are "connected to their own prospective futures" may become suicidal, according to Michael Chandler and his colleagues, who studied First Nations Canadian teens exposed to dramatic cultural loss and apparently certain personal decline.[26]

Children are conservatively present-minded in this imaginative realm of aging, or only moderately future-oriented. They're not postmodernists, playfully changing identities. One rare cross-cultural study in four advanced societies found that most thirteen- and fifteen-year-olds prefer their own age as "the best time to be alive."[27] (With therapy her goal, Jo Spence intuited that it was best even for college-age students to focus on their own life courses no farther than the age they had attained. For imagining other/future identities, she counseled dress-up.) Children exposed merely to stories of change often stand pat for continuity and dig in or regress when subjected to too much projected difference. The youngest argue for self-sameness on the basis of an essential durable quality: for example, "My eyes are blue," "I *always* play with ponies." As they age, they develop more sophisticated "guarantees" that "different installments of their identity" are related. Finally, Chandler and his associates found, these explanations are narrative.[28]

In the Boston museum, the boy with some chest who liked seeing a "strong" self presumably viewed his future body not as different but as by and large the same, with change characterized more by gain than loss. (He may have stopped watching when the shrinking began.) The other children—except perhaps the girl with the presence of mind to notice redness, my first heroine of resistance—were stricken by more negative change over more future time than they could imaginatively handle. Although their presence in a science museum hints that they are educationally privileged youngsters, they are being prepared, like the socially excluded and suicidal Native Americans in Canada, to relate decline to aging-into-adulthood and to expect it.

FANTASIZING THE FUTURE: DECLINE VERSUS PROGRESS

The children's inarticulate experience of decline in the museum somehow had to be fit into an evolving mental construct—although "construct" is too static a term—that I want to call an "age identity."[29] Even children under fifteen probably have a couple. Age identity comprehends each person's collection of "information" about age and aging in general and stories about their own age and aging in particular, made less random but not necessarily less perplexing by the aging narratives they have come across, since some narratives serve as evidence of their implicit theories and desired outcomes and match their experiences while others do not. Age identity as I conceptualize it keeps a moving balance sheet, evaluating what aging—or, more typically where children are concerned, "growth"—has so far brought the self or its subidentities, as well as guessing what it is likely to bring in relation to what the dominant culture and the child's family and subculture say "the life course" is supposed to bring. The term suggests there is one and only one life course, as universal in its process as the biologized body.

One of the most important vehicles for organizing this "knowledge" may be prospective age narrative. If looking backward is unreliable, as the memoir critics never tire of telling us, looking forward might be considered preposterous. H. G. Wells's classic text of time travel carried his reader ahead into the year 802,701.[30] Our culture's narrative prophecies take us no less fantastically along our putative trajectory. Prospective narrative is now available for all ages. (Novelists writing about ages they have no experience of yet are among the unseen producers of this psy-fi genre.)[31] But children have even more limited experiences of temporality than the rest of us. I started this book with the monitor in the booth above all because it is such a startling example of forecasting: a wreck foretold about each and every tender body.

Prospective age narrative in a normal American childhood is mostly about "progress," not decline. Spence told her students the basic story-structural form: they "had gone through various phases, changing all the time, and were in a state of dynamic progression."[32] Progress narrative has weaknesses, but its intent is not menacing or hostile. It doesn't come to the young in a single dreadful flash of affect (as decline can be learned) but in a surprisingly coordinated humdrum and reassuring way, through myriad comments, stories, and nonverbal practices, in family, social, religious, and institutional contexts.[33] Many people will recognize something like the following reminiscence.

> I remember a dinnertime when it was Christmas. . . . Sometimes there
> would be other kids over and we would have a little table in the corner
> where we would eat, the kids, while the adults had the big table to them
> selves. And I remember that being a specially nice time. A lot of laughing,
> and cutting, and scraping, and eating and talking and all those kinds of
> good things.[34]

My family too practiced this holiday division between adults and children. Other people may have hated it or learned something else from it than I did. It taught me that I would grow up eventually—all in good time—to find myself at the big table, with my cousins also grown up, sharing it with my parents and my aunts and uncles (in my mental picture they were unchanged: robust, dazzling talkers, leaning forward in one another's faces, intensely gossipy and political). Was this my first experience of age hierarchy? In any case, age hierarchy seemed appealing. My husband's first age-memory, still fresh from when he was six, is of stroking his chin like a thoughtful grownup and being mocked by an aunt. His introduction to age hierarchy had a stick in it (ridicule at precociously presuming to act older) as well as a carrot (an image of impressive masculine maturity). Both of us were learning that life could be a progress.

The kind of prospective age narrative each of us internalizes in childhood can be foundational. It may be no more than one sentence deep and yet as salient as Pike's Peak. When I was about five, I cut my knee on some metal sticking out of our new used car. The wounds bled profusely and my father held the cuts closed with his two hands until they stopped; I didn't get stitches. My mother used to say, about the two scars, "They'll be gone before you're married." Today's readers—trained to think of auto/biography sociologically, up to a point—are likely to note first off the way compulsory heterosexuality is built into my mother's prophecy, because sexuality is a main narrative we are currently being trained to read for. But in this book we are in training to read differently, in an unaccustomed way, for the age and aging that are ubiquitous.

In this context, the basic notion that my mother conveyed was about healing through time. The body (married or not) would always heal. By itself, without constant scrutiny and tinkering: health was its default. The message she read off *her* crystal ball was, "Be calm; don't worry; all in good time." This optimism comes, she thinks, from her father, a first-generation Jewish immigrant ironworker who put his daughters through college in the Depression. The postwar boom assisted: That battered car was our first. In this and many other powerful normal sentences and anecdotes, my mother invented for me a trustful progress story about "the life course." The message went bone deep; it has functioned in all my recoveries, lifelong. It gave me a bias toward aging that had no sentimentality in it. The two scars in fact never disappeared; I can see them now. But it didn't matter that she was wrong. Her soothsaying—coming from a parent, it was true aging *knowledge*—strengthened me. It may have enabled me to become an age critic. It may be part of what made me bold enough to identify myself with the term "age studies."

"Progress" is defined here as beginning in a personal relationship to time and aging, a willingness to get on the life course as on a train, for a lifelong journey, and an anticipation of staying on the Patagonian Local because the future seems worth it. Progress is latent in all developmental metaphors of psychological, physical, and moral "growth," as critical psychologist John M. Broughton has pointed out.[35] Since my first book, *Safe at Last in the Middle Years* (1988), "progress narrative" is also the capacious term I have been using for stories in which the implicit meanings of aging run from survival, resilience, recovery, and development, all the way up to collective resistance to decline forces. The genre has been an influential engine of soul-making since the French Revolution, from Goethe's *Wilhelm Meister's Wanderjahre* to Toni Morrison's *Beloved*. Progress novels can be found in children's literature, the so-called coming-of-age story (of aging-into-adulthood), or in stories about aging-into-the-midlife or aging-into-old-age. Their implicit effect is to prove, through the readers' experience of fictional time passing, that faith in aging is justifiable. In *Declining to Decline* (1997), I tried to say what made the form culturally valuable and how writers could make it less vulnerable to criticism on the grounds of what it ignores.[36]

Progress is implicit in the age grading that children learn by entering school and by continuing through the education system, in the merit badges of scouting, and in other institutions in which status is conferred as if it depended primarily on aging.[37] The Massachusetts Comprehensive Assessment System exam in 2001 offered this essay topic to seventh graders: "Age has a funny way of making changes. It is probably easy for you to look back and see that you and your friends have made some major changes [friends, teachers, interests, are suggested] since you left the elementary grades."[38] The implicitly benevolent age-system that children are taught to rely on could be called "seniority."

In the twentieth century, if not before, "growth" and "progress" became America's semiofficial life narrative for children.[39] In normally protected circumstances, where these exist, children absorb into their age identity an increasing sense of control over things, authority over juniors and over themselves, and trust in the future.[40] In adolescence, many convert the trend of predictable improvements in selfhood—"Next year you'll be riding a bike"—into positive expectations of the next stage, adulthood. Even dropping out of school to get a low-wage job and prematurely rushing into maternity may display a naive faith in the restorative power of aging-a-little-bit-further-along.

Children under fifteen nevertheless have weak equipment with which to counter the feeling that horrified helpless regret is the only response to "aging," especially when decline narrative is imbued with medico-scientific certainty. Their age identity possesses too few *records,* and they know it. The "Face Aging" exhibit abused them spiritually, in the most delicate part of our age identity, the concept of the personal meaning of time. We're used to thinking of child abuse in other terms: malnourishment; inferior schooling; coercing poor children into labor or sexual slavery; inducing rich children to become premature consumers, mother naggers, and dysfunctional pleasure seekers.

"The discourse of hope is replaced with the rhetoric of cynicism and disdain," Henry Giroux declares, warning about institutions that fail youth.[41] Prospective decline narrative brings fatalism home: "You'll grow up to be a bum like your Dad"; "We can't get ahead." Some adolescents are exposed to domestic middle-ageism. When they are sunk in miserable adolescence, someone says glibly, "*These* are the best years of your life." Or, "You'll be old/have gray hair/be wrinkled too someday." But not all such messages are internalized. Even if such sentences are said out of bitter "realism" by an authority figure who feels he or she is "fastened to a dying animal," in Yeats's malignant phrase, destined for an age-adjusted pink slip, or immiserated by prejudice, some children find a way to mishear the words or fail to identify or reserve a hope that their fate will be different. They may continue to fantasize richly about their own future and about social change. But not in front of the science museum monitor. When I saw that exhibit I felt the temblor of a seismic change in American age socialization.

←——→

What of adults? In invoking the figure of a "threatened child" with "weak equipment" and new "needs," I have no intention of isolating children.[42] On the contrary, I have been preparing to make a move fundamental to the emerging field of age studies, which believes that no age class exists in a capsule, insulated from whatever is impinging on the other age classes—younger *and* older.[43] The move I am making at the end of this chapter, from the vulnerability of children to the vulnerability of adults, consolidates us all imaginatively as stakeholders in age ideology and the politics of aging, with a powerful interest in secret life-course narratives.

What happens to the sense of rising through an institutionalized and secure and progressive age hierarchy, as those brought up in its expectations age beyond childhood and adolescence and, for some, their college years? Adults continue to build ever more complex age identities, and progress is supposed to remain a pursuable goal. Progress means that over time some people have acquired by some means a degree of what Anthony Giddens calls "ontological security." (Bracket the specifics. Some acquire this security by agency, some by luck, some by inheritance. Some conceive progress in masculinist metaphors, of overcoming less fit adversaries or cruising directly on time's arrow. Some envision it through a version (relevant to their class, race, gender, ableness) of the life-course narrative called "the American Dream."[44] Some satisfy this narrative desire in base ways: progress can mean exploiting sweatshop workers more invisibly.) People need to feel, Giddens says, that they can "colonise the future with some degree of success."[45] Historian Tamara Hareven calls this "life-planning": for people who parent, it involves children and even grandchildren, not the individual life but family time reckoned in generations.[46] Even people who don't know literary forms or who face serious obstacles may do this planning and want that progress.

But aging-beyond-youth makes any sense of security more elusive, starting earlier for the disadvantaged. Life storytelling becomes more edgily poised within the binary of progress versus decline. To deal internally with the threat of deprivations, to keep their particular narrative going, adults respond on many levels, including a recurrent "drive toward identity stabilization" or "self-continuity."[47] In our culture, adults too want to maintain a subjective sense "of having reached a higher level of self-knowledge, of having become more self-confident, of having gained more control over one's impulses," in the words of cultural psychologist Amos Handel, studying Israeli immigrants, nurses, army recruits. He concludes, "Stability and progressive aspects of the self-narrative are not inconsistent and may actually coexist."[48] So if you ask, with Zygmunt Bauman, "What possible purpose could the strategy of pilgrim-style 'progress' serve in this world of ours?" one answer is that stability and progress are felt as interior needs, essential to the survival of the self.[49] Another answer lies in how the life-course opposition of progress and decline constrains narrative options in our culture. Age studies might help explode that binary. But until it does so, progress narrative—as the only apparent alternative to decline—is almost obligatory.

The paradox is that in many ways and for many people, aging-past-youth is increasingly *becoming* a decline. I argue in the first half of this book that the structures that support progress and progress narratives are slowly being withdrawn early or late in middle life from all but the most privileged. My research uncovers bad news about the economics of the life course—detailed in chapter 5, "The High Costs of Middle Ageism": the age/wage curve peaks low at midlife for white and black women, for black men, for those with low educational attainment.[50] Even for well-educated men now at midlife, the most privileged class, there are disquieting signs of loss of employment, stagnant or declining income, erosion of respect. Our age ideology presents us with an overarching contradiction. It constructs a tension—the subject of chapter 2—between two pressures: "Change, dammit, in subjection to ineluctable laws, while simultaneously never getting older" (because being young is the single best promise of being able to succeed in the future). This can be an irresolvable and frightening conundrum for anyone who is no longer young. The tension increases over the life course. But it can be a buried terror even for those still young (even ideally young: male, single, highly educated, and child free), reading their own prospective decline in the ads and through their nightmares at 4 A.M. The losers are little better equipped than children to explain why progress is merited in their case.

The unconscious belief produced by these circumstances—that decline is as inevitable as disease and has an early onset—is now so widespread that it seeps willy-nilly into artifacts like the booth in the Boston Science Museum. In light of this, the booth is what the joke calls a second opinion:

> Patient: "Doctor, doctor, you tell me I have a terminal illness. I want a second opinion!"
> Doctor: "Okay. You're ugly too."

Everyone should be aware of the economics of the life course, the cult of youth, and other forces of middle-ageism. But should people who parent use this knowledge to "predict" decline to their children? Or say how early it began in their own lives? (Plan their surgeries in front of the kids?) Many, including me, would argue for defensive optimism: "You'll have a good life whatever happens." It would require a heart of ice, a false realism, a poor understanding of my data, or a failure of will to be more menacing. Children also need a foundation of heightened age consciousness on which to build their future age identity and confront future risks. Adults need to become good enough age critics to explain the joke.

←———→

The rest of this book disentangles—as only a reconceptualized age studies can do—other central, toxic, unrecognized stories about age and aging from the welter of age culture. It will demystify their sources. As we identify the harms, we can figure out how to protect ourselves better—the children who sat in the booth, others waiting their turn to be exposed, the rest of us.

We can resist more effectively only by changing age culture. Chapter 2 discusses why change should be possible, and the whole book suggests how. Activists can frame better arguments—building on a wiser, progressive form of age consciousness—to keep the concept of decline from becoming a reality for more people. There are socioeconomic contexts and political choices that might enable more people to attain more security over longer periods of life time, and there are narratives that can tell their full story more honestly. The overarching question is, How might more people of all ages develop a collective identification with the whole life world—especially the ages of life ahead? Only through such imaginative solidarity can we maintain our precious sense of self-continuity and possibility within the dangerous age ideology we confront in the twenty-first century. (Shades of another prospective narrative.) Is it too blissful to imagine, as our goal, being able to feel at home in the life course at every age?

True Secrets of Being Aged by Culture

A CULTURAL WAR ABOUT AGE AND AGING

There is another reason why this book begins in that nook in the urban north-east of the United States, in the year 2000, in a setting into which William But-ler Yeats ventured with sixty "winters" on his head: among schoolchildren. Rich cases are detective stories: they reveal more than anyone initially imagines, and they go on yielding. The place where the children scurried away from age anx-iety turns out to be an ideal site from which to analyze and resist American age ideology in its latest historical manifestations. A good theory of ideology must begin, Stuart Hall suggests, from a place where power "hails" a class of subjects and gets them to invest in a position.[1] Unable to avoid the new kid subjects, we are led to look for the shuttle bus of history that silently dropped them there, at an intersection of intimate experience, mega-mechanisms, and the master nar-rative once intended only for "the old."

The Debate over "Positive Aging"

The museum site punches a big hole through age ideology's cover story: "Progress is *already* the new truth of aging." Progress is merely a cover story when people who think they need hope against aging-past-youth believe they can find it in the form of individual remedies for "getting over getting older."[2] In the entrance to the "Secrets of Aging" exhibit, a worried male voiceover begged, every sixty seconds, "Is there anything I can do to postpone getting old?" The heady rush of "anti-aging" is commercial. "Rejuvenation" is repackaged as posthuman transcendence of decline: botulin parties, solutions to "the midlife crisis" from kayaking to Buddhism, penis enlargers, toothpaste with "rejuvenating effects," all in the rhetoric of "health," "choice," or "take ten years off your life," all underscored by the belief that "the Boomers are changing everything because they have so much power." Web sites, daily e-mails, the health tabloids, media, books, lectures, spas-with-conferences attached, are pumping product.[3] But remedies presuppose defects: "Youth restorers" turn "someone with a particular blemish into someone with a record of having corrected a particular blemish."[4] Americans wouldn't need such "hopes" if aging really equaled progress. Younger people would be tattooing wrinkles on themselves or highlighting their hair with gray.

Using prosthetic youtheners to defy aging as early as midlife proves that youthfulness is symbolic capital (to apply a term from Pierre Bourdieu).[5] As such, it can be a possession only of the chronologically young—and then only briefly. After that, dominant culture soon exposes the aging to the various kinds of identity stripping that come related to the category of age. As more people are known to be undergoing cosmetic surgery to avoid looking "older," especially midlife men (once, not so long ago, considered too "distinguished" to need it),[6] and as people submit to the knife earlier ("preventive" facial surgery before forty, men in their thirties getting calf implants), and as these procedures become less stigmatized, the more deeply even the rest of us internalize the meaning of time passing as the loss of our capital. Lacking age studies, Americans are led to desire anti-aging products rather than age-conscious ideas. *Because* decline has such sharp teeth, "positive aging" increasingly sports a capped smile.

There is a stronger if much narrower argument that American age ideology has changed for the better—that it is bringing "successful" aging for one age group in one class in one period: middle- and upper-class people aging into their middle years in the past few decades. They're in the prime of life: "instead of occurring in the fourth decade of life, declines and losses are now thought to occur in the sixth or seventh decade"[7]—our fifties and sixties. (Not a big claim, since losses used to be thought to occur in the eighth or ninth decade.) This mostly Anglo-American group now includes some African Americans and other minorities. In this image they are healthy and relatively secure financially: when they make life plans they expect to carry them through.[8] They benefit from second chances at work, lifelong learning, and a lessened stigma about midlife sexuality, and they enjoy sharing adulthood with their children. Looking at various longitudinal materials, feminist scholars in many fields have challenged notions of decay or static rigidity over the later lives of women. They have found creativity, cognitive, ethical, and psychological developments (including increased autonomy, assertiveness, political activism), and, for postmaternal women entering the workforce, marked increases in some intellectual domains.[9] "Life-course scientist" Janet Giele, quoting historian Joyce Antler, says many women have experienced "feminism as life process."[10] Benefiting from the civil rights movements, these women earn more than their mothers and more in real dollars than they did at twenty-something. Hope-sponsoring narratives (novels, films, and plays) spin around a group larger than the cosmopolitan elites: midlife women and men of various races, classes, sexualities, ethnicities.

Age as a marker of difference between age classes is getting more salient in popular culture. "Look at the demographic!" now often means age instead of gender or race. Some lined, if gaunt, faces occasionally sell products geared at midlife women, so some of them tell me that age matters less than it used to—not noticing that the ideal age for feminine pulchritude is dropping toward thirteen. Or they take the increasing salience of age to be a good thing. It is called "age consciousness" and is taken to lead to information, mutual tolerance, respect, and desirable public policies. True, women are still aged by culture younger than men are; there was a lot of midlife downsizing in the 1990s. But the presumption, even among some academic feminists I know, is that positive views of aging—which once had to be imposed on the media, government, and business by feminist, gerontological, antiracist, antihomophobic enlightenment and activism—now have stability and momentum. Increased longevity is the clincher.

For any trustful Whiggish surveys, the "Face Aging" booth is an awkward and inexplicable anomaly. If decline is "the truth" that science and mainstream gerontology are offering even privileged boys and girls now, how can progress be the truth for anybody older? Yet this is possible. Hypothetically, the very oldest age class—the luckiest members of the "Great Generation"—could be enjoying a golden age, healthy, wealthy, and wise; while the youngest age class is being prepared for far worse. Many things could make that nightmare projection come true. (It was envisioned in ageist, generation-war terms by Bruce Sterling in his sci-fi novel *Holy Fire*.) The privatization of Social Security could render aging-into-retirement for those eight- to fifteen-year-olds a journey "over the hill to the poorhouse"—as it was before the 1930s and still is for the poor old, the majority of whom are women.[11]

There is no one-way flood of history. Progress in any dimension can be rolled back, or back and forth, in the era of neoliberalism and postindustrial globalization. The fact that "successful aging"—invented to counter geronto-phobia,[12] as well as to improve the lives of the old—is now defensively pursued by people in their middle years or even younger, should itself be a striking proof that decline has been backing down the life course.

←———→

The critique of positive aging does not deny its researchers' main contention: that human potential continues after young adulthood across many domains. And their unstated assumption is correct. "Progress-versus-decline" does frame life-course issues. I have shown that this already happens across a longer stretch of life than they think, and later chapters show how it works across a wider range of issues. As well as querying the binary itself, age studies looks much harder at the lifelong obstacles put in the way of enjoying that potential: the ways our life chances get doled out by age, as well as gender, class, and other biases. The ways our just desires smash against history.[13]

Consider longevity, our foremost metaphor of progress. Some scientists now promise what religion used to: a biblical span. But longevity too is subject to rollbacks. AIDS, the twentieth-century cancers, obesity and other "diseases of affluence," combined with a growing lack of health care, could actually lower life expectancy for those now at midlife in comparison with their longer-lived parents. Political scientist Victor Wallis foresees "biologically [as it were] dis-tinct communities, in which those with the necessary resources will attain for-midable physical resistance and longevity, while the excluded sectors . . . will sink to previously unimagined depths of misery."[14] The United States already suffers from gaps in sickness and death rates between economic classes. Wealth-ier individuals may suffer the onset of health problems as much as thirty years later than those of lower socioeconomic status. As death rates among American men dropped overall, they remained unchanged for poorer men.[15] Within each class level, African Americans receive inferior health care and are sicker. The saying of those nineteenth-century doctors still rings true. "In no one thing do people differ more than in their aging." Indeed, as people groan over higher in-fant death rates among the excluded, aging-into-old-age itself comes to seem less like a "universal" condition. Life and the timing of death are more like dis-tributed chances. *Whose progress is it?*

When the brunts of history strike, they hit differentially by age class in tan-dem with other social statuses.[16] Thus, people who were young adults in the North American workforce in the 1995–2000 period—whether they were high school graduates or college educated, women or men—experienced a more thrilling run-up in wages than any other age group at the time, accompanied by an adoring media embrace.[17] Then came the NASDAQ collapse, 9/11, the long recession. For some, the age of thirty may turn out to have been their wage peak. Progress narrative could stop making sense to these brief favorites of *Fortune*.

As always, we should simultaneously compare other age classes, in this case the midlife group. In that same boom period in which wages were finally rising after decades of stagnation, the "premium for experience" was lowered for workers in their middle years. People may not know the term, but the idea that there is such a reward for aging-past-youth begins with the child's observation, "Adults have money." At entry level it supports the hope, "I'll earn more later." When I myself was in my thirties, after I had been working at a prestigious but low-wage job for some years, I remember gritting my teeth and repeating to myself, too often, "I'm not earning enough more than my starting salary; I can't make my time be valued highly enough." (My salary had barely been rising, and one year it went down.) At the time I felt frustrated and pitiful for not escaping. Now I see that I was thinking and feeling in terms of the premium for experience.

One way to measure the premium is to find the difference between what people who are between the ages of twenty-five and thirty-five earn and what those between thirty-five and fifty earn in the same time frame. In the 1973 to 1995 period, the premium for being a midlife man hovered in the buoyant 21–27 percent range, according to economist Larry Mishel. For women, suddenly given a chance at professions and other careers with ladders, it leaped up from a puny 8 percent in 1973 to a robust 21.8 percent in 1995. Such a premium makes the American Dream credible. The midlife is *supposed* to be the prime of life.

Over the 1990s, however, mainly between 1995 and 1999, the premium-for-experience differentials for midlife men actually dropped 1.7 percent. They went up only a much slower 7 percent for midlife women. As the wage of the young rose, the differential for midlife workers went down.[18] And if you measure by actual experience—by what a median man who was in the thirty-five to forty-four cohort in 1990 *actually* earns ten years later, it was only $2,844 more (7.4 percent)—far less than the more than 20 percent that aging-into-the-middle-years had previously brought.[19] Such statistics also hide the fact that some few were earning billions by the time they were ten years older, while others had lost ground after a peak occurring between thirty-five and forty-four. (Most inequality occurs within rather than between age groups.)[20] Although a midlife peak can go on rising for the fortunate into old age, for others it ends early in midlife.

"Half or more of male workers lost ground as they aged from their 30s into their 40s, 50s, and 60s," notes economist Jeff Madrick.[21] Over the last twenty years, each successive male cohort between the ages of forty-five and fifty-four has been worse off financially than the preceding cohort of the same age. The age of the typical age-discrimination claimant in the United States has dropped steadily from the fifties to the forties, and the number of women filing claims has risen significantly.[22] Although feminism has helped shape a modest midlife prime for some women, the deteriorations experienced by other women and by men go unpublicized. Macroeconomic and representational factors are two major externalities that an individual cannot control alone. No one can afford to overlook them. The collective effect is a spreading form of discrimination: I call it middle-ageism.[23] If the premiums for experience can be rolled back, whose progress is it?

People tell stories of their life course in conditions not of their own making, to tweak one of Karl Marx's famous dicta. The late Glenda Laws urged age critics to consider as "the most important issue" "the degree to which the labor market shapes one's identity."[24] Their financial profile over time becomes part of the way people intuitively judge whether they're likely to have a "prime" or how long it will last. They fit their ups and downs in work, as in love, into their age autobiography, oscillating between "It's too late" and "Just try again, harder."[25] My arguments in chapter 1 have made it clear that I want *fewer* people to be edged into living a decline story as they age past youth. But as we move through the chapters that make up "Cultural Urgencies," part 1 of this book, it will become apparent that more of us are being forced and likely will be forced in that direction.

Yet in the United States, telling progress narrative in middle life and even old age has become almost obligatory. "The official definition of reality is part of a full definition of social reality and . . . has very real effects," Bourdieu points out.[26] As we saw in chapter 1, Americans—and Westerners in general—are "humans as subjects of autonomy, equipped with a psychology aspiring to self fulfillment and actually or potentially running their lives as a kind of enterprise of themselves," as cultural theorist Nikolas Rose says.[27] People are flexible and persistent in the utmost adversity, survivors' testimonials show, including in their storytelling. To maintain our progress narratives, we "invest in select areas of individual growth," and we minimize others.[28] It is also allowable (especially for women) to say we dislike or fear "aging" as long as we are referring to our bodies; and individuals are permitted to be "depressed" when they lose jobs at midlife and of course at "being old." But such limited licenses prevent us from seeing decline as systemic. We can thus neither resent decline nor take steps against it, especially in apparent boom periods like 1993–2000, when midlife people were losing ground in an America more than usually hostile to failure.

←——→

This book is for anyone who distrusts the commerce in aging and dreams of re-making age culture much more to our advantage, for anyone who has noticed other anomalies in our celebratory age ideology but not understood them, for anyone who is strong-minded enough to look decline in the face. Some, having experienced age-linked bodily loss, may be surprised to see cultural hypotheses pushed so hard that some of those links snap. Some readers, who feel person-ally comfortable with the complex life-course narratives they tell themselves, are curious about broad trends in age culture. Others, already having acknowl-edged the powers of cultural decline and having found successful resistance harder than anticipated, will want wilier defenses than currently exist and ef-fective offensives on more fronts. Some will want a book about "age" today that is not about just one of the ages—old age, "the BoBos," youth in crisis, children at risk—as if age classes were utterly separate from one another and age were separable from any of our other identities. Some will know quite a lot about the intricate interactive work of gender, race, class, sexuality, and ethnicity in cul-ture and selfhood and will therefore find the work of age (as I do) even more fascinating and mysterious. Today, the most inaccessible layer of our social for-mation may be our formation as subjects-with-age being aged by culture. All readers, I hope, will begin to anticipate the insights and new motives for social change that come from asking, persistently, with the new tools age studies pro-vides, "What has *age* got to do with it?"

CRIMES AGAINST THE LIFE COURSE

"Age ideology" is now rather like the elephant in the fable. In the present emer-gent state of age studies, it's too early to survey the beast. But calling the system that produces such indeterminacies around age and aging an "ideology" can in-spire work of all kinds—as do terms like "patriarchy" or "global warming," which have been functional, however contested. Revealing hidden ideologies is one of the most amazing faculties of recent critical literary and social theory.[29] In age, as in gendered and racialized constructs, relations of difference depend on the din of representations, unseen internalizations, unthinking practices, economic structures of dominance and subordination. Age theorists will have to show, as Erving Goffman said about one of his topics, "how this material can be economically described within a single conceptual scheme."[30] Meanwhile "the material" is changing. Ten years hence, will the forces identified in this book have become more crushing, or will they have been challenged by coun-terforces, including the visionary antidecline movement this analysis calls for?

←——→

I have spent more than twenty years being personally and professionally attentive to American culture's progress narratives as well as its decline narratives. To tell the truth, I started from the former. Exhilarated by the novelty of "midlife progress novels" in the 1980s, and by my own ability to "grow," I was convinced that the proliferation of positive representations signaled a new paradigm. My book *Safe at Last in the Middle Years* (1988) records that heady moment. I thought the sources of decline had been the high-art melancholics like Samuel Beckett, the Waugh of *Brideshead Revisited*, the Nabokov of *Lolita*. Decline's power over readers came from their prestige. I thought decline was a philosophy and an esthetic genre, not an ideology. By the time of *Declining to Decline* in 1997, I had changed my mind. I saw that the narrative of decline involved unconscious habits of thought and affected every subidentity, ways of seeing bodies and holding one's own, explanations of history; that it distorted visual culture, was supported by institutions and dollar signs. If you fought it alone, that fight sapped your energy.

One reason I could see this was that I had controlled my tic—a cultural tropism—of looking primarily for signs of progress. It was psychologically uncomfortable to block this tendency, but cognitively useful. Tracing decline's forces troubled and then revealed my own unconscious allegiance to having progress roll forward. This realization made it possible for me to notice many other perverse new time machines. Originally both my historical research on the 1880–1930 period and my contemporary work on the period after 1980 was in what might be called cultural studies of the midlife.[31] This focus was fortunate, because in both periods the midlife was suffering great alterations: in the first, the term "middle years" was invented, and in the second, comparable transformations were occurring behind a silly diversionary label, "midlife crisis." Following current trends—and raising a child—forced me to look backward, as it were, down the life course—not the typical one-way direction life time supposedly runs. I had had no prior professional interest in young adulthood or childhood. But understanding the workings of American age ideology means considering age as integral everywhere, "in contrast to formulations of [it] as analytically outside of other systems and impinging on those systems only at certain points."[32] In the conceptual breakthrough that resulted, I realized that midlife studies was another arbitrary division of the whole life into bits and that what the world needs is age studies. Intellectually and spiritually, doing this new comprehensive kind of age work made me feel less like Cassandra amid the joggers.

My current view is that we must be willing to consider the harsh reality that forces that make the life course bearable for some can unmake it for many more. Although the politics of optimism and resilience is appropriate when we focus on resisting age ideology, at this stage of our examination of culture and the economy we must be nuanced and precautionary. We do well to see this as a war over age and aging. In the war there are a thousand sites of skirmish. If my preliminary observations are correct, the sides are immensely unequal. Decline muscles on, yielding here and there when enlightened forces shove back. When age critics choose terrain for a combat we openly declare, age ideology is fortifying the ramparts someplace out of sight.

Constructing Age Anxiety

Many cultural critics are concerned about what we call postmodern or postindustrial time; we believe that a "slow but palpable transformation of temporality is at stake," as Andreas Huyssen put it.[33] As an age critic, I note that increasingly in ordinary speech "time" means, not eternity or history, but "a time of my life" (as in book titles like *A Map to the End of Time*, about later life, or *The Last Gift of Time*, about the writer's sixties).[34] Age studies method, foregrounding age, justifies itself by noticing how our culture increasingly foregrounds "life time." "Temporality," from the vocabulary of an earlier paradigm, cannot reckon with life time at its most grippingly personal: the Aging *Me*. Many transformations of selfhood make better sense if studied through the everyday mediations of age culture.

The urgencies I am concerned with are drastic biases in postindustrial/postmodern age ideology. They further naturalized themselves during the long 1990s, an eventful—and silently devastating—era. "Our culture is essentially periodical: we believe that all that is deserves to perish and to have something else put in its place," Randall Jarrell wrote in *A Sad Heart at the Supermarket*. It can't be said too much: this "perishing" is not about death but about the furtive power of decline to instill a masochistic belief in human obsolescence. The children in the booth are being prepped to accept age-graded competition: that in time someone yet younger and thus ipso facto more deserving will be put in their place. As Americans reach, say, their early or late thirties, this comes to seem common sense. A fact of life. An emotion like age anxiety, which changes our relation to life time, is simply one highly invasive effect of our age ideology.

The *speed-up* of the life course is another force that alters our relation to life time negatively. Jürgen Habermas thinks that after the Industrial Revolution "time becomes experienced as a scarce resource for the mastery of problems that arise—that is, as the pressure of time."[35] Speed-up has since sped up more. Many mechanisms produce it. It is that button catapulting the children through the spooky faces to come. In the workplace it is manifested in the trend toward 24/7, the adult life dominated by work. (Even the professional classes, once protected, are not immune to this historic increased pressure: in the 1960s the norm for lawyers was thirty-five to thirty-seven billable hours a week; now it's almost double.)[36] Speed-up is operationalized by just-in-time production; the feeling "it should have been done yesterday." The crunch steals from all of Juliet

Schor's "overworked Americans" the leisure that slows down our biorhythms and widens our time for reflection, giving the passage of time its rhythms and personal meanings.[37] Speed-up means the loss of Sunday, hobbies, family time; for some, the time to raise a family. Speed-up divides the overworked more markedly from the retired—some of whom respond by claiming to be still overworked—and from the unemployed, who are allowed no dignified claim.

Speed-up also creates the bitter paradox that what should be a longer midlife in a longer life span is actually becoming shorter at both ends of adulthood.[38] A feeling of haste and fear of failing comes to some younger adults partly from the belatedness with which certain signs of maturity now arrive, if they ever do: a permanent job, a life partner. The age at first marriage has never been higher. Professor Carol Fleisher Feldman found that at New York University between 1995 and 1999, at the height of the boom, her students were worried about whether they would succeed in having a spouse, children, and a house, as adults.[39] The interwoven concepts of the long-term job and mutual loyalty of employer and employee have become insecure as work becomes more transient, contractual, part-time, and seasonal. Ageism may be an ancient prejudice, but middle-ageism is our own postmodern toxin—like Chernobyl's fumes, spreading globally. The worklife is being shortened at the far end by cultural means in tandem with the economic system. Dispatching midlife workers is slowly becoming postindustrial policy.[40] I call unemployment or underemployment of this midlife class "premature superannuation." Many who lose jobs in their middle years can't find another and, discouraged, stop looking for good work or full-time work. "Early retirement" has a Procrustean effect as well. While some get golden parachutes, others are forced to depart without pensions. (With full Social Security beginning later—age sixty-seven for those born after 1959—the number of those who will have to work after "retirement" may grow.)[41] Surely longevity appears to promise that there will be *more* time for using our midlife powers. That's why it is used to clinch the faith that aging-into-the-midlife *equals* progress. Speed-up makes that mantra seem naive. The scarcity of jobs and life time spirals into accusations against midlife workers. In the press they are called "aging," which makes them seem too old to worry about. They are told to drop out to make "room" for the young, while retirees, who do make room, are made to feel that their "dependency" harms their "productive" juniors. Our very own Catch 22: people are rushed through their working lives to suffer longer, competent and energetic, from constructed gerontophobia.

Speed-up and these other workforce mechanisms have profoundly inhuman consequences personally, on those considered to be aging-into-the-middle-years and their families. Fear of the squeeze—and the reality of early exit—curtail the time for developing a sense of accomplishment, a career, accumulating savings. When speed-up is symbolic, it is being treated as if it were just normal fun—as the makers of "Face Aging" probably thought. The writers of the popular TV cartoon *Rugrats* decided to attract the preteen market by aging the preschool characters. A co-writer asked rhetorically, "Who wouldn't like to put a baby in a time machine and see what they look like in 10 years?" [42] Its parents, for starters. Processing life at our own pace—digging boredom on a vacation day, relishing variations in the flow of time, feeling that life is long—ought to be an outcome of American affluence for more people. Instead, this psychological essential becomes more endangered. Everything is made urgent. To respond to socially constructed time-panic attacks, I want, among other things to be announced, a vast Slow Time movement, like Slow Food in Europe.

Speed-up and physiomental, economic, or social decline—alone or together—can also construct the feeling called nostalgia quite early in the life course. [43] Nostalgia is an emotion recognized through narrative. Indeed, nostalgia, as I discuss further in chapter 8, is a main affect—sometimes the point—of retrospective decline narrative. This common but unnoticed genre is pithily encapsulated in adages like "Youth is wasted on the young" and jokes like "Inside every old person is a young one going, 'What happened!'" Such expressions purport to be insider wisdom-of-aging, sharing the sense that decline is a *biological* fate and the only way to beat it is *to have known this sooner*. This subterranean feeling is probably widely influential. Remember the mother who said, "That's when you look the best—as a little boy"? We should be shocked that decline, already speaking through that primary caretaker, turned off the visionary MRI of her love.

Nostalgia is troubling when the regret in it becomes a primary emotional coloration rather than the good feeling of being "part of a community, even if it was only a community of previous selves." [44] Nostalgia can even be dangerous, when adulthood itself comes to seem—as it more and more does in an exploitative global economy—an exile. [45] One outcome to avoid is a First World equivalent of the horrifying nostalgia of Rigoberta Menchú anticipating during her skimpy childhood that it would soon end in the intolerable hardship—"la vida amarga"—of being a grownup like her parents. [46] Installing nostalgia is a mental injury, a viciousness of our economy and our age ideology. Longing to be younger grows acute over time, daily deepening "like a coastal shelf." Constructing nostalgia for children is utterly wrong. But it is also contemptible to create conditions so that masses of people—last-hired first-fired, prematurely superannuated, disabled, old, people whose age/wage curve has already peaked, or those who anticipate such things—are forced to believe that reminiscence must be their dominant emotional relation to life time. It is stupid to write about nostalgia as if it were an ahistorical feeling.

This book also provides evidence of the hardening of age divisions. Decadism, generationalism, and named age cohorts are other mechanisms that construct an obsession with age—aging, age classes, or the ages. [47] The decade anniversaries—fifty, forty, thirty—are increasingly flamboyant and critical dates, potential "crises" decorated with black balloons. ("Sixty," however, at least in the middle class, has some of the cachet it had in China.) Markets become age-niched. Even AARP has different magazines for its different age groups and has started up *Secunda Juventud* for the Americanized Latino market that also thinks the answer is *Second Youth*.[48] We have news shows and documentaries for "older" viewers who can sit still and still vote; violent films and Letterman aimed at those thirty-five to eighteen with shorter attention spans; Disney for junior sensation-seekers. Each cluster—not just that of later life—touts how much more delightful it could be to be the particular age you happen to be if only you would buy the lifestyle goods produced for that age. Fruits and vegetables, once recommended for everyone, are now labeled "fountains of youth." "General interest"—a category which united all adults, often around the choices of midlife tastemakers—wanes.

The means seem harmless—mere infotainments—but the salience of the stages, especially youth, does not enhance anything that critical age studies would want to call true "age consciousness." Marketing by age requires stereotyping the targeted age class and other age classes in relation to it. The rise of named age cohorts (like "the Boomers") hardens the stereotypes. Youth ads for fashion, high-tech, music, and movies imply that there are no other age classes in America: no children, no parents, no elderly—just "Generation Xers" or "Ys" partying together. I show how age is being used as race and gender have been, to construct unarguable and unbridgeable relations of difference; to create misinformation, subjective inferiority, disrespect, and animosity between groups; to serve as another displacement of anger, away from systemic solutions, another defense of damaging public policies, another set of obstacles for political activism, family solidarity, and rational explanations of historical change.

These are some of the time machines that revved up in the 1990s and that operate today to naturalize our age ideology. I try to show how discourses, real-world facts, and practices infuse our interpretations of the meaning of time passing and time to come. As I hypothesize their mode of action, these are not "messages," received as sent (as in a simpler apprenticeship or direct-communications model of ideology). Rather, the mechanisms that affect us do so by raising, time after time, personalized questions worryingly worded by decline: "How long can I keep my progress narrative going?" "How likely is it that I can?"

If age studies develops as I hope it will, researchers will measure these effects in creative ways across various populations. I would look for the greatest concentrations of such feelings in people now *younger than* forty-five who are not in unions or other seniority systems, because each younger cohort is increasingly exposed to the postindustrial pressures on life time. Women and minorities may find or expect more insecurity at younger ages.[49] People are not always conscious of such effects. Philosopher Thomas Nagel says that "psychological states, like knowing, believing, and intending, need not be immediately experienced to exist; nor are they usually present in consciousness, though they can have large conscious effects."[50]

Age unconsciousness is held in place by tenacious sources. If some mechanisms (such as the relentless cult of youth) come to us explicitly connected to age, others (like the increase in working hours) appear to have no connection, and some (like Social Security) are obviously linked to age but in misleading ways. To acknowledge the deeper psychology of decline, we would have to investigate people's struggles against age apprehensiveness, their attempts to continue to feel resilient and in control as they age past youth in an ideology that appears youth-obsessed. Both progress and decline narratives can isolate and privatize life chances so we can't see the forces behind them. Decline narrative in particular often lacks the polyphony of characters that shows inequalities among people of the same age, similarities among people of different ages, and diverse responses to similar historical fates. Age theory can point to other missing levels of analysis, as I suggest in chapter 6, "What Is Age Studies?"

With slight pointers, many people are skillful at noting discrepancies in the official story, distancing themselves even from their own experiences and storytelling to reflect on them. My plea for true age consciousness is for us to think, *Age too could be different.* Reading this book involves active self-reflection. Inquire whether these alterations in "temporality" have been affecting you, and if so, whether you feel more like reporting or hiding them. Has decline invaded your jokes, your vocabulary, your secret autobiography? Has it leached into your vision, "aging" those parts of your body that have been highlighted by magic marker as vulnerable and making other unchanged or improved parts invisible? Have you thought all this was "natural"?

Backing Down the Life Course

The social history of the life course in the twentieth century will be, when it is written, in large part the history of the culture's attempts to resocialize adults to "recognize" themselves as "aging" by applying the lore personally, starting at ever younger ages. Decline, nostalgia, speed-up, and age obsessiveness used to be the landscape of the very old who were also helpless. For their "condition," passive "wisdom"—rather than anger and resistance—was long considered the appropriate or standard "rhetoric of emotion," as age critic Kathleen Woodward has brilliantly shown.[51] Looking over the last thirty years, "Cultural Urgencies" concludes that this privative condition, along with its built-in passivity, has been sliding backward down the ladder of years. Its effects are not uniform, but it threatens people in two directions: at ever younger ages and in ever higher classes.

Decline has long been targeting people at "midlife." Although people by that age have records as children do not, the button operates for them too. It can be punched faster by menopause discourse aimed at women of thirty-five, by the new use of the term "seniors" to refer to people over fifty, by William Safire's use of the term "near-elderly" for people forty to sixty, and of the term "elderly" to refer to people as young as thirty-seven.[52] The phrase "senior moment" is applied to themselves by ever younger people, and each time its less of a joke. Although the little research on memory at midlife shows no inferiority to college-age subjects in comparable contexts, people somehow believe that memory lapses are mainly age-graded. The allegations of cognitive loss may overlap with what Huyssen considers a growing "fear of forgetting." That is no light fear if your job depends on cognition.[53] The term "middle-ageism" recognizes that powerful forms of stereotyping and bias are moving backward from old age.

The button is going lickety-split even when we don't know it. Many people are unaware that the Supreme Court's decision in *Kimel v. Florida Board of Regents* gutted the Age Discrimination in Employment Act. Justice Sandra Day O'Connor wrote for the majority, "States may discriminate on the basis of age. . . . [a] State may rely on age as a proxy for other qualities, abilities or characteristics that are relevant to the State's legitimate interests."[54] Midlife stereotyping is being legalized. This is "arguably . . . the harshest limitation of civil rights law enacted in the past twenty-five years."[55] Middle-ageist discrimination has been sanctionable the way racist and sexist discrimination are, proved by finding a "disparate impact" on the age class. "Employer groups and conservative legal organizations have recently taken aim at the disparate impact theory across a variety of civil rights statutes," warns Linda Greenhouse in the *New York Times,* writing about another Supreme Court case, in which 70 percent of the employees who were laid off were over forty.[56] O'Connor's decision is itself precisely the proof she opined was missing from the historical record: institutionalized discrimination. Even the media that hasten to inform us about losses of affirmative action in gender and race made little of *Kimel,* or of the loss of seniority that the right wing accomplished in creating the Department of Homeland Security.

Seniority gives maturity its value, as a word and an experience. Seniority is the system that supports age-graded ladders, job security, rewards like the premium for experience, later and higher age/wage peaks, and midlife progress narrative. Seniority through the worklife is one of the few remaining supports of a democratic age hierarchy throughout life. "Age hierarchy," as I use the term, has nothing to do with the authoritarianism of gerontocratic patriarchy or sentimental relics of traditional piety. It means the system that makes respect for "aging" people (those otherwise being aged into decline by culture) credible and effective. Seniority should be more widely available and much more highly prized.

"Premature" aging is downwardly mobile. In the 1990s, chillingly, I watched my son and others of the "cohort" called Generation X being sent signals that they were getting "too old" before they were even thirty. In the ambience of the bared umbilicus, the alleged technogenius of "Generation Y," the youth of advertising agents and the producers of MTV, twenty-something is no longer so young, no longer so promising. Where skills depend on schooling and deteriorate rapidly, people only five years after earning a degree can find themselves at a disadvantage against those younger. College women look back nostalgically to high school, before they gained the "freshman fifteen" (pounds).[57] One junior told me, "I feel like I am past my prime." Before I saw "Face Aging," I couldn't imagine that decline would reach subjects as young as fifteen or ten. Since then, I have read about a class in modeling and self-esteem for girls no older than thirteen and as young as six, warning them how bad their skin might look at "fifty" and teaching them the importance of facials.[58] Girls and women are the shock troops of age anxiety, but boys and men are being shoved after them more promptly.

The Hurried Child, David Elkind's 1981 book, argued that the increasing value on precocity was driving "the readiness" concept out of child rearing.[59] Rather, Americans are simply being "readied" at earlier ages for whatever the dominant system requires us to face. Psychoanalytic theorist Adrienne Harris noted fifteen years ago that "[c]entralized day care and its particular programs [are] geared to the production of children skilled at analysis, self-control, conceptualization, and abstract reasoning," and that developmental researchers were effectively pushing "intentionality, and purposive functioning . . . deeper and deeper into infant subjectivity," anticipating what I call the "preprofessional" child.[60] Adult eyes—including those of working-class parents—have learned to see in the toddler with his computer a future New Economy worker. Are our eyes being trained to see, in the robust infant in the cradle, marks of weakness, wrinkles of woe, precursors of "aging"? As if our culture were reinstating a postmodern puritanism, the Fall—the original sin of age, distrusting the declining body—could begin for us not at three-score-and-ten but soon after birth. Americans are becoming obsessed by age, not because of increasing longevity but because of premature decline. Age is becoming an overriding constructor of difference and an alarmingly ubiquitous focus of subjectivity throughout the life course.[61] Age is the new kind of difference that makes a difference.

I document these contentions in part 1, "Cultural Urgencies." Chapter 3, "'The Xers' versus 'the Boomers,'" looks first at the lingo of the claptrap business media, starting with the term "slacker" and following the twists of power that have caused everyday speech to be invaded by the naturalized practice of naming and characterizing age cohorts—with everything that follows. Chapter 4, "Perilous Parenting," shows how literary discourse—through novels of wide circulation—constructs linked lives so that child rearing becomes a fearful anticipation. Chapter 5, "The High Costs of Middle-Ageism" traces the undoing of seniority, social status, and age identity. Throughout these opening chapters, I am doing as Stuart Hall recommends.[62] Add, add, add the different levels of determination together—and integrate them as they overlap. Taken together, they suggest decline's increasing prevalence. By the end of part 1, readers should be better able to judge the regimes of power and decide what kinds of help they need in order to resist the overlooked, underestimated, and misread forces manufacturing age.

Speed-up at any age, the dominance of decline narrative, early nostalgia, age apprehensiveness, slicing life into mutually hostile stages—these are crimes against the life course. We need a term to define this new category of ideological crime and ethical injustice. Just as critical race studies points out the roots of racism, and gender studies the roots of sexism, to eliminate them, so age studies focuses on the sources of these manifestations of . . . But we don't even know what to call this -ism that is akin to ageism and middle-ageism but even more rapacious over the whole antecedent, or anticipated, life. For this book, the term is "decline." It unites gerontophobia, middle-ageism, and the threat of early hopelessness offered to people below forty, thirty, or even twenty. Exploring the sources of decline has made me ever more unwilling to use "aging" as its synonym.

←——→

The local examples of "Cultural Urgencies" are linked to their nearby and their distant perpetrators. In this book, some of the suspects are unexpected, like the wise heads of the Boston Museum of Science show, pollsters presenting their inevitable age-cohort graphs and charts, novelists penning touching books about the deaths of children, cartoonists commenting wryly on economic trends, pundits of fifty attacking "Boomers," academics carrying on their customary theory moves where "age" appears in the better lists of differences and never again; postmodernists trumpeting "young" technofeats, you and your friends gassing over the water cooler. (I try to be a spoilsport where decline is concerned, like those people who don't laugh at tit jokes or let the "n" word slip by.) Most of us are "innocent" of our grassroots complicity in building an unlivable age culture. It is easy and ordinary to flaunt jocular ageism or fall in line with the cult of youth.

But no common sense gets disseminated around the water cooler—nothing major happens in age ideology—without the business and entertainment media, pharmaceutical industries, advertising, the current form of patriarchy, the weakening of state-centered alternatives to global capitalism, the smashing of traditional counterforces like unions, and the reach of the decline logic of megabusiness into the presidency, Congress, and the Supreme Court. For decades, American business and multinational capitalism have deindustrialized, downsized, outsourced, deregulated and self-regulated, and hyped the New Economy, striving to drive wages to the bottom and the workweek to 24/7, increasing insecurity, attacking seniority systems, and promoting the commerce in aging, in the normal pursuit of profits, income, or market share. Aging under globalization with fewer safety nets than in the past makes the difference between progress and decline ever more tense.

What makes the regular heavies interesting are the long chains of evidence that link them to decline invisibly, negligently, or ironically. That all this business-as-usual distorts American age ideology (or French or Indian or Samoan) is simply collateral damage. It used to look as if a larger class toward the top—and their children—would be spared. Now the near-privileged look more like the canaries in the coalmine. If *they* are being aged by culture early, what could spare the rest of us? Patriarchy? Global capitalism might fail worse in installing age-related decline here if American patriarchy still cared to defend seniority in its current avatar. Do midlife white men care less to defend a system of seniority because it is increasingly shared by men of color and women? Or have the cult of youth and midlife decline discourse demoralized even the dominant class, who—if they discovered how age hierarchy was going under—might be willing to defend it out of self-interest and habit?

Yet there seem to be counterforces: whatever maintains seniority or delays the triumph of decline. One sign of this is that the war over the "value" of people age forty-five to sixty-five, or forty to fifty-five, or wherever the scrimmage is now, is still undecided. (There is indeed a "midlife crisis," only not the kind we were led to believe. The term seems to have disappeared, although the crisis grows.) In the United States, premature superannuation from the workforce is not as widespread as it is in some European countries, despite the fact that the EU countries have far stronger labor traditions and safety nets. American democracy may need to maintain enough public midlife progress narratives to keep our mythic Dream alive, and that need might limit capitalism's downward pressures where the midlife spread of decline is concerned. More positively, there are still many countervalues, interests, discourses, practices, and institutions that attach symbolic values and material gains to the process of aging-beyond-youth. The desire of adults to continue to tell progress narrative, younger adults' anticipation of premiums for experience—these are part of our implicit seniority countersystem. Perhaps decline can still be rolled back. My goal in every chapter is to introduce practices and concepts that combat insidious decline ideology at levels that go as deep as its own. Insofar as the counter-system can become more self-reflexive, egalitarian, united, and effective through age studies, there is hope.

←——————→

Age studies has been called into being in the twenty-first century by such emergencies, perplexities, plans, and dreams. The discoveries of age critics confer cognitive and emotional benefits on those who take them to heart. They make people want to stand up, object, strike back, make change. People who are superstitious about decline avoid whatever smacks of "age," particularly when they are on the verge of being considered no-longer-young. Age hasn't been their issue. Now they can know in their hearts that only the seniority counter-system (not their innate potential alone) makes it possible for them to derive intrapsychic, interpersonal, and material benefits from becoming older, whereas decline strips them of such benefits. Younger people may leap clear over the propaganda to recognize themselves as stakeholders and agree that the system must be fortified at all the points along the life course where it is being damaged. At no age would anyone be able to say, of being aged by culture, "Not my issue." Of no identity could anyone say a priori, "Aging-in-culture has nothing to do with this."

A thoroughgoing response, some readers might already have decided (in answer to the question, Whose progress is it?), would require a large-scale activist movement and redistributive changes from the federal government that no one in her right mind can foresee today, alas. I agree, but ethical visions in themselves can have influences that are unknowable in advance. Political action on the feasible agenda that I detail at the end of part 1 could restrain some of the worst institutions of decline. From the practices described in part 2 could come psychological strength, intellectual and narrative flexibility, and teaching materials for the cultural combat.

As age studies reveals the ideology's vast range of resources, being aged by culture into accepting decline as inevitable (and being compelled to produce glossy public autobiographies of progress) will seem effects of a wealthy, prepotent system. But age studies also spots the leaks and metal fatigue of this Rube Goldberg system, fault lines that can be widened by critique. To avoid shame, even the relatively secure must watch for the psychic residues of age-linked stress and try to determine what mechanisms produce them. Only then will more people—including midlife male writers, who produce so many naive decline films, novels, poems, and plays—be able to declare out loud how they displaced age anxiety, economic woes, relational failures, bewilderment, and conflict onto essentialized aging-as-decline. Young adults could feel freer to complain of woes (impotence, exhaustion, burnout) that now signal "aging." Such moves could wrench us out of the progress-decline binary into liberating jeremiads, respectable complaints, satires, thrillers, and manifestos. This would make possible full-voiced heroism, more convincing progress narratives, and tragedy.

Suppose that many midlifers, even in the middle classes, were to begin gravely qualifying their progress narratives or redescribing some of their allegedly age-linked losses as cultural, out of broadened age consciousness. Critical age auto/biography, research, and analysis would make it harder to conclude that American democracy and economic globalization are benign systems for the whole life course, or that decline can be explained primarily by biology. The American Dream serves as a lure into the workforce and a rebuke to those who "fail" there. But it can be turned 180 degrees to measure the injustice of allocations and the age-linked structures of opportunity at a time when the United States is the richest country in the world by a commanding lead. Inequality is growing but anger at age-linked unfairness is not commensurate. "All serious human moral activity, especially action for social change, takes its bearing from the rising power of human anger," in the words of feminist philosopher and theologian Beverly Wildung Harrison. Anger "is a feeling signal that all is not well . . . it is a mode of connection to others, and a vivid form of caring."[63]

The American cover story needs to be revised to read, "Progress can be an important truth of aging"—during and after childhood—"*if* we do something about it." Narratively, psychologically, historically, economically, cognitively, ethically, politically, and ideologically, we need this new field of age studies to help us care and to believe we can succeed. Little by little, reacting to age ideology in America will willingly involve our hearts and minds and bodies and speech, inspiring those who believe in social justice. It could make a revolution.

"The Xers" versus "the Boomers"

A Contrived War

> And the children's teeth shall be set on edge.
>
> —*Ezekial 18:2*

Soon after our son graduated magna cum laude from Harvard in 1991, he was fired from a new job as a waiter. His employers told him he didn't smile enough. Having taken advantage of the recession to hire more young people than they needed, they had to expel some without cause. Our son was a self-confident adult with wide opportunities, but even so I lost my postmaternal cool.

Sean moved to New York to launch an independent magazine and a writing career, supporting himself through day jobs. His struggles gave us a window—a big, drafty window—on the hand-to-mouth life of the 1990s job market. He worked evenings making cold calls as a telemarketer; he freelanced as a "content provider" (the belittling new Internet word for writer). Simultaneously he joined the growing army of "consultants" and began working for a temp agency, doing computer-assisted design. One such agency, Manpower, was the largest employer in the country.[1] Within six years, he amassed 1099 forms from over a hundred companies bent on outsourcing, none of which paid his Social

Security or gave him a health benefit or participation in a pension plan. Despite the high quality of his work, he was often stonewalled on fees.

Thirty percent of workers have similar—"nonstandard"—new American jobs: contract or other short-term work, with less security, fewer health benefits and pensions, no ladder, less clout.[2] "Permatemps" describes the status of most workers in the computer industry, but at Microsoft they must leave after one year.[3] Isolated and competitive, nonstandard workers must seek employment continually. Unemployment and underemployment are endemic. Whether "Old Economy" or "New Economy," nonstandard conditions are gaining ground. This degradation of work in the First World may turn out to be as profound an economic transformation as the Industrial Revolution.

Meanwhile, how is the postindustrial order being explained to us—not only to parents and adult children, but to the American public? Not, except in progressive circles, as a contestable trend in the treatment of workers, not as "the race to the bottom" or "class war from above," NAFTA at home. Instead, the rhetoric shaping the public record depended heavily on the skillful deployment of two imaginary age categories, "the Xers" and "the Boomers."

NAME/BLAME

During the recession of the early 1990s, when our son joined the workforce, the media cannily invented the term "slackers," meaning lazy, apathetic, cynical, young adults, apolitical "whiners" who were dependent on their parents and did not have the drive of "our" generation.[4] This was classic victim blaming. Having dissed kids with high school degrees when manufacturing jobs disappeared, now they started dissing college-educated kids when professional and managerial jobs were inadequate to demand.[5] Nevertheless, the term "slacker" spread from coast to coast. The media reported parents berating their kids for not trying harder to find work. (My husband and I were telling our son to get more sleep, take a day off—poor palliatives for our rage at being unable to counter the terminology, let alone the economy. I was also saying, "Watch out for the spin.")

As the recession tailed off, press coverage changed to defend the young, now called "Generation X" or "Xers." (In every future reference to either term, imagine them in quotation marks.) The young writers getting published now were those who resented being called slackers. Slackerdom, they said, was a malicious "myth" or "hoax."[6] Although Xers were still discussed as if they had a single homogeneous character, that character possessed values central to America and was capable of changing and improving through time: sympathetic, *human*. Xers were quoted talking earnestly about growing up, wanting to marry, even—clinching proof that they are human—*investing*.[7] Although they had been called "the Hard-Luck Generation," we began to be told repeatedly how aggressive, competitive, successful, and ruthless they were. A 1997 *Time* magazine cover story gave an order to midlife workers, "Well, move over," and warned, "So boomers, beware. There's a whole bunch of kids with scores to settle." "Who would have thought the kids would start taking over so soon?"[8] Inciting the economic aggression of "kids" against parents, and warning parents about power loss, was *Time's* humane mission that week.

After the recession ended, "Xer" as well as "slacker" might have become as passé as shoulder pads. Yet hundreds of articles about Xers (that included Boomers as well) continued to appear, intent on bringing yet more justice to the allegedly still vilified young. The phenomenon of columns or articles turned over to young writers qua young began in this period. (A column in the *Boston Globe* was called "Whatever.") Editors who swear they scorn political correctness gave indignant Xers space in which to speak from their aggrieved point of view.

But what if young adults are too diverse an assemblage to be sorted together as Xers? When I asked fifty Brandeis students what gender, race, and class Xers are, I found the connotations to be whiteness, maleness, higher education, potential for job success. Women with the same economic characteristics may be members of the club; so too "model Asians," gays, and upwardly mobile African Americans. (Had I asked whether Xers can be fat, I think few would have said yes, so large a role does advertising play in the "youth imaginary" of young people.) "Xer" thus does not seem to include "youth in crisis"—crack sellers, violent offenders[9]—or fast-food servers, teachers, or union organizers. The term is as class narrow as "Yuppie" was but not pejorative. In short, although Xer is the opposite of Boomer in this binary, it is by no means synonymous with "the young." Yet its claim to be scientifically encompassing, to represent *a demographic cohort,* is precisely what authorizes age generalizations.

Now for the other side of the story. Eerily, as "Xers" became sympathetic individuals, journalists turned to maligning a group they identified as "Baby Boomers." When Boomers are present in Xer discourse, they serve as the Other. *They* exist without question. They were said to hold all the good jobs, gobble the perks, and dominate the media, harping on themselves. In the stock market run-up of the 1990s, economic "boom" echoed richly inside "Boomers." They are the plutocratic sellouts with dental plans and pensions. Powerful but undeserving: "deadwood."

"Boomers"—for those who have been living in Siberia—began as a neutral demographic term referring to a birth bulge that between 1946 and 1964 reversed a century-long decline in the birthrate. But it soon became rhetorical, inconsistent. In contexts where power or income or size is the core attribute, the Boomer label bulges out to include war babies of the early 1940s as well as others still active in the workforce. "Boomer" nevertheless quickly became imposed as an identity. Pop writers—and now a few university press authors—address those who consider themselves Boomers. Midlife industries rely on the wealth of some and flatter their supposed cultural power. It all provides a soft "positive-aging" cover for the other discursive strategies I am examining.

These strategies are hostile. Conservatives use the term "Boomer" to belittle the "generation of '68." (Whether they mean the antiwar protesters, counterculture, or the druggies, these were small subcohorts, not a generation.) The media has been describing them as "the aging Baby Boomers" since 1982, when the youngest were only sixteen.[10] "Aging" isn't neutral either: its decline elements are up front. "Now that they're in their 40s, boomers are finally feeling old, and they're blaming you," wrote one woman who identified as an Xer.[11] A "Talk of the Town" piece in the *New Yorker,* ignoring the thirty-somethings in the group, blithely asserted, "Now, in 1998, every baby boomer is middle-aged"; death is "a major item" on their agenda.[12]

Boomers didn't grow over the 1990s except to get older. "Aging" in a world of Xer hustlers, people in their thirties and forties were told that they were "clinging" to youth—or should try to. (Boomers are reminded of their mortality more often than the Puritans were.) The commerce in aging depends on "denial" or "defiance"—blurring signs of physical change. Women were once supposed to be more slavish about this. Now—in a unisex blur, only a little later—men too compete with younger men, fetishize youth, buy rejuvenation. They're ugly too. Age is overriding gender.

Boomers too have a character, but not a perfectible one. Pictured as essentially rich, greedy, self-righteous, unwilling to share their vast economic and cultural power, reckless, undeserving of their luck, and of course *aging,* they possess a not-so-mysterious grudge against photogenic Xers. The jealous elders have acquired a pseudobiography. A *Boston Globe* article described them as "idealistic longhairs" who became "Yuppies" and are now "ready for the glory days of the menopausal and the bald."[13] They are usually depicted as if they were all male, white, and overprivileged: Bill Gates, not women, minorities, or the homeless. They are undeserving because unpleasant: "whiny, sarcastic, narcissistic, self-indulgent, cold, bloodless people."[14] Few writers feel the need to point out that Boomers are too heterogeneous to have a single "character" or opinion.[15] Even some social scientists ignore their diversity. What exactly are people aged thirty-eight supposed to have in common with people aged fifty-six that they should regularly be polled together?[16]

Such omissions make it appear that all middle-aged people are rich and powerful and wield power uniformly. They can thus be more easily objectified as secure rule-makers and oppressors of the young. Envisioned as male, they function as a patriarchate, ergo, intent on playing out—in the words of psychoanalytic theorist Kathleen Woodward—"the oedipal familial logic of struggle and recrimination."[17] As Goliath to the Xers' David, they're responsible for the most important problems Americans, especially Xers, have faced in the last quarter century.

What I noticed—because our son was being shoved into Xerdom and his parents were being made perverse new characters in the social text—is that the media have been creating a war between these two age groups. (That's one reason I start this chapter with a family anecdote: age politics is personal. Somebody hurts. Everybody hurts.) Before long, as a cultural critic in age studies, I began following the construction of this difference closely. Preposterous as some of the generalizations have been, they have proliferated beyond the right-wing politics of the alleged twenty-something "movement" and other heavily funded youth groups, moving into major monthlies, mainstream newspapers, and the influential weeklies that younger readers rely on for news more than they do on the dailies,[18] not to mention fiction, nonfiction, and everyday speech. Age stereotyping has been made more than respectable: cohort difference is becoming common sense.

In this chapter, I try to make readers warier about how age cohorts are branded and generation gaps manufactured,[19] about using the terms "Boomers" and "Xers," about age-related language in general. My theme is the politics of the representations of age—from a location in any of the life-course imaginaries of our time. This is a necessary perspective for age studies. I'm explicitly avoiding the slice-of-life approach, offering a case study of not one but two age classes, the history of their discursive relationship, and the conjuncture out of which this emerged.

Often, as we know, what fences in a lumpy, heterogeneous bunch of people so that they can be treated as an integral group is another internally diverse bunch constructed as an opponent. It takes two to make each one one. As that opposition is accomplished, age-as-stage constructs subjectivities and can be used to divide the workforce and the body politic. When immensely consequential ideological work is underway, age can do it imperceptibly. One effect of the Xer-Boomer war is to make age hierarchy seem unfair. Listen in what follows for the insinuated question: "Why should there still be a premium for experience?"

CONSTRUCTING THE ENEMY

In the guise of defending Xers, the media constructed midlifers as the enemy: the generation "that sucked up too much of the oxygen" that Xers need.[20] "Defying stereotypes and misconceptions doubtless nurtured by insecure baby boomers, the twentysomethings on parade here are an idealistic and defiant bunch" (this, from the *Washington Post* in 1992) compresses a typical maneuver.[21] Overtly, sentences like this sum up positive views of Xers. Covertly, they stigmatize the Boomers. Reporters sic the young qua young against the Other by representing Boomers as bullies. Fight imagery prevails. In *Fortune,* a writer asserted that "Boomers are more than willing to take on twentysomethings in what's shaping up as a generational grudge match." In "Talking Trash about My Generation," a writer in the *Dallas Morning News* noted, erroneously, "The great bulk of what I find is commentary by Baby Boomers bravely attacking their brash youngers."[22] A 1997 *New York Times* op-ed piece said "Crybaby" Boomers "hate their kids."[23] In the first full-length book constructing the age war, *13th Gen* (1993), which has been much ventriloquized, Neil Howe and William Strauss asserted that the Xer phenomenon was a "one-sided assault from elders."[24] In fact, neither Howe nor Strauss nor anyone else provides evidence for this charge. It would be difficult, aside from three nasty mainstream articles in 1993 and 1994 that represented "whiny," "crybaby" Xers as overreacting to the recession. At first these articles were regularly cited in the just-doing-justice campaign—as if three men from the *Washington Post, Newsweek,* and the *New Republic* spoke on behalf of the alleged seventy-odd million Boomers.[25] Since then, nobody's bothered.

Perhaps because evidence of Boomer hostility was slight, the tack changed from what Boomers said to what Xers felt Boomers believed. One young woman asserted that Boomers "sneered at our McJobs."[26] "It's hard to find an Xer who doesn't believe that . . . the baby boomers see them not as human beings but as disposable incomes in sneakers, and that all this Xerbashing is just another boomer power trip," a *Newsweek* writer "reported," although he'd certainly not done a national survey.[27] Xers are *told* how they feel. "They hate baby boomers, and they're sick unto death of reading about them," the *Utne Reader* editorialized.[28]

Since the articles don't appear to be *about* the elders, fairness doesn't demand that malice toward them be denied or qualified. Editors find individual young people to publish and review who feel that there is no point in looking further than Boomers for objects to blame. Some editors are manipulating the war for known conservative agendas. Others intuit the needs of the business class, support niche advertising, or are dazzled by the wicked simplicity of the age binary. If older, some cling to Xers out of youth-cult envy (despite the self-flagellation this requires). If younger, they sport their Xerness. The war has widely fostered age chauvinism. Younger writers who deploy identities other than age, who praise aspects of the midlife generation, and who use categories like gender to disaggregate the Xers (David Greenberg in *Next* comes to mind) are rare.[29] The feminist press publishes articles about crossing age borders, but feminists regularly use the terms "second wave" and "third wave," markers of excessive age-cohort difference, without noticing the overflows from the Xer-Boomer war.[30]

Midlife people with secure Old Economy jobs can be represented as useless (as academics know well). A character in Doug Coupland's *Generation X* says bitterly, "You'd last about ten minutes if you were my age these days, Martin. And I have to endure pinheads like you rusting above me for the rest of my life."[31] Imagined as a class of employers, Boomers can also be represented as the force responsible for "management by the numbers and downsizing" and shipping the jobs overseas, rather than members of a midlife generation made widely vulnerable to having their wages cut at their peak.[32] In a 1999 article in *Modern Maturity* (published by AARP, which should have an editor more skeptical of age-cohort attributions), Mark Hunter is allowed to state that "Baby Boomers, who came of age shouting their contempt for the man in the gray flannel suit, have done more than any other generation to erase the line between work and private life."[33] Name any deterioration of working conditions and it can be blamed on "Boomers" rather than seen as the next wave of global capitalism's power over labor.

Using the term "Boomers" adroitly hides the fact that the people in question are often parents, and that not all of them are doing so well. But a startling 1997 Roz Chast cartoon glances at the meaner reality with three Fathers' Day cards "For Today's Dad" sent by kids-with-jobs to their unemployed fathers. The first says, "You always thought I was such a slob. Well, guess what, Dad? I got your job." The second boasts, "I'm working full-time, You're still lookin'." The third offers Dad a job "as my personal assistant!" Presumably these are sons, not daughters, who are allowed to voice such nonchalance, resentment, and glee at the overthrow of age hierarchy. It's their fathers who have lost. Younger male–older male competition used to be conceived sexually, as oedipal. The age war relocates it (and sanctions it) within the workforce.

No one could imagine boys jeering at their mothers on Mother's Day, even in jest. (Many young people, girls as well as boys, have watched their single mothers struggling and felt abandoned by their fathers. Even at their midlife peak, women earn only half as much as men.) Mainstream discourse finds it easy to forget that black women raising their grandchildren and last-hired first-fired Latinas are also "Boomers." With women omitted, Mom's precarious work situation and her relentless boss—whatever his age—are muted in the blare of media assertions about Boomer power.

Some journalists have noticed the war the media has created. In the *Boston Globe*, Matthew Grunwald joked, "If Libby Borden repeated her hatchet job today, we would undoubtedly be deluged with think pieces featuring the ax as a metaphor for Generation X's disenchantment with baby boomers."[34] But the warfare has been minimized by being lightly termed "Boomer-bashing." According to that *Fortune* cover story, it's just "the new national pastime."[35] "Generational Flagellation Lite" is what John Gregory Dunne called media attempts to belittle the Boomers with the "nobility" of older groups.[36]

As a menace to the young, Boomers have to be fought. Their superpowers

"For Today's Dad," by Roz Chast.
© 2003 The New Yorker Collection
from cartoonbank.com. All rights
reserved.

make economic revenge appealing: "Let's yank away your cushy day job, your dictaphone and your dental insurance," Ian Williams was trapped into snarling in *13th Gen.*[37] Intellectual historian Louis Menand cites "the revenge fantasies of [the Boomers'] younger siblings" as if they were a fact, just as Chast does.[38] Calling the Boomers "aging" amounts to revenge. It implies that the enemy are has-beens. To younger workers, it hints that the unjustly rich group may be on the verge of decline, powerful but not omnipotent: a Goliath that David can beat.

Privatizing Social Security is the revenge suggested to the anti-Boomers. The terms "Boomer," "Xer," and "Social Security" constantly appear in combination: in one two-year period I found 282 such articles—an induced panic. Peter G. Peterson, a Wall Street banker who long ago started using the age war as an argument for privatizing Social Security, early predicted "ugly genera-tional conflict" once "[our kids] understand the size of the bad check we are passing them." [39] "The coming 'entitlement wars' over how to pay for the old age of 76 million baby Boomers may make the generation gap of the 1960s seem quaint," said *USA Today*.[40] The *New York Times Magazine* tried to diminish the sense of danger in 1995, but the author wound up warning of future "shoves." [41] And in 1999, editor Charles McGrath imagined "impoverished 20- and 30-somethings massed outside the gate" of "our" deluxe early-retirement commu-nity, "tennis rackets and Big Berthas in hand," unwilling to "foot the bill." [42] Metaphors like "bad check" teach the young to be anxious; group pronouns like "we" and generalizations like "paying for Boomers" focus their anger in an age-graded way. A friend of our son's snapped at me, "I pay 15 percent into FICA, and Social Security won't be there for *me.*" [43] I'll wager he had read some of those ar-ticles. The ground has been so well prepared that the young can plausibly be rep-resented in the mainstream press as a worried and cohesive group of potential antagonists.

According to the late Robert Eisner, a past president of the American Eco-nomic Association, the "crisis" in Social Security manufactured by the right wing was never plausible; there is none looming in the future.[44] On the con-trary, people in their peak earning years were providing Social Security with al-luring surpluses for the first time in its history—the direct cause of attempts to privatize. Meanwhile, people are distracted from the true weakening of pension plans (an important source of retirement income for union members and the middle class). If the young can be constructed as a cohort defensively for itself, the right will find it easier to split family solidarity on Social Security and tatter the major remaining safety nets.

The staging of work scarcity is also serious, especially in any downturn. Age-cohort explanation insidiously preps the young to believe that a young person can have a job only if a person at midlife loses one. A standard anecdote came into urban folklore in the 1990s. "The 50-year-old, $75,000-a-year-veteran ex-ecutive who was right-sized out of a company and replaced by a 28-year-old, $30,000-a-year, fresh-out-of-college MBA graduate is not a rare species in to-day's economy," noted a writer in the *Orange County Register*. "This is not job creation. At best, it is job exchange; at worst, it is job loss." [45] "First Boomer" Bill Clinton confirmed the job-swap myth at a commencement ceremony when a student yelled out, "I need a job!" and the soon-to-retire president replied, "Well, you'll be able to get one now." [46]

Jokes and anecdotes do age ideology's work. Imagine countercultural anec-dotes instead: a company pink-slips fifty midlifers and hires only thirty younger people. That would clearly be seen as exploitation. But how satisfactory would it be if the company fired thirty older workers and hired sixty younger ones at half their wages? From a family perspective, a parent's job loss is devastating, even to adult children who are employed. Does it make sense, if American business is unable to produce enough good jobs for all, for anyone in a family unit to prefer to exchange a parental salary for a starting salary? In a nonfamilial, differently othered labor market, this would be called scabbing. The job-swap myth makes "still" being in the workforce at midlife seem unjust, the way the supposed perks of Boomers—like dental plans—are treated as unjust. It conceals the unwillingness of businesses to offer a dental plan and the powerlessness of young people to ask for it at the hiring interview.

Despite the trumpeting of American prosperity throughout the 1990s, various economic problems have had to be "explained." Female competition, black competition: those binaries put the blame on nondominant workers for failures that are systemic. Now the blame game has been moving into an additional arena, that of age. The Boomer-Xer age binary brings scarcity into the heart of the family, where (when not treated as a joke) it operates openly and sadly—as if midlife unemployment had always been an accepted part of the economy, and younger people had never been able to get jobs unless their parents lost them.

IGNORANCE AND SUFFERING

Does anyone take this age war seriously? Do real people repeat the stereotypes and scapegoating—the middle-ageism—they've read and heard? If your main goal is to privatize Social Security, you needn't care if Xers repeat it word for word: they got your point. But the rest of us care, and those who notice are saddened by the accusations. The editor of the Simmons College student newspaper wrote, "Older generations look at Generation X as somewhere between a nuisance and a nightmare."[47] Some of my friends' adult children repeat how easy "we" had it when we were young. They're primed to hold an age group responsible for both the rightward trends that have made their lives so tough (declines in scholarship aid, housing starts, and job creation, the growing prevalence of nonstandard work, and 24/7 schedules) and for the changes that no one controls. My friend Linda reports that her twenty-five-year-old daughter told her, accusingly, "You had sex, drugs and rock and roll, and all we have is AIDS."(In fact, according to a 1988 report from the Center for Disease Control, AIDS was growing fastest among people over fifty.)[48]

I am appalled but not surprised that undergraduates have naturalized the Xer category as theirs. In that large Brandeis sociology class, I proposed first off that age divisions are socially constructed, like the gendered and racialized differences they had already studied. They readily agreed. Then I took a written survey, asking, "Are Xers different from Boomers?" Two-thirds answered yes. Only a seventh offered any critique of the binary. All of them thought they were

"Xers." Family resentments get tied to the language provided by the war. The psychological anthropologist Thomas Weisner interviewed "the children of the children of the '60s" in a part of California where people in the counterculture settled and raised families. He found that some adolescents who had been hurt by their fathers, though preferring not to call themselves Xers, did use the label "Boomer" to explain behaviors they condemned as selfish: divorce, alcoholism, drug use.[49] (Think of Kevin Spacey in *American Beauty*.)

From grade school on, children learn to think of themselves as united by age, but up to a point this cohort identity is modified by looking up to one's parents. The Brandeis students were not resentful of "the Boomers": many regarded them as energetic, successful, or activist. Two students retorted, "The Boomers are our *parents*." While in college, almost-adult children may use war language, but with compassion. "Oh," gasped an undergraduate remorsefully after I'd given a talk at another college, "When my father lost his job last year, I said, 'Daddy, I don't want to have to compete with *you!*'" Age differences may harden later, in an atomistic and competitive workplace. Cohort-cohesiveness, midlife-othering, and self-absorption can congeal, as in the discomfort of a younger man who thinks that at twenty-three, he suffers from "workplace problems" because "many of the people I work with have children who are my age."[50] If job milieus are conceived as ideally young, it may come to seem odd to have midlife workers around. Younger workers are taught the emotions they are supposed to feel toward midlife people: estrangement, resentment, anger, vengeance.

The media do not criticize "Xer" anger; indeed, they publish hate-speech that would be unthinkable in gendered or racialized contexts. The young woman who said the Boomers sneer at her McJob imagined their future in chilling terms. "It seems as if the generation that thinks it discovered everything— from sex to drugs to music to love—would rather not think of itself as a pioneer in these last few battles [retirement, deteriorating health, death]. If it's true, if they have paused here to catch their breath, I can't say that I'm disappointed to see them humbled."[51] Writer Rosie DiManno complains, "You are old. You are wrinkled. You sag. . . . You've had a lifetime of being at the centre of the universe. . . . What next? Sex and senility? A hip-to-be-dying movement?"[52] The passions aroused by the historic downsizing of the American Dream can be turned into ill will against a group too often told it must die first.

The subtext is parricide. As I suggested, parricide is not now sexual. It isn't even, exactly, a death wish. I think cultural psychologists who studied this conjuncture now would find that the emotion being constructed is a compromise formation, a miserable yearning that people who are older-than-young not be there in the workforce. People in their twenties who might feel this way are involved in two difficult processes simultaneously at the volatile turn of the century: forming new adult relationships with their parents and taking their first steps into the postindustrial global system. Handling both tasks simultaneously may be made more confusing and painful by the age war.

These discourses are one unhappy face of a new "structure of feeling" (as Raymond Williams called such waves of historicized emotion).[53] The other unhappy faces are those of people in their middle years. (Here too, there's little research. Who, in our youth-centered culture, interviews fifty-year-olds about the age war, honoring them as ethnographic subjects as they honor people in their twenties?) My friend Linda, never a swinger, was saddened by her daughter's envy. When I was a guest on a Midwestern NPR show, a woman called in to declare, "I may be fifty, but I'm no Boomer, I'm no Yuppie." Hers was the kind of fierceness shown by people who feel that no one has been listening. An acquaintance tells me that her son, a thirty-nine-year-old computer defense analyst, fears he'll lose his job after forty.[54] That's how young you can be and already be "too old" in our middle-ageist culture. But when Boomers lose their jobs, they still can't do anything right. Don Snyder, in a memoir called *The Cliff Walk*, recounts how his college teaching career ended when he was forty-one. One (male) student "let him have it": "Man, not another baby boomer out of work. . . . Every time one of you guys loses his real job you take the crap jobs at Blockbuster and the mall so I can't even pick up summer work."[55]

Midlifers have not been as vocal as I would expect people to be about being dumped into a despised age class and hounded off the stage of life. Pundits make no protest as the generation gap is widened. At readings I gave around the country in 1997, two midlife women and one man said that "we" ought to give up our jobs so younger people can have them. They too have absorbed the anecdotes. The story the media had midlifers following focused on the sufferings of the Xers. Many read not as self-interested parties in their own highest-demand years or as activists angry about economic inequalities, but solely as parents, generously concerned about the futures of adult children. It would be easy (but wrong) to assume that Boomer-bashing comes primarily from our children, who wouldn't knowingly hurt us, rather than from journalism, publishing, advertising, and the business class in general, which have profit stakes in generational otherness. In different ways, the Xer-Boomer war picks off people at all adult ages, separating and disempowering them.

AGE WAR: MANAGING THE CRISIS

Our son's hardscrabble mid-twenties had one intellectual benefit: it taught us to see through the contrived war between the Boomers and the Xers, and to see "in the name of the children" as a dangerous weapon that can be twisted flexibly—against the midlife, the workforce, and the future. Why did this form of age warfare occur in the 1990s? My view is that Boomer-bashing explains major historic, economic, and social changes in postindustrial capitalism in a way that reduces resistance to them. Since at least 1973, Americans have seen declines in quality jobs, real wages for men, employment security, and pension vesting; erosion of seniority systems; a rise in economic inequality; the loss of authority in professions such as teaching and medicine. However loudly the bull market roared in the 1990s, and however many billionaires American inequality produced, such losses affect people *at all ages* below the top 10 to 20 percent in income and wealth, and some at the top too. The age war is one spin put on the bad news the elite couldn't help but release.

Each new group of the young hitting the job market has become a greater potential crisis. Ordinarily, workers just starting out must be resocialized from their adolescent prework values—the relative indulgence and cooperation of family life, and (for those who go to college) the autonomy of collegiate life— into the steeper hierarchies, greater atomization, self-subordination, and insecurity required by work. Employment compensates for such losses with independent income and anticipation of future augmentations of power. If work appeared futureless, some of the young might resist. Monitoring this transition, the establishment press also guides it so new entrants take the impress that will keep them compliant. In the 1990s the media, treating "the young" as if they were a single economic class, said Xers suffered *disproportionately* from scarcity. Ian Williams's diatribe against the midlife generation was frequently quoted. "Boomers have the job market in a full nelson, asphyxiating any hope we have of approaching their collective wealth anytime before the year 2050." [56] Hurry up now, it's *my* time. Xers were told a prospective decline narrative while young people's wages were *rising* (long before the stock market dive of 2000). "And Xers believe their own press. . . . 75% think they will be worse off than their parents," reported the *Economist.*[57] Prophesies foster resignation.

The age war sometimes lays the griefs of the young on Boomers' behavior (their high divorce rate and high percentage of women/mothers working—the "latchkey phenomenon"), and sometimes on their dumb luck in being born earlier. Ignoring the rich and powerful born before 1946, a *Chicago Tribune* writer declared, "The 77 million Americans born between 1946 and 1964 are now 'it.' There's nobody left to take care of things. Worse, there is nobody else to blame for whatever goes wrong." [58] The midlife generation is being scapegoated for History—the history of postindustrial, post–Cold War capitalism.

Age, you could say, manages many crises. Silly as this may seem, the constant noise of blame distracts people from thinking about power, class, or protest. It enables younger people who feel they cannot advance to attribute their woes not to the economic system but to Boomer piggishness. It manipulates history so other unfairnesses seem more equally shared. Boomer-envy deflected the anger of new entrants away from the much-touted members of their own cohort who became millionaires overnight. The age war turns all of us rhetorically toward the "natural" world of generations (seen as cyclical, with a time to start work and a time to bow out) and the little world of the nuclear family (seen as rivalrous). There, the best that adult children can do is to wait with impatience, and the best their midlife parents can do if they can't afford to retire early is to survive with guilt.

By magnifying a youth crisis, the age war disguises a real midlife crisis—the erosion of seniority, meaning not just the economic rewards for aging-into-the-midlife but the psychological and social ones. I sketched the patterns of loss in chapter 2. I come back to their effects in chapter 5. As Anne Monroe pointed out in *Mother Jones,* discrimination against the middle-aged "is the dark underbelly of downsizing."[59] Even college-educated men between forty-five and fifty-four, a once privileged group, are targeted. Corporations and state and city governments operate as if the only way to raise profits is to cut the wage base, pensions, and perks, not of the bosses but of the next-most-expensive employees. People downsized at midlife have the top cut off their expected age/wage curve. Nothing more needs to be at stake than the bottom line, once cutting "Boomers" also coincides with the young needing these jobs.

The Xer–Boomer war has increased middle-ageism. This system of bias minimizes or even justifies harms inflicted on people as long as they are older-than-young. It imputes to aging no experiential gains. Nothing but decline: slower reflexes, memory loss, burnout, techno-retardation. Through discursive, economic, and legal means, interactively, the midlife itself is being devalued—even as Boomers are beguiled by being told how much power they have. Viagra, HRT, and being vilified by the press are not perks of power. Most people in this age class are entitled to say, "*We didn't eat the goodies; we've been helpless to save them.*"

If such complex losses can befall people as young as fifty—people who are allegedly so omnipotent—the life course can be poisoned for each cohort as it turns forty-five or forty. Or even younger.

To those under the spell of the age war, whatever their age, middle age may now seem to be an unjust proxy for power and wealth. Seniority produces apparent life-course "inequality," in that the young start out earning less than their elders. Age studies has a responsibility to clear up any misapprehensions about whether "equality" would be better for the postmodern life course. It would not be.

Thinking that there must be something wrong with the *relative* affluence of the midlife generation is an intellectual and political mistake. Seniority through age hierarchy is not empty veneration; it's a countersystem that brings improved conditions to people as they age into the middle years. Over the past thirty years, more women (white and minority) and men of color have gained this complex seniority than when the American Dream was intended only for some white men. Now that this is a more democratic system, it's more worth defending than in the past. Like any economic distribution it has some problems, but the alternatives are devastating.

If deterioration in life-course expectations cannot be stopped, more current young adults will age without being able to look forward to the wisdom, respect, and higher income supposed to attend the middle years. Without some of these rewards, keeping a progress narrative going is a herculean task. If there is a small rise or no rise in wages for half the people now aging-into-midlife, it's a good bet that conditions will be worse for people who are younger when their turn comes. Even in times of high employment, insecurity depresses wage gains (as Alan Greenspan has admitted) by weakening isolated employees, and even unions, in negotiations. As midlife people who still have good standard jobs retire or are forced out, younger workers find that employers eliminate the benefits and raises they used to offer.

If the current midlife generation of workers do not resist middle-ageism for their own sake, they permit a flattened, foreshortened, proletarianized system to pass to their children. *Without seniority, the first wage a young adult earns could be the highest wage she or he ever earns.* Not many of the young ever started at $80,000 a year. They are more likely to begin in the bottom quintile, and 47 percent who begin there stay there.[60] Certainly more young adults need help rising. Without a culturally inscribed seniority system, fewer would get out of their starting quintile. Do even the rich young want an age/wage curve that peaks before they have children or the habit of saving and that declines thereafter? (Would those who are now at midlife have wanted any earlier peak for themselves? If a peak at thirty had been their fate, would any of them have been able to tell a progress narrative as they aged?)

Those currently at midlife hold whatever structural and social advantages they have only temporarily, in trust for the workforce as a whole. The seniority "trust" is turning out to be more fragile than anyone my age ever imagined. A few more shoves like the age war and seniority may disappear forever. The "revenge of the Xers" on the middle aged—if capitalism destroys age hierarchy in their name—will in due course destroy them too.

HOW NAMED AGE COHORTS WORK

The war depends on a supposedly neutral and scientific concept—that of age cohorts based on birth date. Wars take two sides. But a binary based on ages should be harder to manufacture than racial and gender oppositions, if only because the life course is usually seen, subjectively at least, as a continuum. Male-female difference has been fabled in song and story, but Boomers and Xers were never natural objects. The entire infernal machine was jerry-rigged while we watched.

The term "Generation X" came into currency during the early 1990s to refer to people who were first joining the workforce then, those born, roughly speaking, between 1968 and 1972. For a while the term "Xer" flexed to embrace individuals born soon after 1972. Thus, for the age war, a cohort that spanned nineteen years was arbitrarily matched against a cohort that spanned about fourteen in order to prove statistically that Boomers are a giant army (76, 77, or 78 million) and Xers a tiny defenseless one (37 or 40.5 or 45 million). "Couldn't the Baby Boomers pick on a generation its own size?" *Newsweek* asked, playing the bully card.[61] In fact, the first wave of Boomers—the tsunami threatening Social Security—numbers only 35 million. And the Xers will never be configured as a nineteen-year cohort, because the next youngest have been given other names (the "Y" or "millennial" generation) and their own crazy characterizations.[62]

To be describable at all or useful to social science research, cohorts need definitional rigor.[63] The dean of cohort claims, Norman B. Ryder, warns that birth cohorts are "more random in composition than any other cohort type."[64] So future data will have to be disaggregated by class, race, gender, and other identifiers. Until the Xers turn fifty, we can't have the data that might make possible sensible comparisons and contrasts with their parents' generation: whether they will suffer as much income inequality as current fifty-year-olds do, whether their wage peaks will differ as much by gender and race, what their rate of divorce will be. But no amount of data can help—according to sociologist Melissa A. Hardy, editor of an excellent book on aging and social change—with "fuzzy, gradual, or disputed transitions."[65]

No previous named cohort has been so dogged throughout life by its label as "Boomers" have been, on so trivial a foundation. (When earlier age cohorts were designated by name, those names alluded to catastrophes: the Lost Generation after World War I, Depression babies). The characteristics, although unprovable and tendentious, seem stable: Xers don't *want* job security. Boomers just want to have fun![66] How can age cohorts appear to have essences when they're random and the diverse people in them age and change? This illusion depends on a familiar, widespread linguistic trick for othering. Theorist Mary Louise Pratt describes it: "This abstracted 'he'/'they' is the subject of verbs in a timeless present tense . . . an instance of pregiven custom or trait."[67] "Boomers are narcissistic" is a generic noun phrase like "Girls love dolls." According to feminist development psychologists Susan A. Gelman and Marianne G. Taylor, learning generic noun phrases suppresses in-group anomalies ("I know generous Boomers") or similarities with the out-group ("Xers also like to have fun").[68] Using the binary suppresses the intelligence of most journalists, writers, editors, and pollsters.

A cohort-replacement interpretation of socioeconomic change can be made plausible.[69] But even applied cautiously, the age-cohort concept may be too simple, providing little insight into the underlying causes of change. Sociologist Karl Mannheim, the most brilliant theorist of cohorts, attacked those who "'discover' fictitious generation movements to correspond to the crucial turning-points in historical chronology."[70] Such fictions are one-sided, he warned, like "race" or "national character." Mannheim called for multifactoral history, a regard for uneven developments and respect for the power of elites to produce "truth."

That each named "cohort" in the age war is irrational and misleading makes the dissemination all the more striking. Adding one new age class to the language in such a way that undergraduates and (eighth-grade level) readers of English-language newspapers have learned it, is no mean feat. Validating two incoherent cohort terms in such a short period of time demonstrates how effective media teaching can be when highly motivated, persistent, and well funded.

Putting these two well-established new characters in the social text, piggybacking on the prestige of demography and history, seems to have stabilized the media habit of constructing pseudo-cohorts. These terms are never just marketing labels, although the biggest development in niche marketing is to sort by age. They are collective identities. People of all ages are now interpellated by cohort. If you identify with the label (who can deny his birth date?), you are henceforth urged to identify with waves of untestable, inflammatory characteristics. Not all do, but many do. People born on a frontier—say between 1962 and 1966—don't get an age name; some feel deprived. In a few short years, our son's cohort could be called "the aging Xers."

A "generation gap" is not ahistorical and universal, as writers innocent of history like to declare. Long periods can go by—"periods of social equilibrium and stability, when the environment and experience of successive generations remain pretty much the same," historian Al Richmond noted—when no gaps are perceptible.[71] Generation gaps are constructed, rhetorically shaped for their moment. Audre Lorde warned that such constructions are a tool of a repressive society, facilitating historical amnesia.[72] Middle-ageism now functions, for example, to make parents' work experience seem irrelevant and their impotent pain seem like useless nostalgia. It helps to construct younger people nervous about their futures, ignorant about economics and public policy, and selfish about their age class's alleged interests. The young raised in this embattled environment would be unlikely to feel that midlife job loss was an unmitigated evil.

Ethically, the worst evil of the age war may be that it undermines commonalities between parents and children. It pits them against one another as if they were unrelated social groups: silenced audience versus dominators of discourse, small fraternity against huge horde, poor youths versus rich adults. The setting is a particular stage of the family life course, when two generations are in the workforce together. Middle-ageism and contrived scarcity raise the emotional stakes. For the younger people, the war cruelly depends on a poignant mix, of their youthful desire to be independent and their increasing need for help against market forces. For the midlife parents, it cruelly takes advantage of both their devotion to their children and their anxiety about their own decline. We have to look back to World War I's carnage, and Freud's *Totem and Taboo*— which imagined a prehistoric state in which sons had to kill fathers literally— to find a constructed war against the midlife taking a form more extreme.[73]

Getting "the young" to parrot negative, dismissive feelings against another age group has strengthened age as a category. When age dominates, as we've seen, it obliterates differences within a cohort: gender, class, race, ethnicity, sexual orientation, physical ability. Age difference may help override intergenerational solidarity within feminist, antiracist, and other groups united by shared political goals. The age war has been so naturalized that "age" has been invisibly consolidated as a primary explanation of life-chance differences and justifier of contemporary feelings, personnel practices, legal decisions, economic conditions, and understandings of the future. Age war obscures the cult of youth, class war from above, and globalization, world-historical facts that would otherwise seem both more dire and more resistible. Resentment of aging provides "mental software" for experiencing life's contingencies passively.[74] And cohort naming breaks the sense of life-course continuity, which underlies any hope of generational unity. Thus, although "young people" can become "midlife adults," "Xers" can never become "Boomers." They can only become aging Xers in their turn. This is the culture war that nobody noticed.

AGE STUDIES AND ITS FAMILY VALUES

As members of multigenerational families and as political persons, we can resist age war by refusing to identify ourselves primarily, or at all, as members of named cohorts or (heaven help us) age "subcultures." Each of us gets to choose, after all, how to speak of our multiple identities. In writing as in talking, we can eschew all such terms, even in jest, put them within scare quotes, or, as here, subject them to relentless scrutiny. "Boomer" and "Xer" have become almost unusable. Editors' style sheets ought to forbid such terms unless they come with a justification.

I taught a class of first-year college students in a course called "Culture Matters," where my assignment asked them to find out what the media say "Generation Ys" are. Some came out saying, "I'm supposed to consider myself a 'Y,' but I don't." Others said flatly, "I'm a Y." Ys are being praised in order to disparage the Xers. One subgroup of Xers, the DINKS—double income, no kids—are being set up as the next Goliaths, kitted out to bully the younger Ys. As the mass media move on, Generation Y are the next victims of its meretricious and deceptive "cult" of younger youth. However thoroughly the theorizing class demolishes cohort naming, this frenzy may well continue. For many people, the dominant media provide the *only* draft of history. Can its writers obtain enough intellectual freedom "somehow not to collaborate with the centralizing powers of our society?" in the words of Edward Said. Can they "make the connections that are otherwise hidden"—and investigate their own age politics?[75]

←——→

The stage of life when two generations are in the workforce together can be a long moment of economic strength and mutual support, in which we stress our proud solidarity—kin united by love and concern over the future. Fortunately, the family is at a point in its history when many midlife parents earlier disowned traditional and "oedipal" patterns (filial obligation, children-as-property, sexual jealousy) and raised their offspring in more egalitarian and less rigidly gendered ways. At midlife, such parents feel they deserve a better covenant and embrace the ideal of "becoming equally adults together."[76] So do many of their children. The "individuation" of young adults, coinciding with the time they join the workforce, can be managed in reasonable, humane, nonsexist and connected ways. Having a solid economic premium for experience is compatible with friendship between two adult generations—as long as everyone concerned understands its value. Age hierarchy finds its democratic culmination at this moment, which can last for decades.

The so-called Xer complaint has a hidden emotional core: disappointment that there is not more resistance to "the firestorm" of the New Economy. "No one is coming to rescue our future, not our parents, grandparents, or political leaders,'" Nelson and Cowan wrote plaintively (and self-centeredly) in *Revolution X: A Survival Guide for Our Generation.*[77] If we can demonstrate the spuriousness of blaming parents, we can imagine turning that disappointment into politics. Together we may rescue our *mutual* future.

Building a strong multigenerational front starts at the dinner table long before it begins in school and college classrooms. Whether or not they have children, trusted older figures and younger adults can start the conversation at a new place. By sharing age analysis, we can end the state of ignorance in which these cultural combats occur, undo contrived emotions, invent tactics for resisting the assumptions about age that print and visual culture inculcate. We can develop a grand detailed vision of an age politics. Only as the analysis of age comes to be practiced as widely as the analysis of gender and race can we begin to estimate the long-term negative consequences of using age as a wedge issue and having age terms become such peremptory linguistic categories.

From the dinner table and the classroom we can, if need be, step out together into the street, arm in arm. Adding activism to age consciousness, we can try to save the structures and values on which we must all rely: the age/wage curve, seniority, workforce solidarity, life-course continuity. A first step toward mutual rescue is to unmask the war between "the Xers" and "the Boomers" in all its mendacity and malevolence.

Perilous Parenting

The Deaths of Children and the Fear of Aging-into-the Midlife

Life-course pessimism, so canny, so savage, so intimate with our age apprehensions, so entwined with our secret superstitions, so devious in linking itself to the world's undeniable evils. Inevitably in our culture, writers would shape life storytelling by foregrounding the deaths of children.

←——→

There has been a steady stream of child deaths in North American fiction since 1960, when the publication of John Updike's successful *Rabbit, Run* seemed to give important American writers permission—after a long gulp of hesitation—to appropriate the plot: among them, Updike again (*Rabbit Redux*, 1971), Joseph Heller (*Something Happened*, 1974), Rosellen Brown (*The Autobiography of My Mother*, 1976), John Irving (*The World According to Garp*, 1978), Lynne Sharon Schwartz (*Disturbances in the Field*, 1983), William Kennedy (*Ironweed*, 1983), Lisa Alther (*Other Women*, 1984), Anne Tyler (*The Accidental Tourist*, 1985), Maureen Howard (*Expensive Habits*, 1986), Richard Ford (*The Sportswriter*, 1986), Toni Morrison (*Beloved*, 1987), Oscar Hijuelos (*Mr Ives' Christmas*, 1995), and Barbara Kingsolver (*The Poisonwood Bible*, 1998).[1] In the 1990s, child deaths moved into film. (Add to this a recent and puzzling phenomenon: the deaths of *adult* children in film.)[2] The writer who chooses to plot a story around the death of a child knows its potential to shock and disturb the reader. But leaving aside the esthetic or marketing choices that went into the making of each novel individually, what might be the cultural sources or effects of having the deaths of young children represented by so many major writers at a fairly frequent rate over a period of thirty years, so that cohort after cohort of novel readers is likely to have been exposed?

To answer this, it helps to start by emphasizing the fictitiousness of the event when it is taken up to motivate these plots. Novels involving children who die are not often about the social and economic conditions that cause actual children to die in alarming numbers: infant mortality, inadequate health care, the suicides of adolescents (many gay, lesbian, or bisexual), the murders of teenagers by teenagers in conflicts over drug business, turf, and respect. In one sample of African Americans between the ages of forty and forty-five, almost 10 percent had lost a child, versus 6 percent of non-Hispanic whites.[3] True, Howard's *Expensive Habits* is set in a world of urban criminality: the sixteen-year-old white son, Baby, is stabbed by a Latino burglar in New York City. In the same predictable setting, the seventeen-year-old son of Hijuelos's Mr. Ives is shot by a fourteen-year-old Latino with attitude.

But the other novels with contemporaneous settings deal death to children who are not at such risk: white middle-class children well under the age of majority (several are infants), who have good life chances and life expectancies. Most of the novels were written well before *Boyz 'n the Hood*, Marian Wright Edelman, and the daily news had told mainstream America that the social conditions of parenting were worsening for many low-income people with children. Three of the novels deal with historical risks. The infant death in Kennedy's *Ironweed* is set in the Depression and linked to poverty and drunkenness. The child's death in *The Poisonwood Bible* is the result of a father's obstinacy and religious animosity in a foreign county. The infant death in Morrisons's *Beloved*, set before the Emancipation Proclamation, results from the heroine's intense dread of slavery, and the reader's judgments are contingent on knowing that historical context. But even when specific social, economic, or political problems are causally necessary and important to the author, they are not (as they might be in nonfiction) the focus. The main interest of the death of the child is conceived as domestic and psychological.

In the most sensational cases, all written by men until Morrison's *Beloved*, a parent (usually the father) kills his own child accidentally or is somehow complicit in the child's death. The deaths of children growing up in sheltered circumstances often have to be contrived, but plots that contrive parental complicity are more unlikely than usual. In Heller's *Something Happened*, the son has been slightly wounded in an auto accident, but the father, overreacting and hugging him, smothers him to death. In *Ironweed*, Frances Phelan drops his thirteen-day-old son while changing his diaper, and the infant dies. In *Rabbit, Run*, it's a drunken mother who drowns the infant while giving it a bath, but because her husband has run off and left her, he too is guilty. In *The World According to Garp*, one son dies and another loses an eye in a bizarre accident for which both mother and father can be said to be at fault, but the reader is asked, I believe, to blame the mother more. I think that hostility toward women, who produce children, is involved in these stories where male authors construct plots so that it is women who kill the children (many readers will recall Medea). *Beloved* goes back to the Fugitive Slave Act to find the desperate circumstances in which a mother might be driven to kill her own child. And there is one plot written by a woman in which a grandmother is at fault for the death: Rosellen Brown's *The Autobiography of My Mother*.

On a scale from innocence to guilt, there's a complete range in these novels, from cases where the parents are clearly innocent and doubt it only in the first moment of grief, to cases where they are clearly guilty and know it, with cases of moral ambiguity or fudged responsibility in between. But in a sense that will need to be expanded later, by making the children so young and so vulnerable, all these novels take it that, even in the most innocent, accidental cases, parents are somehow responsible. Always already responsible. That's why the plot can disturb readers so. It starts tremors of apprehension in parents of young children. And in films in which children have reached adulthood safely, the plot decision to kill young adults (Larry McMurtry's *Terms of Endearment*, *Godfather III*, *The Grifters*, *In the Bedroom*) can evoke memories of that earlier fear or startle into life unimagined dangers. In stories that imperil adult children, the possibility of death ratchets up parental dread.

No novelist in this group had, as far as I know, lost a child. But we always want to pay extra attention to plots that strain the mimetic: real psychological pressures (and beyond them, great cultural pressures) must have been at work in their production. I suspect there are many more novels containing or concerning the deaths of children than I have listed. I want to direct attention to what these have in common.

After their fictionality, the next thing to note about this group of novels is that they are not about the children themselves. Often the children have only walk-on parts with few or no lines. In many nineteenth-century novels, the treatment was quite different. Charles Dickens and Louisa May Alcott and other writers gave personalities to the children who would die, and the reader was asked to sit by the deathbed, taught how to behave in a last illness, and led to shed tears for that particular child. We now label such scenes sentimental, and they have vanished from contemporary fiction, depriving us of an emotional outlet and one valuable form of elegy. But the main point here is that it is not now credible for fiction, in our culture, to focus on the death as belonging to the child.

RAISING THE RISK

If these novels are not about the children, whom are they about? As my reference to parental responsibility implied, they're about *us*—the fictional adult character (I or she or he) who stands in for readers as the lightning rod of experience. Then why do authors writing about us kill "our" children? I'm going to try to answer this question, understanding that analyzing culture as it evolves is fraught with complexities. With age culture, these are more intractable than usual.

My theory begins with the idea that whatever various functions the figure of the child serves in this set of novels, the plots fundamentally report on *aging*. In one sense, of course, all plots do. Aging is what characters *do* in narrative, whatever else they appear to do. Paul Ricoeur has said, "Narrativity [is] the language structure that has temporality as its ultimate referent."[4] Put in terms of age studies, "temporality" in fiction is the sense of the movement of time produced by the author's ways of representing the characters' lives in time, especially that of the protagonist. This holds true even if the two times that a narrative contrasts are less than twenty-four hours apart. How characters react to the passing of time—most of all, whether they feared the future initially or welcomed it, and how they feel about it by the end—contributes largely to a novel's attitudes toward aging in this larger sense. Even if a main character doesn't finally learn to fear a blow from the passing of time, the plot may surreptitiously teach us that *we* should.

Often without knowing it, then, we are receiving from fiction constant signals about the life course and the meaning of time's arrow. Even if there is only one indirect mention of a protagonist's age, through its thousands of touches a form as expansive as the novel may establish the effects of personal change, the contents of memory, what events or shocks of the life course are expectable, what reactions to the future are likely and approvable or freaky. In short, novels report on age as well as aging. In this context, aging means into-the-midlife, sometimes only early midlife. Novels in a given era build upon and contribute to, affirm or modify or deny, their culture's life-course imaginaries. This is my term for the simplest and most widely diffused narrative patterns, or arcs. Most people living in the same socioeconomic/symbolic system share some of the available imaginaries, whether they read novels or not. As we've seen, out of these shared patterns children are taught, from them adults borrow meanings, and against them we contrast our own lives. Decline is the imaginary that all these novels threaten.

At the time they were publishing these books, the novelists I'm talking about ranged from age twenty-eight (Updike in 1960) to fifty-six—not old even by the sped-up standards of the late twentieth century. And almost all the characters in the novels are even younger than their creators. It is striking that in the postwar era in North America, someone as young as twenty-eight can have been worrying about aging into the next phase, possibly since adolescence. In fact, even before a person has gotten a first full-time job or a first apartment, the subjective clock has begun audibly ticking. Psychologists know this concern from interviewing young adults, in part by using a "fear-of-aging" scale.[5] (Nota bene: not a "hope-of-aging" scale.) At large in the culture, the idea that people so young fear aging may seem peculiar. Instead of persistently yoking this fear to the end of life and bodily decay, we do better to conceive of aging at any age as an issue of consciousness and a relationship to personal change informed by age culture's devices.

The novel itself has had a major part in constructing the Western vision of the life course, at least for fiction readers. One way of writing this history is to say that during the past two centuries, particularly since 1900, the novel grew up through the life course. In the earlier era, from *Tom Jones* through most of the novels of Austen, Dickens, and Eliot, and up through Harlequin Romances, the novel's main characters have been young, and the crucial event that has served as the marker of adulthood has been their courtship or (if male) their travels. By the marker I mean the event that spelled forward movement in the life course if you achieved it, and implied failure for life if you didn't. The so-called Bildungsroman was actually a Youth Bildungsroman. The date movie—it used to be called "the romance"—is one of its current forms. It is still mostly a youth form, although occasionally a Jack Nicholson is put together with a Helen Hunt to remind us how good it can get for a cranky older male celebrity.

Eventually, however, there began to be novels about what goes on after the youth-ending. At first these over-the-threshold novels were about adultery or the mere threat of adultery. It's notable that as soon as there are novels about even the threat of adultery (or cuckoldry), children are at risk. In Rousseau's *Julie* (1763), the eponymous heroine dies after rescuing her child from drowning, and on her deathbed confesses her repressed love for an erstwhile suitor, whom she was not allowed to marry. Similarly, in Goethe's *Elective Affinities* (1809), a child's death by drowning is one of the punitive outcomes of another repressed adulterous passion. Franco Ferrucci, a literary critic who has studied child death, thinks that earlier writers from Goethe to Mann (all his examples are male) identified their creativity with child figures and that when a child is killed off in their novels, it expresses a man's fear that he is losing precious qualities such as creativity and energy.[6] This confusion—aka allegory—arises from a fear of aging, considered as an exile from the creative peak of the life course. The peak, in this nostalgic, Romantic view, comes in childhood or adolescence or young adulthood.[7]

Since aging past childhood leads most of us, female and male, into a multiplicity of roles and institutional relations and new co-identities, we cannot a priori know what aspect of the life course appeared so terrifying in a particular adult writer's retrospect of his youthful anticipations. Sexuality is a good first guess. Just as in the nineteenth century, many late-twentieth-century novels about young adulthood still express guilt or a warning about sexuality. Although our era is considered sexually freer, most people over the past forty years have traveled through sex-starved and/or sex-obsessed periods. We can read into fiction or draw from fiction many different (and most often gendered) anxieties: the awareness that sexuality is hedged with social restrictions, the prospect (in certain classes and temperaments) that sex after marriage is likely to involve transgression; the belief that punishment *should* follow sexual wrongdoing.

Nowadays, arousing vicarious guilt requires a plot in which real adultery rather than heavy flirting precedes the child's death. *Rabbit, Run* has such a plot and so does *The World According to Garp*. In the first case, it is the man's sexuality that is dangerous and needs to be controlled, and in the second, although the man has had affairs (treated as mere harmless flings), it is the woman's adultery that causes the trouble and is dreadfully punished. But today, many people in our culture have thrown away the links between sex and sin, sin and punishment, and death. In general, the children being killed off in fiction are increasingly unlikely to figure as instruments through which parents are punished for sexual offenses. Writers write, and readers read, in quite historically specific and, at times, rapidly changing contexts of values and assumptions.

Instead, the kids now more often figure as signs of the burdensome responsibility of adulthood, a common fate. Novels concerning the deaths of preadult children construct and reinforce the notion that the scary process of child tending begins at the birth of the vulnerable infant and goes on until sixteen or eighteen years later—at whatever age the child becomes responsible for herself or himself.[8] These novels imply that our culture envisions the middle of the life course as a period of perilous parenting. Once this connection is generally established in the culture, of course, a writer need not be a parent to use the material. It could be said that the theme of the death of the child is part of the price we pay (some may decide that it's part of the gain we get) for the fact that fiction has now finally written itself into this later arena of the life course. Novels often need risks that the rest of us are happy to avoid.

In case some think the focus on *this* risk perfectly "natural," let me point out that fiction could conceive of adulthood's troubles quite otherwise. Not all adults marry or raise children. If risk is wanted, there's no end of others. There's job loss, as in *Death of a Salesman* or Donald Westlake's *The Ax,* or nuclear holocaust, as in Carolyn See's *Golden Days.* Novels could conceive of this span as primarily solitary, spousal, fraternal, or filial rather than parental. Or the protagonist's love, care, and dread could go toward kin, a community, foreigners.

But in such midlife fictions, the death of an underage child seems most urgent. Children in these novels are irreplaceable in a way that no other human being can be. Caring for them is obligatory. The loss of a child can presumably be read by all novel readers, even those without children, as an unmitigated loss. For this well-known subset of novels, the worst "unscheduled event" has its source in the generation we produce and are responsible for. Why do we need to read about this more now, in the last thirty years?

←——————→

Novels about the deaths of children utilize more than normal anxiety about parenting and then heighten it further. Normal anxiety about parenting responsibility and caretaking and adult unreadiness produces a different plot, less intense and dramatic—plots like those Margaret Drabble and Anne Tyler produced in their young adulthood, in the '60s and '70s: Drabble's *The Garrick Year* (1964) and *The Millstone* (1965); Tyler's *Celestial Navigation* (1974) and *Earthly Possessions* (1977). These novels are about women who cope. Maybe the babies *almost* die: in *The Garrick Year* they are almost asphyxiated, and little Flora falls into the river, but both times the children are saved—by their mother. She gives up a tasty adultery so she can fix her full attention on her children. Tyler seems to have taught herself how durable babies are. After her second novel, *The Tin Can Tree,* she does not put them at risk, but she certainly gives a complete picture of the unremitting attention they require: the paraphernalia of childhood lead to all the thickenings of life.[9] But these are novels about being good-enough mothers: adults who find through practice that they are capable mums. Women survive parenting handily. Fathers scarcely have a role, but mothers can manage even alone. This is adult fiction in which through aging-into-parenting, women become independent, competent, and successful at a central life-course task. Later on, as the cultural risk became having adult children leave the "nest," Drabble and Tyler each wrote postmaternal novels from the point of view of the mothers. The women protagonists are not invariably successful at forming friendships with their offspring, but they are never guilty: Tyler in *Searching for Caleb* (in 1975, when her children were in fact not yet in their teens) and in *Breathing Lessons* (1988) and Drabble in *The Middle Ground* (1980).

Plots in which children die, on the other hand, emphasize the vulnerability of everyone concerned. They heighten the sense of risk that comes from proceeding even this far in the life course. They are contemporary expansions of Francis Bacon's saying (so mysterious to me when I was younger) that children serve as "hostages to fortune." These novels assert that we ourselves create terrible risk and are thus to some degree responsible for dreadful consequences even when they are out of our control. High responsibility, low control is a recipe for excessive strain, whether in parenting or in paid work.[10]

Danger begins with the arrival of the vulnerable child. "I was responsible for the survival of this creature," Lynne Sharon Schwartz's heroine says (ominously) when her first is born.[11] When Tyler's Macon Leary starts fathering again, a child not biologically his own, he feels

> a pleasant kind of sorrow sweeping through him. Oh, his life had regained all its old perils. He was forced to worry once again about nuclear war and the future of the planet. He often had the same secret, guilty thought that had come to him after Ethan was born: From this time on I can never be completely happy.
>
> Not that he ever was before, of course.[12]

In *Beloved*, Sethe decides not to have another baby: "mostly she was frightened by the thought of having a baby once more. Needing to be good enough, alert enough, strong enough, *that* caring—again. Having to stay alive just that much longer. O Lord, she thought, deliver me. Unless carefree, motherlove was a killer."[13] We don't realize at this point how ambiguous her wording is.

In these fictions, the most anxious parents are the very ones who kill their children; anxiety itself kills. In *Beloved*, Sethe, only twenty-eight days escaped from slavery, fears the future for her children so much that she hastily tries to kill all of them when the slavers arrive to drag them back into humiliation and suffering. Hers is the most rational anxiety: there was no way to know in 1855 that if she let Beloved live as a slave, the Emancipation Proclamation would free her while she was still a child. But other novels show that the peril for parent and child is created by exaggerated fear. In John Irving's *The World According to Garp*, this becomes explicit in one of Garp's own stories: "The World According to Bensenhaver is about a man who is so fearful of bad things happening to his loved ones that he creates an atmosphere of such tension that bad things are almost certain to occur."[14] Male fear of not coping with the responsibilities of adulthood would seem to account for the father-caused death in *Something Happened* and indirectly for those in *Rabbit, Run* and that other runaway's story, *Ironweed*.

If we revise classic psychoanalysis, we arrive at a related, more disturbing explanation for why parentlove can be a "killer," especially for fathers. Some parents repress a fear that a new child means a kind of death for themselves. To avoid this possibility, the child has to be killed first—a preemptive strike. This is what Laius tried to do when he heard from the oracle that his son Oedipus would grow up to kill him: he had Oedipus put out on the mountain to die. The oracle voices a new father's anxiety for himself, a fear that something awful and uncontrollable will happen in the future. In *Something Happened,* when Bob Slocum gets angry at his nine-year-old son, he says explicitly, "I wanted to kill him. . . . That's the part they all leave out of the Oedipus story." [15] Male writers revising the Oedipus story allow us to locate the source of the tragedy in the Laius complex. Male midlife subjectivity dramatically moved the psychic center of the life course from childhood to its own time of life. (As that shift occured, Freud's oedipal fable was losing its totalizing power, to become one more competing story of the way baby boys develop.) [16]

Ambivalence about children is certainly not limited to men, who until recently in our culture have been distanced from children and have also deprived themselves of the remarkable life-course benefits that derive from parenting. Pregnant women often have severe ambivalence about becoming mothers. Being a mother of young children on the typically intensive American model creates ambivalence too (small wonder). The gender-based difference—and advantage—is that women, in most cases, cannot escape the unremitting hourly, daily, activity and attentiveness to children's developing capacities (and their own) that helps to overcome irrational anxiety. Some women writers, living close to poverty during their child-rearing years, may on this account have faced or dismissed other reasonable but nebulous fears in their fiction, as Grace Paley has done. Women's double dose of reality may begin to explain why the *Rabbit, Run*s and *Something Happened*s and *Garp*s have male authors.

The high level of anxiety in these novels gets transformed by the plot of death and its sequelae into fear of time. In some novels this is historical time, which unites the characters' lives with group or national or global destinies, but, with exceptions already noted, history is underreported in highly individualized and family-centered dramas. "Time," through the curious twists I am examining, comes to mean "aging" in its common sense of the probability of experiencing decline and loss. In our age culture, this can be recognized as the anticipation that something awful and uncontrollable will happen in one's *personal* future. In narrative, it's produced by suspense confirmed by disaster.

In our cultural conjuncture, with aging backing down the life course, it is perfectly expectable that some writers will abbreviate the entire parental journey at the very outset. (In Donald Hall's poem "My Son My Executioner," the parents who "start to die together" when their baby is born are twenty-five and twenty-two.) [17] Consciousness of mortality was once a high-art theme, but this kind of speed-up fits into portraits of ordinary domestic life. The birth of a baby, the rearing of a toddler, the development of an adolescent child—or mere apprehension about these events—can be confused with floating unnamed fears and oppressive experiences that have nothing to do with children.

I'm talking about displacement—how it works in novels about the deaths of children and in our own minds as adults. Anything that makes adult responsibility feel long and too hard to bear can be displaced onto individual aging-as-decline. Anything: idiosyncratic losses, like the end of an affair or the failure of an enterprise. Widely shared social problems: lack of day care; the defunding of public schools, the cost of raising kids to adulthood (a repeated theme in the mainstream press, which prints the staggering dollar amounts that my generation of parents never knew), teenage pregnancy, AIDS, debt; the proletarianization of middle-class professional jobs, the destruction of smokestack industry, a growing two-tier economy, government carelessness about the safety nets that cushion suffering; or any of the other crises of the '70s, '80s, and '90s that impinged on the author or the reader. Displacement occurs when tangible factors like these are omitted from novels, as they can be excluded from ordinary consciousness. Children's death books can convey and trigger a range of inchoate anxieties about personal decline insofar as their pure concentration on sorrow for the lost child puts any other considerations in the shade. One could argue that readers need such works as the objective correlative of their own necessary losses: they are consoled, or can dwell awhile in self-pitying and healing pain. But displacement may help conceal something *un*necessary in their losses.

One final feeling that can get displaced onto the aging of fictional characters is being aged by culture. If feeling "older," for whatever combination of private and cultural reasons, becomes dreadful, some writers will deal with it by reaching for a young-adult or midlife disaster plot, and kill children. We can't be surprised that women too have produced novels about the deaths of children. Women certainly can have plenty of reasons to feel that their aging is negatively charged—that they are being "punished" discursively, sexually, or economically for aging-past-youth. And mothering is both an experience of responsibility in high-risk circumstances and a trope for it. Even less will readers be surprised that some women produce novels in which the surviving mothers are not allowed to recover.

AFTER THE WORST

When authors kill children, they construct the question, "Can I survive the worst that life can shove at me?" When a plot acutely poses this question as "Is time on my side or against me?" in our culture the reader demands an answer to another question very closely allied but not exactly the same, "Should I damn aging or value it?"

Novels are presumed to deliver a universal answer, an answer good for every case. If we look to these novels, they can be divided roughly into two tracks on the basis of what happens after the death of the child. Recovery novels, however painful and elegiac, are a form of progress narrative.[18] They show protagonists surviving the harsh events encountered as time passes and demonstrating some continuity of selfhood. Decline novels convey little more than the fear of aging. The existence of borderline outcomes complicates the issues (I come back to mixed genres at the end of this discussion) but should not obscure a rather binary division on the question of "survival": that is, on whether a person can recover from the worst and begin life again, and perhaps even recognize that she or he has recovered.

The narratives I prefer in the current conjuncture are the literary cure stories. I hope to justify this preference—not on the grounds that meliorism is per se for each of us a better belief and attitude than pessimism's quiescence—although I do believe it is, as do (according to therapists) most therapists, and most activists. Rather, I start by making a case that the cure stories walk us through the condition of grief and loss with more imaginative completeness. Their fuller accounts include the experiences of believing that one will have to live permanently in a state of loss—and outliving that feeling. (Meliorism deals with pessimism more persuasively than pessimism can ever deal with meliorism.) Most cure novels exclude the parents' reception of the news of the death of the child. But even the recovery novels that exclude that first and perhaps worst moment of loss nevertheless also tell us what mourning is like afterward and how to deal with it.

Recovery plots do not hustle us into consolation, as some people think the culture at large does: They're not "positive." They say instead what Frank Bascombe says at the end of *The Sportswriter,* looking back at the four years since his son died. "Grief, real grief, is relatively short, though mourning can be long."[19] No recovery novel recommends oblivion; on the contrary, they all value memory. But they trust time, or rather aging. They count on it to bring relief from the most hurtful parts of loss: the self-blame and the ingenious self-punishments, the irrational anger at a spouse; the sense that nothing of one's self is left (that one's identity is constituted solely by being a parent), the inability to enjoy, the shock of the rediscovery of loss over and over. Novels that describe recovery admire the human spirit and often its multiple selves. They show that we have big shoulders. Novels with older characters who have aged and suffered and yet have resilience in the face of the worst vicissitudes of adult life, carry considerable conviction. Even in our culture, these subversive texts whisper, when the going gets tough, it helps to have aged a little. At thirty-four,

Updike described as a discovery an observation he had made, via aging, about aging. "We do survive every minute, after all, except the last." [20]

Decline narrative doesn't say right out that we succumb. It isn't heavy on falsifiable expository comment. But it implies directionality by various narrative strategies. One of these strategies is to end right after the death of the child—still in the nightmare, before any healing has begun. In *The Autobiography of My Mother*, Rosellen Brown has the protagonist's only child vanish into an abyss only three pages before the end. The grandmother should have been holding the four-year-old's hand. Just before the child vanishes, the mother shouts to the grandmother to hold onto the child, but she isn't heard above the circumambient noise. The three pages left don't provide space even for the beginning of grief. They don't try to: they're holding us in the shock of the first moment. There's only enough time for the protagonist to get an awful kind of revenge on her seventy-two-year-old mother. The daughter has always been a "mess"; the mother is a respected lawyer, well organized but chilly. The revenge, in the last page, is to see her mother, no longer omnipotent but guilty at last, collapse and cry. The daughter's self-pitying helplessness is another revenge. It's also a prognostication about her life course: My life fails forever because you failed me and you continue to fail me, and now it's your fault I don't have my daughter: there wasn't much before and now there's nothing at all. How can I bear to survive adulthood?

Something Happened also ends shortly after the doctors tell Bob Slocum that his boy would have lived if Bob had not smothered him. The child's death illustrates the adult's neurotic identification with him. Slocum has told us that the "the boy" (whom he never calls by name) is the only person he truly loves. He too has put all his eggs in this one basket. "I have this constant fear something is going to happen to him. . . . I think about death. I think about it all the time. I dwell on it. I dread it. I don't really like it" (321). Even the boy's tonsillectomy was a narcissistic horror for Bob: he had to leave the boy alone at night in order to try to escape from the child's pain. "I identify with him too closely, I think" (317). What he identifies with is the child's vulnerability—not his sweetness or docility, but his failures at school, his fear of the dark, the way he expects the worst from time and longs to have it come "just to get it over with" (205).

The likeness between them almost makes one think that Slocum needs his son to die to kill his own (our own) midlife vulnerability magically by proxy. Heller shows us that for Slocum, the child figure signifies not creativity, but weakness. Before the boy's death, Slocum already feels guilty. "I think I'm in terrible trouble. I think I've committed a crime. The victims have always been children" (519). In *Rabbit Redux*, three years earlier, Updike's title character had recognized a similar guilt: "He knows he is criminal, yet is never caught." [21] Indeed, Heller could have been talking about the two first Rabbit novels—and forecasting the whole genre of adults stressed by responsibility—when Slocum notices that the victims are always children. If one weak small victim dies, will the grownup be less weak and small? In the few pages after the boy's death, Slocum achieves all his financial and status ambitions, but of course none of it matters any more.

I think writers should consider a moratorium on killing a child in, say, the last quarter of a novel, not to mention any closer to the last page. Such a plot structure not only refuses to conceptualize recovery, it can barely register grief. Its tones after the untimely death are fictional equivalents of shocked silence: the blank page or the intentionally inadequate response: Heller's "I miss him." The implication is that this state of absolute loss is what goes on forever. Worse, like thrillers, such a fictional structure can be filled with fearful anticipation all the way along, up until the death occurs or is revealed. Even if the death occurs relatively early in the novel, room can be made to construct fearful anticipation. In *Rabbit, Run*, as soon as Janice gets drunk and decides to give the baby a bath, every reader knows what will happen. There are some excruciating pages to get through, as we approach the inevitable with horror and aversion. (A friend of mine with a first baby closed the book at this point and didn't pick it up again for twenty years.)

Disturbances in the Field is ultimately a moving recovery novel, but the first half is full of classic decline elements. Retrospective dread foreshadows some awful event. "Everything had the chance to be so beautiful, and look what has happened"(29), the narrator moans, when nothing has yet happened, and Schwartz won't let her tell us for another 150 pages. Hopes do not come true. At one point, at a pot party, Schwartz's Lydia Rowe imagines her midlife-to-come as a relatively "safe" space of life. "Perhaps my greatest problem would be boredom . . . the relief of growing up and believing that . . . things will happen, but you will be so ripe with experience as to be unable to feel wonder or terror, knowing that anything is possible and everything finally subsides. That was what I thought, high and ignorant, in Nina's purple apartment" (177).

We're being warned to level down our hope and bring up our anxiety level; as another character says, "You can't afford to get overconfident when you're hot. The gods don't like that" (155). As if an attitude like midlife self-sufficiency (which was being advocated by the feminist movement, anti-ageism, and psychotherapy) could itself call down punishment. One page after she has dared to say that she will be unable to feel "wonder or terror," two of Lydia's four children die. That's as quick as retribution comes in fiction. Not sexual sin but *trust*—normal modest trust in the "ripeness of experience"—can be the crime in our age ideology. If Schwartz had made this explicit—as a novelist who was an age critic might want to do now, thirty years later—it would have been a devastating critique. And yet Lydia recovers: so that while half the plot punishes her crudely for anticipating midlife "safety," the overall structure recovers equilibrium. By midlife people usually have learned that fears don't all come true.

Even parents discard anxieties as their children grow beyond the period when they were appropriate.

Decline novels force us through the same fictional experience of time as recovery narratives, that fears come true and hopes do not. But they maintain the dread, keeping it fixed on the future as that over which we have lost control. Their pessimism is superstitious. If you want to be safe, anticipate the worst. Don't cheat by trusting your powers; *really* despair. Decline narratives are advisories about how to scam the future psychologically. Along the way they opportunistically haul in what is scary about the innocent dying in the affluent First World in the century of public health advances and Dr. Spock. A sensitive reader is washed in helplessness over a fictitious loss, while in another part of her mind, her displaced forebodings churn on, unnamed and unhindered. Such novels construct passivity by picking a situation where there *is* nothing for adult responsibility to do.

Many readers love and admire *Disturbances in the Field.* I think this may be gratitude because the novel opens up a small space in which it makes partly conscious the irrationality inherent in decline's pessimism. Lydia remains observant, and Schwartz's style intelligent, even soon after the worst. The recovery novel at its best doesn't reward passivity even when it shows that we can't control everything. We have no magic powers, as we may have thought when younger. Our children may die, but not because we wanted them to.

SLOW TIME

Time is a friend in recovery novels, restoring the energy we need in order to confront crimes against the life course or any other resistible evil. But friendship can work slowly. In most of my examples—*Disturbances in the Field* is an exception—the death occurred years before the novel opens, sometimes ten or twenty years before, giving the protagonists a long retrospect. These recovery narratives are constructed so that the accident or the crime occurred in the protagonist's passionate, dangerous younger adulthood, while the healing takes place in a more contemplative midlife. These are, just barely, safe-at-last stories. Francis Phelan in *Ironweed* dropped his baby and left his home twenty-two years before. It takes that long before he can bear to remember Gerald and think about his other crimes; then in two days at the age of fifty-eight, he absolves himself and stops trying to run or die. Sethe in *Beloved* killed her baby when she was nineteen; having punished herself for eighteen years by solitude, celibacy, and forgetfulness, at thirty-seven, with the help of a lover, she finds the courage to make a good wish for herself. She decides she wants "to launch her newer, stronger life with a tender man" (99). It takes a long novel to chronicle the process: she must remember, expiate, forgive herself, exorcise the ghost of the murdered baby, reintegrate herself into the community. Only on the very last page does it appear that she will recover. Sethe has said that her memory of her daughter was her "best thing," and her lover, touching her face, answers, "You your best thing, Sethe, you are" (273) and she responds, doubtingly, "Me? Me?" The first stage in recovery could be self-trust, believing we are worthy to survive.

Hannah Burke, the sixtyish therapist in *Other Women* whose children died several decades before, finds that she has been punishing herself unknowingly. She has deprived herself of the risk of new relationships because of an unconscious fear of "the inevitable aftermath": withdrawal. Her cure at sixty takes the risky form of making a friend who is the age her lost daughter would have been. As a therapist, she argues most wryly and explicitly for the value of time. The passage reads: "What about her own despair? It didn't seem to be around much anymore. . . . The older she got, the less anything could upset her for very long. Maybe the only real cure for her clients was the aging process. But that could take years" (230).

Even where recovery does not take so long, midlife protagonists can be grateful to time. As Lydia's marriage to Victor begins to disintegrate because they mourn so differently, she prophesies, "This land of ours, coarsened by blight, cannot endure. It's only a matter of time" (241). And they do separate. But other things too are a matter of time: Lydia buys a coloring book, one of the ways she already knows of making herself feel that she can get things back within their proper lines. She starts playing music again; she calls friends; after a while she plans to ride on buses—and eventually she wants her husband back, and he returns. When you start using the strengths of your multiple identities in your favor, the healing process is underway. Where decline narratives threaten parents and nonparents alike, recovery novels are written as if to sufferers of any loss, offering practices of healing.

Recovery novels differ in showing how active their characters can be in managing grief, regaining control, restoring self-esteem. Updike treats recovery as a rather passive process. Ten years after Janice Angstrom drowned her baby, she acknowledges "that was terrible, the most terrible thing ever, but even that had faded, flattened, until it seemed it hadn't been her in that room but an image of her, and she had not been alone, there had been some man in the room with her" (*Rabbit Redux*, 54). Ten years after the other death for which he is partly responsible, Harry Angstrom in *Rabbit Is Rich* thinks, "But the years have piled on, the surviving have patched things up, and so many more have joined the dead, undone by diseases for which only God is to blame, that it no longer seems so bad, it seems more as if Jill just moved to another town, where the population is growing." [22] The recoveries happen *between* the novels (which Updike in fact wrote ten years apart), so that we don't see the intermediate stages of the cure. It looks all the more as if aging itself has done the trick.

The Sportswriter makes Frank Bascombe a self-conscious, generalizing optimist: a man who goes into his familiar mental gymnastics whenever anything bad happens to him. It is open to us to believe that he has learned these routines from the process of surviving his little boy's death. "All we really want is to get to the point where the past can explain nothing about us and we can get on with our life. . . . [Most pasts] should be just uninteresting enough to release you the instant you're ready (though it's true that when we get to that moment we are often scared to death, feel naked as snakes and have nothing to say)" (24). In the end, Frank expresses a belief in the future that has him sounding, in his grungy, hedged way, something like Drabble's rhapsodic heroine in the final pages of *The Middle Ground.* "There is mystery everywhere, even in a vulgar, urine-scented, suburban depot such as this. You have only to let yourself in for it. You can never know what's coming next. Always there is the chance it will be—miraculous to say—something you want" (342).

Less self-conscious mental manipulations appear in the recovery narratives of other writers. Thus, in Lisa Alther's *Other Women,* after Hannah Burke's surviving children have grown up and left, she could use this to create a catalog of postmaternal, postmenopausal losses she has suffered. Instead she transforms her feelings: "Occasionally she felt lonely, but it was easy to convert that into a sense of delicious solitude." [23] No progress novelist treats such conversions for the sake of recovery ironically; many admit a category of what we might call valuable illusions. To help console himself for his son's death, Macon Leary in *The Accidental Tourist* creates an image of Ethan aging in heaven.

> And if dead people aged, wouldn't it be a comfort? To think of Ethan growing up in heaven—fourteen years old now instead of twelve—eased the grief a little. . . . The real adventure, he thought, is the flow of time; it's as much adventure as anyone could wish. And if he pictured Ethan still part of that flow—in some other place, however unreachable—he believed he might be able to bear it after all. (354)

By giving his son an independent, parallel life, Macon gives himself permission to have such a life: it marks one end within the ongoing continuum of mourning. The recovery novel uses its painful subject to invent ways of imagining a life we might still want after loss.

←——→

Oscar Hijuelos's *Mr. Ives' Christmas* floats between the genres of decline and recovery for most of its length, challenging this binary from curious directions.

The death of Ives's seventeen-year-old son occurred when the father was forty-eight, and we learn about its having happened in the first pages. This placement hints that this is going to be a recovery story—perhaps the slowest of them all. Yet the pivotal sentence of the book in this context is, "but for Ives, Robert's death had become the defining event of his middle-aged life."[24] What a salutary shock explicitness gives, when typically the connections with decline are shadowy, irrational, immeasurable—and thus unarguable. As time passes, Ives loses his faith, his joy in the world, his interest in love. In such ways, the novel appears to support unmourned loss as Ives's truth, and really, the only truth possible.

But—and this is why I save it for last—the novel ultimately has the curious indirect effect of commenting not just on its own explicit judgment of midlife but on all summations made in the shadow of intense events. Hijuelos carries his protagonist into old age, so that it is not a midlife novel (another reason to treat the book apart) but a retrospect written from very near the end. Its last comment appears to be that, although of course people have the right to sum up their life's narrative to date at any age, middle age is too young to decide on life's defining events.

Somehow, without much drama, Ives regains his simple faith. Although he is incapable of acting on his own behalf to change the judgment he made ("self-help" is beyond him), his tenor of life mysteriously changes it. Although his later life is not as rich as he once had the right to expect, neither is it a collapse of all value. Ives's earlier summation isn't dismissed, but the sense in which he qualified it himself at the time becomes meaningful. In fact, what saves Hijuelos's "Un coeur simple" is the explicitness of that single sentence. Read the first time, "his middle-aged life" seemed to mean something close to "his destroyed life." But retrospectively, "middle-aged" was not an epithet, only an acknowledgment of a place in the life course. That judgment was, of course, only the view from his "middle-aged life." It may have been inarguable at the time, but it wasn't final. It is as if, because his religion refuses to deny the future, faith prevents a believer from falling into decline's distracted ventriloquy. Explicitness turns out to be a grace of language, reason's salvation, recovery's truth.

By showing recovery coming in time, the "antidecline" novel manages—sometimes almost imperceptibly—to put time on our side. Once we know that, we put ourselves on the side of time. We may thus find ourselves, to our fine surprise, also praising aging.

←——→

Instituting a moratorium on killing children in the last pages of novels is neither in my power nor one of my long-term goals. But suggesting it is another way to shock readers into holding certain skeptical concepts in their minds long enough for the ideas to become more familiar: that psychic wounds and social grievances get displaced onto midlife aging, and that fictions of the later life course per se are not only *not* solutions to problems of generations, aging, and the future, but may misstate the problems and distract us from our real cultural quandaries.

No revolution in age-consciousness can occur unless writers participate. They may at first hesitate to disentangle different kinds of pain, assuming that intensity comes from there and knowing intensity is their prize. But perhaps they can achieve that prize in other ways. Perhaps some will decide they can no longer live with metaphoric collapses and representational breakdowns—the train wrecks of being aged by culture without knowing it. One intermediate effect of age studies might be that responsible writers poised over narrative decisions would think more critically about their own age-related contexts and motives and internalizations, and finally, about the consequences of their narrative choices in an intertextual world where discourse shapes the consciousness of others. If "blackness" has been changing in the white imagination (and the black), if "woman" is now changing in the male imagination (and the female), then "midlife aging," and indeed "aging" altogether, can begin to change in the imaginations of all of us.

The High Costs of Middle-Ageism

Middle-ageism is a one-two punch. Age ideology assails its victims in narratives and images—coming at us surprisingly often from the direction of the family, as many chapters have shown. And such assaults on individual well-being, social status, and confidence in the future are given brass knuckles by the economic system. I'm not an economist but an age critic who became curious about the economics of the worklife. What have been the effects on people in their middle years (still a privileged time of life in some ways) of speed-up, downsizing, outsourcing, capital flights, technological advances, and court decisions that permit midlife discrimination? Economists have not, as far as I can tell, produced studies that answer this question. Such forces affect people of all ages, it is true. They are the outcomes of vast economic and political developments: corporate attempts to be globally competitive by gaining more power over labor, and "a conscious, decided shift of national policy designed to unleash market forces."[1] Perhaps this chapter will encourage more concentration on the immense ramifications of midlife vulnerability.

In the labor market, the power of employers over employees has been magnified at that point in working life—the middle years—when employees traditionally have most to offer and most to lose. Relevant data that I have collected suggest that over many decades (even prior to the market collapse of 2000 and the recession) the economic value of aging-into-the-midlife has been eroding for many while all concerned are being trained not to expect better. Millions of Americans in their middle years experience job insecurity, part-time "flexible" work without benefits, longer unemployment, early forced "retirement." Those in the danger zone are testing their midlife reality against the American Dream in an era of premature superannuation. As it happens, they include the first wave of the postwar Baby Boom: the "aging Boomers" who have been promised automatic advantages from turning fifty: the dismantling of sexist ageism, power over the media, wealth. This is, to my ears, derisive.

The "midlife" is not an innocent "fact of life." It is an ideological construct fraught with consequences for selfhood, life-course narrative, families, the workforce, democratic society, and the economic and political systems. We need to understand much more clearly how this construct is being manipulated. In this chapter, I try to estimate the total costs to the nation of the economic trends that point to loss. When enough midlifers lose, it jeopardizes not only their futures and their children's but also the future of everyone who follows them. If middle-ageism becomes institutionalized for increasing portions of the workforce, the midlife will lose more status and the life course as we know it may be irrevocably changed. That's why the *agon* is occurring *there*. We can be facing right toward the elephant—particularly if we're holding the bullish business pages up against our face—and still miss it.

CONSTRUCTING FEAR OF FIFTY

Losing Work

"The decrease in the age of exit from gainful work has been one of the most profound structural changes in the past 25 years. It has occurred . . . in all Western societies," according to Martin Kohli and Martin Rein, two of the editors of a magisterial cross-cultural study of premature superannuation.[2] Data now suggest that full-time work is gradually becoming a privilege denied to midlife women and men in the United States, with fifty being the crucial turning point even for well-educated men. In the mid-1960s, only five out of every thousand men as young as fifty to fifty-four years old were not working. In a 1987–88 sample measured the other way around, only 77 percent of white men were employed full time at the same age; more than one out of five was not.[3] "Participation rates," as they are called, are considered an index of exit from the labor market but in fact "underestimate its real extent."[4]

Some of the privileged ostentatiously choose leisure after fifty, but company programs for "early retirement" are not always "voluntary"—that is, for workers in poor health or wanting more freedom. Formerly called "termination programs," they are typically devised to get rid of these relatively young but higher-waged employees.[5] Between 1993 and 1995—before the big bubble but within the period referred to in the mainstream as the "long economic recovery"—7.4 percent of all working men aged forty-five to fifty-five were "displaced" (economists use this to mean that they did not leave voluntarily). Of men in professional and managerial positions between those ages, the best protected class, 5.5 percent were displaced. Women of this age were actually treated slightly less badly—perhaps because they cost less to retain. Still, 6 percent of women forty-five to fifty-five were displaced, and 5.3 percent of professional and managerial women.[6]

We want to pay particular attention in the data to the effects of these economic trends on the category quaintly called "median men." Since the wages of women and black men at the midlife median are historically only a percentage of such men's earnings, the public should be following much more closely what is happening to those men and to college-educated men in particular, who are mainly white. As soon as these once privileged classes can be harmed in new ways (by lower workforce participation, continuing real-income declines, or less wealth accumulation), the rest of the population is less likely to be spared.

The media's focus on Angry White Men (for a while identified with militias) was actually a red herring. It implied that deindustrialization was the major cause of midlife displacement (and deindustrialization was a hopeless rusty story), that only the male working class was injured, that only kooks would be angry, and that anger could lead only to terrorism. Many of us know someone who is not a terrorist who had accrued substantial seniority but still lost that once-secure job at good wages with benefits, someone who has searched fruitlessly even for lateral mobility and settled into subemployment. Their hard lot has not been seen clearly; they tend to be silent about being axed. Among all workers exiting before age fifty-five, only 14 percent received any kind of employer pension (including private-sector, government, or military). Most of those receiving pensions are men: 44 percent of married men exiting before fifty-five received an employer pension compared with only 7 percent of married women.[7] Midlife single women had a significantly higher poverty rate, at 27.4 percent, than other women.[8] A staffer at the Massachusetts Commission against Discrimination told me that at Westinghouse a woman had been fired two weeks before she would have been vested in her pension. She killed herself. Only a third of the unemployed qualify for unemployment benefits, which in any case last only a short time. Many people lose their health insurance.

Midlife discrimination complaints to the EEOC are rising rapidly, from fourteen thousand in 1999 to sixteen thousand a year later.[9] Most midlife-discrimination claimants have been white males, and more than 50 percent are professionals or managers. Women's complaints have gone up to 36 percent of the total; and though the age of claimants has been dropping in general, the women are younger than the men.[10]

Like the Supreme Court siding with employer power, some state judges handling suits have been deciding that employers may legally fire workers *because* they are high-salaried, without other cause. What midlife workers experience as they job hunt is not a glass ceiling but "the industrial equivalent of capital punishment."[11] It takes longer to find a new job. In the summer of 2001 (which was before the bombing of the World Trade Center and the worsening of the recession), the median duration of job seeking was 6.5 weeks for those twenty-five to thirty-four compared to 10.6 weeks for those fifty-five to sixty-four.[12] Those who do find jobs again typically recover only a percentage of their salaries (those Blockbuster jobs); some need two jobs. By contrast, when younger workers are rehired they tend to receive higher pay.[13]

Looking around at the bewildering postmodern economy, at a time when the market was still climbing, 46 percent of the entire workforce feared losing current employment, according to Alan Greenspan.[14] For people at midlife as unemployment rises, fear can reasonably verge on dread.

The Age / Wage Curve

Aging-into-the-midlife in America is *supposed* to mean a curve of earnings that rises. And income should be highest at midlife if need is the moral criterion, since midlife can be the neediest time in the family life course. When a midlife worker's income flattens or declines, that shortfall often crushes the family's long-term ambitions. Children cost more as they age into adolescence. They know that the penalties for earning only a high-school diploma have drastically increased, and that if they are able to attend college they may enter the job market with high debts. They rely on parents to boost them into the workforce. Parents, especially single mothers, need rising wages, particularly if they want to provide higher education in a time of skyrocketing tuition and decreasing scholarship aid. The tensions in families with teenagers can be agonizing. The food pantries in the suburbs show hunger rising up the class ladder. For the immiserated it can be a time of despair. Doing a report on CETA for Congressman Drinan in 1974, I interviewed a gaunt black man, father of four, being knocked off his one-year job, who said bitterly, "I can't put my body on the table to feed them." One fictional response to scarcity that refuses such helpless bitterness is Donald Westlake's thriller *The Ax* (1997). Having been fired, the white-collar protagonist, a married man who is the father of a teenage child, coolly sets about murdering all the men he knows will be competitors for the single job in his field that is about to open up.[15]

The stresses do not necessarily end because children are old enough to be in the workforce. Parents want to help adult children start out as well as save for their own retirement. They may also need to help their own parents. Family income can be highest when two generations are in the workforce—a blessed relief after years of high dependency. But now, more and more, the older generation is being forced down or out while the younger has yet to find its niche. In the same 1993–95 recovery period, almost 10 percent of workers in their twenties were also displaced. When I hear a postparental voice say, "You can't be happier than your unhappiest child," I think of the helpless pain the first time your child is laid off. And the second. In addition, some of those young people had parents who lost jobs. The adult children rebound while their parent sits home over the want ads for another month. And the afterlife of those displaced at midlife? Why haven't we heard the painful true stories (as well as the relieved progress narratives like Snyder's *Cliff Walk*), and learned the consequences in intergenerational misery, lost self-esteem, lost leadership at work?

A steep rise on the age/wage curve once betokened a white male middle-class life course, what was really signified by the word "career." Entering a "career" implied some security and the likelihood that your remuneration would rise substantially through most of your midlife. You would become more "valuable" (now we are led to say "productive," with its threat of quantification) with age. Although each employee might personally need to justify his raise, at some deeper level beneath individual performance there was an expectation of progressive wage increments. This progress narrative could be described as a stout residue of patriarchy, if patriarchy is understood as the age system that privileged midlife men ("the fathers") over younger men ("the sons"), the class system that privileged the middle class, the race system that privileged whites, and the gender system that required touting a "family wage" to maintain male dominance and keep women out of the workforce. On both sides, where patriarchy worked, economic actors were predisposed to expect employees' wage "progress." Since individual productivity can be hard to measure, employers (who shared these values) would tend to assume that employees' value increased over time. They expected to raise salaries as a reward for experience, firm- and industry-specific knowledge, loyalty—in a word, for *aging*. Midlife workers *should* cost more. Seniority is the something—the value system—that counters the bottom line.

Since the labor movement began, the ideal of age-enhanced progress also reigned in classes where the word "career" did not: in the expectations of union officials and members. In fact, progress marked by income growth (seniority) was more aggressively demanded by the organized working classes. That energy may have been beneficial to the middle classes as well. An expectation operating at this unspoken cultural level boosts entitlement, not for all but for many classes. It is more powerful for being unspoken. A core of American men benefited, albeit differentially, from seniority.

The major progressive change over the last few decades in the economics of the life course is that the system of later, higher peaks has been shared more widely, by white and African American women and African American men. Patriarchy's dress suit had coattails pinned onto it by the civil rights movements, by affirmative action, antisexist and antiracist training of teachers, equalizing access to quality education, entry-level opportunity, and ladders. Before 1992, women's median incomes peaked between the ages of thirty-five and forty-four; since, they have been peaking between forty-five and fifty-four, the same age as men. Over the 1990s, women in their mid-forties to mid-fifties saw their real income rise 32 percent (from a low start). Their wage percentage rose from 50 percent of men's to 59 percent. In 2000 they earned almost twice what women forty-five to fifty-five-years-old had earned in 1980. African American women of the same age saw their earnings rise from 75 percent of what European American women earned in 1967 to almost 93 percent in 2000. African American men and women now also see their incomes peak between forty-five and fifty-four.[16] The expansion of the middle class has been democratizing midlife advantages. The premium for experience is real to its beneficiaries.

But the midlife peak is still unequal and still, for many, inadequate. Those with professional degrees peak in the next older decade, fifty-five to sixty-four, with six-figure incomes.[17] Some in the remaining, mostly modest seniority systems—in unionized labor, government, academe—peak at retirement. In 2000, men aged forty-five to fifty-four peaked at a median income of $41,072. The midlife mean even for college-educated women is only 60 percent of their male peers'. Poverty is lowest for that age group, but no one should make too much of that: 1,429,000 women and 1,015,000 men forty-five to fifty-four live below the government's low-set poverty line.[18] "The employment situation of too many midlife women is characterized by involuntary part-time and seasonal work, undervalued skills, little upward mobility, few or no decision-making tasks, and low pay."[19] In 2000, median African American men between ages thirty-five and forty-four earned 60 percent of what white men that age earn; between forty-five and fifty-four, that rose to 72 percent; at the next older age interval it dropped to 67 percent.[20] Middle-ageism laced with inequality now renders the premium for experience ironic for those who have loads of experience but not much premium. And "middle class" can mean something much more modest for families of color or women-headed households than it does for white two-earner couples. Nevertheless, once excluded from "careers," many members of these groups are now reaching midlife with access to the underlying system of age enhancement.

Money may not be everything, but the economics of the life course affects the way it feels to age into the middle years. Respect in America partly depends on *how much* one's income rises as one ages into the middle years. Positive media attention seems to depend on the height of the peaks. Rising age/wage curves, however modest, accompany and anchor elevations into responsibility and new social roles: as parents, teachers and coaches, mentors of the young, moral authorities, political guides. Respect from one's adolescent children is threatened by discursive middle-ageism, which teaches rudeness, dismissiveness. (Respect can also come to those whose incomes peak at low levels, thanks to family love, human resilience, and remnants of respect for the midlife, but it comes harder. So does self-esteem.) Despite sexism, racism, and middle-ageism, aging-into-the-middle-years should confer increasing dignity and prestige. When parents say they want their children to do better, they refer not to their respective entry-level wages, but to the income and level of seniority at their wage peak: the midlife high.

Intangible midlife benefits are an unspoken part of the American Dream—an unacknowledged hope for some, for others an unacknowledged entitlement. "Seniority"—a word resonant with values—sums up the unstated psychological, familial, social, economic, ethical, and political promises of the life-course imaginary. Many people achieve enough of it to tell pollsters that the midlife is sweet. As long as we live in a classed society, as long as there is no guaranteed annual income, as long as adolescents may be doomed to immobility and the hidden injuries of class by their parents' midlife failures, no one should dismiss the concept of a democratized well-being at midlife as materialistic. Offended by inequality, we should point to the gross inequality between the rich and the poor at midlife.

A nation's fairness could be judged on the age/wage peaks of those below the median or in the lowest three quintiles. In any attempt to expand wealth to include now-excluded classes (as in, say, federal legislation to establish matching savings accounts for low-income people to use for house purchases and educational advancement), the continuum of the life course should be stressed. Democratizing midlife outcomes, and thus family and postretirement outcomes, should be explicit goals. Social justice demands that we lay out the principles that support these life-course values now that they are threatened.

The fact is that over the past twenty years the American Dream has been worth less and less in raising the peak age-wave curve for average and even for privileged men. "In 1950 a thirty-year-old man with an average salary could expect a paycheck 58 percent higher ten years later. In 1977, he would see his pay rise by only 21 percent during the next decade," Andrew Hacker writes.[21] By contrast, look at the premium for experience granted the median men who were between twenty-five and thirty-four in 1980. They saw their reward for aging go up nicely until they were thirty-five to forty-four, not 58 percent but 23.3 percent. But over the 1990s, as they aged into the forty-five to fifty-four bracket, their income went up only 7.9 percent.[22] The incomes of these "rich and greedy Boomers" have been, at best, what economists call stagnant. In fact, members of the forty-five to fifty-four age class earned more between 1986 and 1989 than they did in 2000.

Richard Barnet points out that the median earnings of the 2 million American men between forty-five and fifty-four with four years of college (all but 150,000 of them white) fell in constant dollars from $55,000 in 1972 to $41,898 in 1992.[23] If you look at what economists call "wealth" (house, car, savings), one sees widespread wealth erosion at midlife. The wealth of those who were thirty-five to forty-four in 1984 grew from $51,780 to $60,913 by the time they were ten years older in 1994. That's the kind of positive accumulation we expect during those prime working years. But $60,913 is much less wealth than the forty-five to fifty-four age class had achieved in 1984 ($82,894).[24] Women between forty-five and fifty-four have saved in their retirement accounts only 52 percent of what men that age have saved.[25] The middle classes, "whether blue-collar, white-collar, middle-level manager or professional," are being made to "disappear."[26] Whatever forces formerly protected men at midlife if they were middle class now seem to be weakening.

It's hard to say when the ideal of age-enhancement began to fail for wide numbers of middle-class men. One periodization describes the eighties as the time a "core" of Americans began to lose a sense of security because of deindustrialization and technological innovation.[27] Many obliquely noticed systemic failures during the early nineties. The creator of the syndicated comic strip *Dilbert* probably speaks for many when he says,

> But if you look at prior to downsizing, every year you'd come to work and your life was a little better, you'd look forward to a good raise or if there was a new announcement about your health-care system it was usually adding a benefit.
>
> After downsizing, the trend changed. Now every time there was an announcement that had anything to do with your well-being as an employee, it was usually chiseling away something.[28]

When the progress story that traditionally boosted entitlement weakens, it is replaced by a decline story. The expectation of decline lowers resistance and thus helps business continue to chisel away. Lowered expectations make material decline a self-fulfilling prophecy.

The data on white and black women and black men suggest that they are better off at midlife than they used to be. This good news distracts us from paying attention to the trends affecting median men in general. The statistics remind us that even powerfully entrenched systems are not necessarily permanent, and peaks do not remain constant, inertly, without struggle.

←——————→

Seniority systems are based on "tenure": broadly understood, job security, legal protections, modest increases over a working life. Middle-ageism and underlying structural changes in the economy are undermining tenure. In postindustrial global capitalism, the labor market is failing to create enough good jobs— possibly enough jobs at all—for the available workforce.[29] Even in the United States, jobs are becoming more short-term and insecure. In situations of scarcity and insecurity, however constructed (or even imagined), power shifts to employers. Suddenly it appears possible to cut the (next) most expensive employees rather than the cheapest and to overwork the remainder. Middle-ageism pushes wages toward the bottom, because it cuts off the top of a person's age/wage curve and weakens everyone's bargaining position. Layoffs—as the Enron debacle showed—may also do workers out of a pension.

Tenure narrowly defined—life tenure spelled out in a contract—is the model. It is under attack in schools and universities. Unions and government, with their own seniority systems, are being challenged in different ways. Other ingenious mechanisms help to lower age/wage curves and diminish the rewards for aging-in-the-workforce: refusing promotions to midlife people, squeezing them into less exciting work, cutting their departments, their desire to be loyal, their pay. New requirements that professionals be retested (as in education) also undermine the concept that aging means acquisition of cultural capital and characterize aging as obsolescence rather than experience. This is not the moment to abandon tenure. Seniority is a practice to be cherished, fought for, and expanded to other groups and classes.

The Future of Middle-Ageism

We are in the midst of a historical change of immense consequences, an era when capitalism is silently clashing with patriarchy over seniority. Why should capitalism let patriarchal midlife privilege endure if it gets in its way? Or extend traditionally male midlife privileges to the clamoring others? When privileged groups are vulnerable, who can stop the drive toward the bottom? The unorganized middle classes may begin to experience the lower income peaks that the working classes suffer. Women and black men, now slowly pulling up closer to midlife men in general (as men's incomes drop or stagnate), may begin to fall back.

As more beneficiaries lose protections, they also lose the power to uphold the entire rising age/wage system. The formerly excluded groups—who can enjoy and expand the system only if it exists—again become vulnerable to the proletarianization of the life course. Deprived of the unstated values of seniority, each worker aging into the midlife becomes an ever more atomized individual, required to justify her or his value within a system that is becoming discursively more middle-ageist as well. The decline discourse that already makes the midlife atmosphere toxic is pumped in more densely. When there's a Viagra to be marketed, "midlife diseases" like male sexual dysfunction are "discovered"; there is rising horror at normal wrinkles; anti-aging "necessities" like preventive facelifts are recommended earlier.

Without seniority, legal or customary, many people aging into midlife internalize their worthlessness. In the working class people say they feel "old" younger than those in the middle class do—and they don't mean they feel more mature. ("You're only as old as you feel," the saying goes. But "how old" you feel and how young you begin to "feel" old may be a function of gender, class, or other prejudice—of lack of seniority in conjunction with debilitating labor, lack of access to medical care, and other avoidable sources of distress) To add insult to injury, mainstream writers are now chanting the delights of "retiring" at fifty-five. Sure, on what pension?

To guess our own future if we do nothing, we could start by critically looking abroad. The news we are permitted to hear from France about age in relation to the workforce describes people cheerfully looking forward to retiring to pleasant second homes at fifty-five. The facts are quite different, as anyone who watches the movies of Laurent Cantet (*Human Resources, Time Out*) already guesses. A full half of French workers between fifty-five and sixty-four have been pushed out of the workforce. Even "50 to 54-year-olds are now caught up in this trend; their employment rate fell by seven percentage points from 1975 to 1988," writes Anne-Marie Guillemard, whose essays are extraordinary in including so much detail about the psychological consequences and about social indifference to their plight. In this harsh new world, even having employment at midlife carries with it permanent anxiety about losing one's job, with any renegotiations occurring from the employee's situation of reduced power. The "preretired" (horrible term, echoing "preseniors") are treated as one with the prematurely superannuated. One way or the other, the social value of the entire group from fifty to sixty-four in public opinion polls is sinking toward zero. Although the young are also seriously unemployed, Guillemard writes, "This is the only age group to which this has happened. The others' positions have oscillated between 13 and 11 on this 20-point scale." [30]

Here in the United States, after unemployment insurance runs out, there is no safety net until Social Security kicks in, perhaps years later. How a needy group fares morally and economically and even legally (as Kimel shows) depends on how it is represented—it depends on "needs interpretation," and that in turn depends on the "character" the group is given.[31] Given the media's lack of coverage—not to mention its misrepresentations of the Boomers—the public has no clear picture of midlife conditions over recent decades. If we fail to prevent and reverse the trends, we will have the leisure to contemplate whether it's worse for midlifers to be invisible or demonized. One tactic that serves the free market's ruthlessness is having the commerce in aging involve us in interminable inner debate about whether at midlife people are "too old" (to be useful workers) or "too young" (to be inactive). People at midlife could be both too old and too young—fixed in a tragic "natural" bind—so sad, but nothing to do. Except defy "aging."

Even before they are perceived as a group, an ideological contest to represent the prematurely superannuated is shaping up, with the left trying to show them as primarily diverse, hard-working for decades, able, and unwilling to go quietly into the jobless future, and the rest portraying them as losers. Susan Sheehan wrote in the New Yorker about a family in which the fifty-one-year-old father had lost a good job. "I know I'll never be able to earn $11.80 an hour again," Kenny Merten recognized. "The most I can hope for is a seven-dollar-an-hour job that doesn't involve swinging sandbags."[32] Although Merten was partly disabled, a victim of a downsizing economy, lacking education and a union, Sheehan discussed the couple's financial imprudence at length, bringing in a consultant to help them with poverty management. (In a confessional mode that Foucault and Richard Sennett have explained, they had given her their detailed financial records.) Condescension could well be the lot of any of us with drooping age/wage curves.

The discursive side of middle-ageism is useful to a system opposed to seniority and trying to prevent the anger of the superannuated. Middle-ageism imputes losses of ability (slower reflexes, techno-retardation) so that layoffs and downgrading of "deadwood" have some show of justification. In an era where computers have phenomenal "memory," memory loss is incorrectly represented as a problem peculiar to the midlife. Middle-ageism takes advantage of the cult of youth. The defects of the middle years are contrasted explicitly with the entrepreneurial, physical, sexual, intellectual, and creative accomplishments of the young. Anti-middle-ageist forces are put on the defensive, trying to argue through *proofs* why midlife workers are superior. Instead of admiring their adult children for doing well, some parents are humiliated or bitterly envy their age class. Middle-ageism teaches us to blame *aging* for the loss of hope and the crushing of dreams, instead of putting the blame where it should lie: on the mechanisms of postindustrial global capital.

Shortsightedly driving wages down, the agents of these changes are also blind or indifferent to their effects. They are not only losing the abilities of midlife individuals and damaging their lives. By tinkering with the life course at the midlife, in the long run they are also changing what it means to be human.

The French example shows how this comes about. Decades of dealing with "early exit" are marked by inadequate planning, demonstrating in part the lack of ethical theorizing about the place of the midlife in the life course. Companies continue as much as they legally can to cut midlife employees from the workforce at the lowest possible cost, and the public authorities refuse as far as politically possible to take responsibility for the formerly employed. Even the patchwork responses are shredded as soon as they begin to cost too much (read: work too well). Programs called "unemployment" and "disability" have been the preferred means of interpreting need, but when it appears that too many "older" workers utilize them, they are reread as "welfare."

Worst of all, once the "logic" of substituting the labor of a younger age group for that of an older has come into play, it is hard to put an end to it.[33] The practice can become explicitly normalized, as when midlife workers are praised for giving up jobs "for their children." France has given dramatic proof of solidarity with labor by imposing a thirty-five-hour week; this might help midlifers. But Guillemard believes that an improvement in the French labor market will not lead back to the situation prior to the early-exit trend.[34] The devaluation of the age class becomes a part of social understandings of the life course, an institutionalization of the work span that seems "natural." Only those who remember an earlier system know in their hearts that this apparently natural succession is false, but their sense of history has been a priori nullified. In an economy saturated with decline, the happy few who benefit from seniority cannot by themselves reinstate it. I know many middle-class educated people in our own country who are aware that their security is fragile. Some are hoping to weather the national midlife crisis without ignominy and exit voluntarily by their own timing, leaving decline behind for the rest.

Once decline has been administered at midlife, we never regain powers that we are unable to exercise. Disempowered, embittered, some people withdraw from action, hedge the generosity of their politics—not so mysteriously turning into the conservative midlife caricatures we were taught to deride and anticipate. If aging were the problem, how could anyone resist *that*? A population clinging to a decline view in a period of fabulous fortunes and painful inequality may not see the contradictions. Many are blinded by the ideology that economic chances are private and natural; they may become yet more self-involved, atomized, and subdued. A nation demoralized in such ways is dangerous— likely to be mean-spirited to "losers" domestically; and, distracted by paranoia, hostile and belligerent abroad. In such ways the devaluation of the midlife constitutes a collective "midlife crisis" for the nation. This is the nightmare we should be trying to avert.

Can the 35 million first-wave Boomers, the 44 million second-wave Boomers, the 37 or 40.5 or 45 million Xers, and the millions now over sixty join together to prevent these dire outcomes?[35] In the face of such powerful forces, can an anti-middle-ageist movement turn the American life course from a deepening national crisis into a civic progress story?

As a first step we need a sense of urgency. Public intellectuals need to explain, publicize, trumpet, the high costs of middle-ageism and develop arguments to make our life-course claims forceful and undeniable. We could argue that American capitalism cannot be trusted to strengthen seniority, that it is failing too many of its workers, and that we refuse to let the life-course be distorted in order to hide this. "A stunning 95 percent majority believes that corporations 'should sometimes sacrifice some profit for the sake of making things better for their workers and communities.'"[36] The wide reach of decline into the middle class and into the future might make it possible to create a democratic populist coalition of progressives and conservatives. That supermajority could help create what might be called a life-course vision.

Shared values come with a more just and precise economic agenda. Continuing to extend seniority to the formerly excluded, raising the dollar peak for those in the lower quintiles, raising the age curve for those who peak below age fifty or fifty-five while restoring modest rises for median midlife men—these could be explicit goals of a country still as excessively rich as the United States. Assume for the moment that a cross-generational coalition convinces the political parties of the urgency. Whatever success we have here might have an influence on other countries confronting similar decline ideologies. But delineating our goals could be effective even if we fail to reach all of them.

To make the hardest pressed visible, their contexts and their characters will need to be narrated—first of all by them. We need surveys of those not in the data (by education, gender, race, and by five-year rather than ten-year cohorts). How many suffer such consequences of midlife decline as illness, divorce, alienation from children, homelessness? We need media exposés, pressure on the Department of Labor to do a national study of midlife conditions. We need writers who can imaginatively integrate data, ethnography, age expertise, cultural criticism, and theory. Before better information is available, critics need to follow the twists of discursive middle-ageism closely, because decline makes discrimination more acceptable.

The idea that the United States could solve the future by *raising* the age at which full Social Security benefits can be doled out to the jobless would be laughable if it were not so malicious. If normal retirement began at seventy, those who need Social Security at age sixty-two would get about 62 percent of the benefit rather than the current 80 percent.[37] As long as there are not enough good jobs for people over fifty and no adequate safety nets, postponing rescue is a refinement of cruelty.

Fairer redistribution and social cohesiveness could start with livable wages for, and reduced inequality between, young workers. We might hold CEOs responsible for restoring the weekend, retaining employees, providing benefits, accepting unions. Young people need to understand that a seniority system is sage and desirable and that—with aging—it will help them in their turn. (They have to be ready to counter sophistical arguments for "equality.") Since many young adults start to raise children only at older ages than their parents did, the wage curve should probably peak *later* than it does now. The elite midlife pattern—six-, seven-, and eight-figure annual incomes—can be remedied by more progressive taxation. Public pressure could expand unemployment insurance and welfare, and permit the long-term unemployed to enter the public pension system as early as sixty, as the German and French governments have done.[38] Or fifty-five. We could consider early Social Security for those taking care of elderly parents or (on the military/fire/police model) for people who have worked in especially difficult or dangerous conditions like mining and manual labor. These are respectable ways out of workforce participation, dependent on coding the recipients as "deserving." But the demoralization of the French life course, or that of the Japanese salarymen, who after retirement often drop a caste, suggests that high participation in work at midlife *of the right kind* is a prerequisite in the United States too for maintaining a socially valued midlife and a bearable life-course imaginary.

One goal would have to be true "full employment," to ensure that there is work, coupled with retraining programs and affirmative action, at every age for those who can work. In Sweden, a model, the unemployment rate runs around 1.6 percent and the "cash-support principle" is considered less humane than the "work principle."[39] The means here could include a shorter work week at steady rates of pay, longer vacations, the concept of overtime for professionals, a restored eight-hour day. Unions, labor laws, the National Labor Relations Board (NLRB), and the tenure system in the academy would be strengthened. We could experiment with ways to make nonstandard employment (especially temping) more secure, more dignified, more comprehensive in benefits, and less prevalent. Companies that repent their overexuberant layoffs and rehire somebody else's superannuated workers or some of their own would have to offer the valued fringes of in-house status, rather than the substandard conditions of most outsourcing. The Clinton administration wanted to provide health insurance for those over fifty-five; the young need it too. This means national health care. Full employment would require regulating jobs about to be exported abroad or compelling departing multinationals to compensate the workers and communities they abandon.

Full employment would reduce job insecurity, which by disproportionately weakening the mature employee vis-à-vis each new employer at hiring, makes lifting the wage-curve so hard to achieve. By satisfying so many constituencies simultaneously, full employment might be an answer to decline that avoids categorizing midlife beneficiaries as a group. If the United States had instituted a Full Employment Act in 1967, when the Age Discrimination in Employment Act was passed, we might have avoided many decline phenomena.[40]

Such a program could be supplemented by measures addressed specifically to middle-ageism. Critical legal scholars could imaginatively counter the employer argument that "earning too much" is a just cause for dismissal. "Disparate impact" arguments could rely on the kinds of data and the explicit life-course vision adduced here. Midlife antidiscrimination laws could be reinforced by a campaign to bring shame on the CEOs and legislators and judges who subvert them.

Once retraining became politically viable, postsecondary education throughout the life course could be revived. It was authorized in a 1972 education act hailed by the then secretary of HEW, Elliott Richardson, as the boldest in history; it was never funded.[41] The government could fulfill unmet needs in housing, health, education, and the environment through a distinguished Senior Domestic Peace Corps that would capitalize on experience and leadership acquired by midlife.

I call such a project, sensitive to life-course needs, "full employment plus." Although full employment could go into effect without singling out people in their middle years, full employment plus would require that the values of supporting democratized seniority and lifting the age/wage curve be made explicit. We have learned why this is urgent from the fumblings in Europe. As our society restores their full presence in the workforce, the collective capacity and untransferable skills of midlife people need to be represented undefensively.[42] Their loyalty becomes precious; they are wooed. Only thus can we eliminate the likelihood that people over fifty-five, and then fifty, and so on, will become stigmatized as a "problem," a curse from which there is almost no exorcism. But at the same time we must avoid the "rich-and-greedy-Boomer syndrome" by showing how contingent their power is and how necessary it is that midlifers have power. As full employment diminishes the contrived "scarcity" that pits whites against people of color, "Americans" against immigrants, men against women, full employment plus would eliminate the scarcity that pits adult children against their parents, and parents against adult children, for jobs and other cultural goods. It could moderate the cult of youth.

To restore and expand a more humane system over the life span, Americans need to understand age conceptually and to think about seniority as an ethical issue—an issue of the "good" life course. Although every familiar public policy I have suggested has been attacked by the right wing, and although much could be labeled "socialism," the broad coalition I envision would be open to social-justice arguments, developed by using new concepts from age theory. The keywords I offer in this connection are "progress and decline narrative," "middle-ageism," the "age/wage curve," "premature superannuation," "democratized seniority," "age hierarchy," "the long adulthood." I hope thinkers will want to refine these terms and imagine more specific political agendas in the context of life-course values. The issues are framed to address people at all economic and psychological positions and all ages. This would be a true "family values" agenda and a powerful organizing tool for the twenty-first century.

HOW AGE STUDIES CAN HELP

Part 1 of this book, "Cultural Urgencies," begins with decline prophesied for children and ends with decline meted out to midlife adults. Once readers have understand that much of recent age history and age politics, it seems to me, they can feel how deep the social construction of age and aging goes in the United States whether they believe they have been afflicted personally or not.

The "middle years" are a test case. The midlife has become as unquestionable a part of the life course as childhood, adolescence, or old age. Empirical investigators reify it: it is now allegedly human to have a "midlife passage."

The changes in the construction of "the middle years" from 1970 to 2000 have been marked. There was a time not so long ago when people in their middle years could have been regarded, to borrow terms from anthropologist Andre Simic, simply as "a loosely defined category of persons otherwise integrated into an age-heterogeneous society, and identifying most closely with the interests of their own families. However, of late a new self-perception and stereotyping has emerged competing with older values." People in midlife had been unincorporated agents; they are now envisioned as a peer group.[43] Simic wrote this in 1978. He was actually talking about the growing age segregation of the elderly, but already his terms were appropriate to the middle years, the phase of life that was for millennia the most indefinable and the last to be contained by nomenclature.

Middle-ageism sometimes seems to shade off into ageism against the retired. But the former has very different means, motives, and consequences because the *agon* occurs in the workplace. There, with the family behind one party and capital behind the other, a war between need and greed has been ongoing. It was in 1967 that Congress passed legislation to provide redress for age discrimination starting at age forty: some wise heads in the postwar boom were already nervously noting and anticipating middle-ageism. In the 1980s, the most interesting sociologists of the midlife thought that "the 'midlife crisis' form by which the middle years are encountered and understood" might disappear, because it was probably "unique" to those born in the late 1920s and 1930s who were being aged into midlife culture in the 1970s after the youth "revolutions."[44] Yet current forms of middle-ageism are being passed on to cohorts aging into midlife culture in very different conditions. Middle-ageism is proving just as adaptable to cohorts raised in expectations of wealth as to those raised with Depression-era expectations, to large cohorts like the Boomers as it was to the small cohorts of the 1930s.

Many phenomena have muddled the connections between economic and representational middle-ageism in the past twenty or thirty years. How oblivion works is a fascinating problem for age studies. In a preliminary way, I can summarize a few sources. The positive-aging gurus tending the affluent middle class declare that "the midlife is a great stage of life" and that "there is no midlife crisis." (One can agree in some sense with both statements, as I do, and feel that they utterly miss the dangers.) Anger at losing jobs is "missing," as the business press likes to remind us, or ridiculed. Data is lacking. Experiencing the "middle years" has been privatized. I borrow a sentence from Nancy Fraser, adding age to her focus on gender. If "midlife" issues are "enclaved" as merely "personal" or "natural," and discourse is channeled to (and from) specialized publics associated with, say, fitness, women, autobiography, midlife-crisis therapy, elder care, hormone therapy, urology, this serves to trivialize the midlife.[45] Cultural critics tend to study youth. Gerontologists focus on wars between "canes versus kids." Feminist gerontologists and other feminists overlook men; and men's studies and the left ignore midlife men. In the progressive media, the attention has been paid to the current postretirement generation.[46]

The processes by which the life course is constructed are never-ending. Through the changes, the social text has quietly been absorbing the heightened importance of a new axis of difference: age. So far, the clearest recent results have been constructing decline as a biological fact of the early midlife, dividing the body politic into warring age classes, lowering our expectations of what the economy can provide, subjectively shortening the life course in the middle. Decline, speed-up, age obsessiveness, nostalgia. Age, in the words of my friend Winston Langley, is "a nice new devil."

There is a lot to try to reverse.

←——→

Adding the "middle years" to the life course means that the age class has a solid existence. But those in it have no name, unlike "children," "adolescents," and the "elderly." "Middle-aged" seems pejorative. "Baby Boomers" is all too solidly established but is useless and harmful. Once those in the years between young and old had no name because they were the most powerful and unclassifiable;

the norm, unseen. Unnamable. Language still betrays the lumpy difficulty of trying to stuff so many who are so diverse into a single homogeneous grouping. Perhaps still having no name is a good sign—a sign of latent power.

With this slippery postmodern thought in mind, it is easier to understand why "the midlife" cannot benefit from being reified in any way. Those who pass through the middle years should not conceive of themselves as incorporated except for the purpose of resisting the forces that make midlife aging a decline. "Midlifers" is an ugly term, but I need it occasionally because it asserts that the targets of middle-ageism are a collective and might see themselves as such. They may unite in their midlife millions (if they can) as long as everyone understands an anti-middle-ageist agenda as cross-generational, a fight on behalf of the life course.

It is not reification, however, to assert that the midlife is central to the life course—too integrated and continuous to be libeled as a stage of fixed ("special," "narrow") interests. A vast population, now and in the future, depends on the fate of those who are passing through it collectively at this historical moment. For the purposes of unity, it might be useful to reconceive the midlife as "a long adulthood," expanding it backward into the decade of the twenties and forward past whatever end ageism currently assigns.[47] The long adulthood would be *intact* in this conception, as that span of maturity in which we try to develop our powers and exercise them within circumstances less and less of our own making.

←——→

The life course should make its claim to a kind of sacredness. This is different from the sanctity of "life," a biological birth gift and essence that inheres in each of us at every moment and makes murder a crime. The life course depends on this original gift, but is distinct in demanding that we acknowledge the increasing value of a life lived in time. Society should be organized to provide the maximal conditions possible for increasing this value in line with each person's potential and desires. Democratically lifting the age/wage curve in itself serves—both negatively as a way of staving off capitalism's relentless effort to infantilize humankind through enrollment as a subordinated "workforce" throughout our working lives and positively in enabling us to fulfill our life-course responsibilities and goals.

A true dream of the common life course transcends the American Dream, as a collective goal does an individual one, a spiritual vision a solely material one. Our joint aging through life must not be stripped of value. *Feeling at home in the life course at any age:* I feel the sanctity of this without being able to explicate it. Perhaps it is best to try to say it simply. If the life course is out there in the world, constantly being constructed, as it is, and we want a bigger share in doing the constructing, as we should, then we had better take this on with a caution that approaches reverence. No other construction concerns every one, or concerns each one so nearly.

Part Two

Theorizing
Age Resistantly

What Is Age Studies?

PRIORITIZING CULTURE

The next provocative proposition of age studies might be that we are aged more by culture than by chromosomes. Such judgments are not of course quantifiable: I put it this way as a teasing into thought, and to recognize a philosophical trend in studying the phases of life. Philippe Ariès implied this priority for childhood, inspiring historians to investigate "childhoods." Simone de Beauvoir, the godmother of age studies, exhaustively documented it with regard to old ages in *La Vieillesse* (*The Coming of Age*). I, as well as others, have done it for the middle years. Cross-cultural anthropologists have shown cultural construction globally for those who have eyes to see. The step that made the proposition more meaningful to many students of age culture in the United States (including me) was scrutinizing the midlife, precisely because it had been an unmarked category. The "middle years" emerged like the other ages—no sooner named than characterized and disputed. By now, the "life course" can be seen "from end to end"—rather than "from beginning to end"—as a terrain for power and ideology. As part 1 showed, age and aging have been overnaturalized.

A culturalist conviction unites practitioners in age studies. Its component disciplines may not agree exactly on what "age" is—or for that matter, "aging"—once all this is put into question. But we all study age culture now or in the past, here or abroad, in dominant and subcultures, with the knowledge that the systems producing age and aging could be different—and that if they were, our experiences of the life course would be too. This conviction separates our work from the self-help guides, the "anti-aging" marketeers, or the positivists. The "natural" is conventionally constituted as the Other to the "cultural"—while the masters of the natural busily erase culture. Age studies undoes the erasure of the cultural in the sphere of age and aging.

Feminist theory denaturalized female/male difference, and then started on older/younger differences; critical race theory denaturalized the sphere of black/white difference. Unmaking an essentialized, body-based ideology, Robyn Wiegman says, "superseded the "nature/nurture framework . . . by yielding primary analytic power to the 'nurture' side." [1] This shift of power is one of the great intellectual developments of our time. However incomplete, it has immeasurably heartened the antisexist and the antiracist movements. Now, in reference to age, it is necessary to any antidecline movement. The mere term "age theory" slightly disrupts our mental habits by implying that we should become wary about every age reference.

Existing age studies has made some headway. One of our collective accomplishments has been in dragging "aging"—arguably the most biologized aspect of the construct of age—away from nature and toward culture. Some "natural" scientists are edging closer toward age studies by declaring that what we think of as aging is really biosocial damage: physical ills caused by smoking, inactivity, poor diet (called "lifestyle diseases" even though some start before birth), or those caused or worsened inter alia by unemployment, by poverty and environmental racism, by caretaker stress, and by lack of access to health care. "By the time you make it to 60," says a psychiatrist who has reviewed longitudinal studies, "health and longevity depend less on your genes than on how well you take care [have been able to take care] of yourself." [2] One of the excitements of epidemiology has been to show that hypertension and heart disease can be caused not by normal aging but by job strain in the workforce. [3] Feminists and public health specialists have proven that menopause discourse and hormone replacement "therapy," as it was called until July 2002, are more dangerous for women than any "symptoms." It was culture that made "the male menopause" into a similarly dire prospective decline narrative and that sells Viagra. [4] As such critical perspectives infiltrate the medical model, the evils that "age" our body-minds often turn out to be like toxic waste or "empty-nest syndrome." Remedies for external inflictions come from not from positive thinking or extreme diets but from better public policy (prevention) and wiser public discourse (antidecline). It becomes harder to blame the body in itself, harder to displace economic or sociopolitical problems onto age, and harder to call age and aging wholly "natural."

I began this book with prospective narratives told to children and with the worklife biography of the American Dream because revealing the unsuspected narrative bases of aging is way of wrenching attention toward the realm of the sociocultural, where power comes from to tell the stories of the body-mind. One of my goals in writing *Aged by Culture* is to make "narrative aging" a fruitful and unavoidable concept. Biological determinism—whether the old hormonal or the new genetic kind—could eventually be regarded as another set of aging narratives imposed on our body-minds. But utopian scientific claims about "cracking the code" of bodily aging still distract attention from the many ways life chances are linked to socioeconomic status and discourse. Biochemistry lines up with God as another acultural source of human nature and destiny.

Because this is so, it is also important that scientists are "discovering" growth processes like brain myelination in midlife. That ability to find "natural" continuities of function confirms that the unspoken assumption—*anywhere you look for age-linked organic decay you'll find it*—is weakening. Academic anti-ageist research—including the MacArthur Foundation's Research Networks on Successful Midlife Development and on Aging—and OWL/AARP/Gray Panther–style advocacy have been convincing some scientists to uproot the ageist biases influencing research protocols and agendas. That some succeed is also proved by the finding that new brain cells keep being produced throughout life (neurogenesis).

Yet which "fact" do you know: that brain function declines after five, that it peaks at eighteen, that it peaks at fifty-five, or that "peak" is a misnomer? This would be a cultural test—if anyone could measure the distribution of your answers—of the weak reach of anti-ageism in mainstream culture. In my newspaper's comics page, readers with even modest levels of education can regularly enjoy and pick up concepts from feminism (Nicole Hollander's *Sylvia*), African American cultural criticism and left politics (Aaron Magruder's *The Boondocks*), ironic self-referential postmodernism (Bill Griffith's *Zippy*), and critique of the corporate workplace (Scott Adams's *Dilbert*). But on this and other pages, from living/arts to news, age-wise commentary is mostly absent or sub par. *Sylvia* has a goddess for "women over forty." Not much to point to. Chapter 3 above includes a cartoon in which the comic oedipal "constant"—resentful sons battling dads—muffled the unfunny news it contained: that during an astonishing boom, midlife men were unable to find work. You may judge from that single example how hard it will be to outsmart age ideology. Swayed by its paymasters and its own propaganda, mainstream culture beats out the bass line "Decline, decline" under its trumpeting of purchased progress. Common sense is still instructed to consider age-linked changes natural, ahistorical, prenarrative, congenital facts of life. Most people interpret their own "aging" through mainstream discourses, not recognizing that's the way gender and race used to come disguised. I have friends even in academic theory who, when I point out an acculturated side of age, feel the need to respond with something like, "But my metabolism is slowing down." I have four responses.

First, as a friend, empathy—and as a cultural critic, conviction that owning up to an involuntary, medically recognized decline must not end the conversation. Rather, it starts the analysis of "age" from the supposedly common body, where a lot of people need it to start. Next I ask, "And so what if it is?" A while later I might get to three: "You can suffer from an age-linked decline (if it is one) and still be quite a thoroughgoing age critic." Fourth, this book, especially chapter 8, the section on fitting your unique socially constructed body into your unique socially constructed life-course stories: "And you might even spin an antidecline narrative out of it."[5]

Culturalist insights and decades of extraordinary work in currently existing age studies have yet to inaugurate a strong theory revolution or a movement around the construct of age. If they had, that bright idea of having a "Face Aging" booth would have been stopped in its tracks. I don't want to belabor the specialists who vetted it. Next time they may apply their social-learning theory to age and think twice about the effects of teaching decline. What makes that single site a hard fact, an indigestible cultural datum, a symbol of our emergency, is that this malicious new time machine was constructed, as it were, by an age ideology against which even most experts among us have little recourse. Although it operates in plain sight, it is almost invisible. Some artists—the Jo Spences, the Feldmanns, the recovery novelists—hack their ways out of the ideology. The age critics are those who recognize, applaud, and do likewise.

In *The Social Construction of What?* philosopher Ian Hacking says that a social construct, to be worth the bother of analysis, has to be nontrivial, taken for granted, and must appear to be "inevitable."[6] Some elements traditionally associated with old age, the midlife, youth, and childhood are no longer regarded as inevitable. Still, to move from a culturalist presumption across a few domains to reinterpreting your own body-mind experiences, and from there to scoping out age ideology, is quite a voyage. Rethinking age may appear strange to those first practicing it, like Alice's thinking three impossible things before breakfast. In the present state of affairs, age still soars over Hacking's high threshold for constructs that require, well, deconstruction.

So, what kind of symbolic/social/ideological/construct is age? The term is maddeningly loose and untidy. It becomes more intelligible if we start by branching into its aspects, like age lore and aging narratives, which organize the meanings of personal time passing. The word "age" as an equivalent to "stage" also refers to those vague categories to which we get assigned and that then become all-too-definite attributes (as in "I've decided I'm old now," or the vehement assertion, "I'm no Boomer!") And that's not all the work the one poor noun does. "Age" is also a set of critical and heuristic theories about the construct and the ideology, analogous to "gender." Is age sufficiently like gender and race, the other allegedly body-based constructs, that age theorists can pick up their analyses, apply them, and expect parallel outcomes? We can't ignore age's confusing temporal component, aging, which other critical theories often ignore. Is the inescapable term "aging"—its very grammar marking a process of difference from oneself—one reason why age-as-construct operates differently from gender or race, when it does? Does the word "age" itself (because it serves also as another euphemism for "old age") weigh itself in too late in the young/old dichotomy to ever shake that binary?[7] The taxonomy I sketch in this paragraph would be arguable to some, superfluous to others. Are these even the right questions?

Reconceptualizing Age Studies

Age studies needs to reconceptualize itself in order to decide on the questions it will ask, let alone answer. Currently it means something like "ongoing parallel work having to do with age in myriad disciplines and interdisciplines, each defining its own objects of study and goals." Much of that work is admirable. I rely on it everywhere in this book and admire its practitioners. There could be no further development without these foundations. Yet age remains an impoverished concept, partly because of its undertheorized relationship to the body-mind and narrative, partly because of its poorly defined relationship to market forces, neoliberal politics, and ideology. Age studies theory is as weak as gender theory or critical race theory were decades ago, when people who said, "*Now* we know how this works!" were fooling themselves. It is not only that age is the latest comer. The case feels like the most daunting. Age critics work (to update Bourdieu) "in the area par excellence of the denial of the social."[8] Theorists have to expand their imaginations to encompass all the situations where the key axis of difference is the one never mentioned—being aged by culture.

This transformation of the academy needs to come along simultaneously, pari passu, with a mainstream cultural and political revolution around age. Right now, without further ado, we could happily front more pundits—publicly connecting, say, Sandra Day O'Connor's argument that there is no history of midlife discrimination in the United States to the mass media's ways of justifying discrimination by calling people over thirty-seven elderly, unproductive, and expensive. But in many contexts, I don't see much difference between "us" where age is concerned. Even a feminist who writes in age studies, long exposed to anti-ageism and an applied anti-ageist in regard to her own body-mind, may find herself vulnerable to positivism outside her zone of deconstructive comfort, subsumed in her age class in unimagined ways, unaccustomed to being on watch for the latest time machines, aware that age is historicized but not fully aware that the meanings of age and aging are invisibly fluctuating and battling around us now. We are all incompletely suspicious, insufficiently prepared.

Age, redefined and deconstructed, is what age studies foregrounds—what makes it a field. Age thus understood could be the next analytic and hermeneutic concept to make a cutting-edge difference to general readers, writers, artists, and journalists, feminists, the media, cultural studies, the socially informed humanities, the narratively informed social sciences, science studies, the medical/industrial complex, and global socioeconomic practices/policy.[9] How can age studies help us all to *think* age (and aging) better, and what kind of field would it have to become to do so? This brief chapter attempts to limn a collective vision, just as the chapters 1 and 2 justified a collective mission.

A STRONG THEORY REVOLUTION

At this stage I think we can make headway only if age studies repeatedly presents to its various publics persuasive evidence of its founding proposition, the priority of culture in constructing age. This can also be done by explicitly changing the objects that people now assume are worth looking at and convincing them that the new objects are worth attending to. From the confetti of the phenomena to the confetti-factories of ideology—that was the first switch of attention I recommended. Here is an ensemble of other theoretical moves that might be strategically useful now (the trouble is, they probably have to advance together, banging cymbals and drums and blowing their own horns). From old age to children, and thus, from the ages of life separately to the whole life. From age as a construct to its aspects, like aging; from "natural" aging to particularized age socializations, narratives of aging, and a culture's life-course imaginaries. Thus, we make the whole set of leaps from the (overnaturalized) body to the body-mind and thence to the embodied psyche in culture over time.

Changing the Objects

If this book starts with distraught children, adult children, and midlife parents, in situations indisputably constructed to interpret age to them, its readers should never again be able to fall back into certain narrow, unquestioned, and mind-inhibiting associations. "Age" will not refer exclusively or even primarily to "the old," or "older people" or "old women," as we have carelessly come to agree. In reconceptualized age studies, "aging" will no longer be either a euphemism for old age or a process that begins at an undecidable period in middle age. The very term will acquire qualifiers, like "aging-into-the-middle-years" or "aging-into-adulthood" (with others to be added as necessary), and these terms will refer not to a fixed chronology but to cultural pressures that stabilize age ideology or engineer its novelties. Age studies will not be synonymous with gerontology or even, as the leading edge of that field prefers to call itself, "critical aging studies." [10]

But probably we *will* fall back, because these received associations are so powerful. Age is not a simple essentialized condition like male/female, or black/white (brown, red), once considered to be set for life at birth. Age may be the hardest of the body-linked constructs to dispute because two of its properties, change and continuity, seem unavoidable and yet, when considered together, contradictory. While subjects are younger and vulnerable the body changes visually (in size), and heavy attention is paid to highlighters like puberty. Yet "[f]or many purposes society sees age as a continuum." This "flexibility" of the category seems an advantage to theorist Judith K. Gardiner,[11] and I treat it as an advantage for identity theory in chapter 7. But it is a pain for deconstruction. The term "age" and the term "aging" in their motion violently tend to jerk away from birth toward the *other* end. There the language of "postponement" peters out. Decline narrative makes aging like a "choice" of tracks only in the middle. Along one we hurtle toward a rocky slope, along the other we saunter toward higher elevations—but both (if all you are allowed to look at is the end) end the same way. Decline always has the death card up its sleeve.

This most speedy of mainstream decline's moves wins without contest when age is treated as only or fundamentally about the naturalized body (shorn of mind). This is not a body in parts (genitals, skin, hair), on each of which naturalizing ideologies like racism and sexism have been yielding bit by bit under decades of reasoned and grassroots assault. No—the use that decline makes of parts (those same genitals, skin, hair) depends on a later-life body that is a purely physical and undifferentiated unit, unidirectional in time and, as the everlasting drone has it, universally subject to an uncontrollable fate. As decline backs down the life course toward children and positive aging raises its volume, the middle-aged are more often swept in with "the elderly" even by gerontologists, quite unreflectively. It's as if the body got gradually *more* natural, more *bodily* over life time. Not slowly more expressive, as I argue in chapter 9, but quickly more fearful. Our metaphors of *gravitas*—"weight" of age, "pull" of death—underlie our associations with "age." Ordinary people shake out the death card. Aging discourse slides into dying discourse without critique, although Baba Copper has called "the age/death connection" "that virulent stereotype." "The assumption that death is a . . . subject of expertise, of midlife or old women is ageist." "Death has become a private buzzword for me, warning me of the shoals of ageism before me." [12]

"Thanatology" shows that the apparently natural association between sickness, dying, and old age is actually a historical phenomenon.[13] Death tightened around sick old age in America only with the lowering of the infant mortality rate toward 1900 as a result of public health and obstetric advances. Before that, the old seemed healthiest because they had survived so much. Death occurred so frequently to newborns and children under five that *they* seemed heavy with it, heavier perhaps than all other categories but the enfeebled. In our modern life course and contemporary metaphoric system, children have become nearly weightless. New practices—by which children are kept from funerals and often apart from the elderly—seem normal because it's right to keep them light.

It would be curious to examine this unconscious metaphor of having more or less body. The concept that children are aged by culture upsets it. Having a body-mind, they ipso facto come to bear the weight of age culture, as, qua girls and boys, they do the weight of gender culture, and qua racialized beings, the weight of race. In the best circumstances, they bear the burden of littleness, weakness, dependency (the characteristics that modern age lore assigns them), confusion and misinformation, the admixture of doubt spooned into their hopeful narratives. The burden is becoming heavier because the future projected for them makes them beings already-about-to-be-aging (ugly and alien). The children in the booth received this additional dread burden. Age studies will not end with children; books that practice it need not start with children (and this book returns to representations of them only a few times). But age theory must include children to be able to emphasize that they too are laden with culture.

Age theory must in general tear up the death card and slow down the speed-up. Once people persuade themselves that such moves can be effective, they can see the whole life as cultural from end to end of embodied consciousness.

Starting the Arguments

Alice Rossi, a sociological doyenne of midlife studies, wrote in 1990, "No one would ague that 'age' is purely a social construction as many do where 'gender' is concerned."[14] I know of no systematic debate in the age disciplines around this issue. This is unfortunate. People should shove that "purely" into a high-profile debate. If not, the body could turn out to be the repressed of age studies. (My friends, by reminding me of midlife disabilities, surely wish me to keep this in mind.) To respond to their concerns fully, I think it helpful to work in the close space between two possibilities: "To speak of nature is always already to be in the space of discourse" (Boal) and "[W]hat is material never fully escapes from the process by which it is signified" (Butler).[15]

Age critics, because they continually become aware of more body-effects produced by our colonizing processes, are also well placed to pay riveted attention to the phenomenology of living in one's body resistantly. (I consider both cultural impositions and resistance to them in chapter 9, where I chose to deal with very sensuous and signifying material bodies, acting age. There I fix on qualities our body-minds have acquired over time that, so far, have partially escaped discourse.) "Interactionism," as this poised position is sometimes called, is quite compatible with arguing that age theory should try out the most radical social-constructionist positions.

Thus what interests age studies cannot start at birth with our genes—whatever heavy lifting they may do—but with children's earliest personal encounters with age lore and aging narratives. The notion of childhood as a social construction has become "the industry standard" over the past ten years, according to two leaders in the sociology of childhoods.[16] Yet that field gives only rare fragmented hints toward a systematic study of socialization into age and aging in particular postindustrial cultures—perhaps because less work is done on aspects of children's lives that are considered hard (adult) experience.[17] Age is certainly treated as one of those. Age socialization clearly needs a nudge from age studies.

To see how far ordinary people are from thinking about childhood this way, ask yourself: What was my earliest bit of age socialization? If you leave out the first birthday you remember, it's probably hard to say. Like me, you may perfectly recall your first discovery of being gendered or racialized or classed, and not be able to recall an early age-related event. There's no discipline yet pressing you to inquire so closely, no movement that tells you remembering is important because the stakes are high here too, no published narratives that jog your recollection. My husband remembered his aunt teasing him at age six because we were talking about age hierarchy and about *wanting* to be older, a strong motive in our mid-twentieth-century America. And you might say he lives in a movement household. (Hint: ask yourself about the first *growth*-related sentence you heard, or your first powerful impression of age *hierarchy*, like bossing or being bossed by a sibling.)

Maybe age studies should argue that subjects have *no* age until that first remarkable age-linked sentence fills their ears. "Prelapsarian agelessness" could be the name for those few years of life. Both ways, as subjects and as objects, we fall into being "aged" because we are social beings. No ideas about age are preexistent in our baby minds. Even in their early months, infants taking on weight and learning to smile are being aged by culture. Although they have no age subjectively, as objects of their parents' acculturations they are already receiving affects determined by their newness and their parents' age identities. Nothing happens to or in or on "the body" over time—not "genetic inheritance," "puberty" or other physical changes, "hormone deficiency" or other medical diagnoses, sensations of pain, even death in anticipation—that doesn't come already shrink-wrapped in the "facts," beliefs, language, visual images, practices, and plots that are available.

The repertory of age notions and aging stories that children acquire is also specific to a historical period and a particular place and family and community and nation. When I was a child, the science museums I was taken to didn't have "aging" exhibits. In fact, the Boston show claimed it was the very first traveling exhibit on aging.[18] For early-nineteenth-century Americans, "age" did not include birthday parties (except in rare upper-class subcultures) or age grading in schools. "Young" and "old" didn't change much in meaning. Throughout any contemporary life, however, age is a continuing education, in which the content matter gets continually updated and we pupils constantly change our minds.

My hesitation to start age studies investigations of age at birth; my refusal to start where gerontologists often stop, transfixed by an elderly subject; my repeated turn to historicizing the life course, including the imaginary of death—these are ways of opening up space. Age and aging as social constructions—this could be as sensationally motivating as Judith Butler's idea in *Gender Trouble* that even the sexuality "behind" gender is a construct. Kathleen Woodward, a pioneer in age studies in the humanities, once said that it lacks "self-conscious debates," and Andrew Achenbaum, a critical gerontologist, said his field needed "an intensified collective consciousness."[19] Their concerns joined my own to inspire this book. As age studies becomes a single, systematic field, it will generate more thinkers who can start the arguments.

Age Is Everywhere

Proofs that age is culturally constructed starting shortly after birth are necessary but not sufficient to found and unify this field. Age as a symbolic system takes on vitality only when the concrete age curricula are suspected to be ubiquitous at any age. The object of study becomes *the whole life* as an imaginary, constructed in our heads where innumerable age-linked influences intersect. This "whole life" is not a linear concept like the "life course" of developmental and historical studies, but rather the full spread across which power sprays its differentials. Calling the entire field "life-course studies"—the name of some courses and departments—would be misleading theoretically and a tactical mistake. It would institutionalize linearity. It would also obliterate my age studies point: that cultures produce multiple life-course imaginaries. Even though my son and I are both offered decline stories, his is different from the one bedeviling me.

Gender studies gained power—and a new name—when it foregrounded "gender" and "sexualities" (rather than "women" or even "women and men").

Critical race theory gained power and a name when its object became "race" and "ethnicity" (rather than "blackness" plus "whiteness," etc.) Each of these approaches, by breaking the binary that divided its object of study, more effectively showed that gendering and "race-ing" were omnipresent in culture, interpreting *difference* to the advantage of certain groups—by no means incidental to the lives of the subjected, but not a special syllabus *for them alone*. As for me, when these ubiquities came as breaking news, they opened my eyes wide, on watch for clues. I was awash with feelings. Everyone I saw was altered. Fixed systems shifted.

The same liberating astonishment could come from theorizing age. But age is a different difference, as I find myself realizing over and over. People who feel stalked by age discourse don't want to see "age" anywhere else! Many think "age" always refers to people older than they are and is thus of no present interest. Writing about age is not taken as an intellectual or theoretical interest, comparable to Chinese history or biological diversity, about which anyone can care and develop specialized knowledge and passionate attitude. Rather, it can only be a brave sign of recognition of one's own advancing age, an admission that puts those who make it at a disadvantage and denies that there is a discipline there. When I say my book is on "age studies," a tenured professor says to me jocularly, ruefully, gesturing toward his face, "Oh, your book is for me!" "For undergraduates, actually," I say, straight-faced, to see if that will help shake out his assumption. Nothing doing.

When I say my last book was about the midlife, even professors jest, "So this one is about old age?" (It's not.) No one would say to the Chinese historian, "So your next book will be about Japan?" because it's adjacent. Do they think that gerontologists can't be young? The linear positivism in these responses may seem inconsequential, but it piggybacks on the body without culture, sliding ponderously toward its end. In the United States, the median age is still the mid-thirties, and in some Third World countries in the teens, but we have it dinned into us through "alarmist demography" that the world is aging dangerously—meaning becoming crowded with old and poor women.[20] Age studies arrives on the scene just when decline ideology is making North Americans turn our heads away—politely of course. Perhaps making age a distasteful topic to study, on top of presenting it as a purely personal dilemma, is another crime against the life course.

People who accept the abstract idea that age is constructed at all ages may think they already know the ways age works. But as age critics reveal what is omnipresent and invisible, culture and our own selfhood will become a treasure hunt again. Once age ideology is the beast we're after, the hunt to discover which way it is lurching gets more intense. The trivial, the brushed-under-the-rug, the hurt the kids didn't quite know how to feel, the "natural" transformed into a new hydra head, the culture-denying body-based stories that the youthful "aging" can obsessively repeat, like Tourette's sufferers: everything grows more vivid. The ruling stars will shift again in their orbits.

People become sensitized, come alive in new ways. They see the magnitude of the effects, the beast's excretions hidden out in the open, in plain sight. Its marks are waiting to be found, scratched into our everyday contexts and all our formulations of life's events: in conversation most of all, even in a single sentence. They're decipherable—as *Aged by Culture* suggests—in the media, fiction, auto/biography; in worklife patterns, technologies; in historical analogies; in visualizations as slight as an old snapshot; in representations high and low, from museums to cartoons to poetry; in our private practices (even walking and talking, as chapter 9 suggests); in social, sexual, and family relations, law, politics, the corporation, the global economic system. Like any other cultural studies, age studies pounces on its evidence wherever it happens to lie.

To show that age is everywhere, and that the processes are not obvious, the topics of this book (refreshed by age studies considerations) include stories my mother told me and novels about the deaths of children; my son's early c.v. and my salary history; practices as far apart as niche marketing, theatrical casting, and midlife downsizing; age-graded emotions like anxiety, panic, envy, revenge. The chapters are not ordered chronologically, by age class. To make the tic of linearity less automatic, age studies benefits from sometimes treating the life course as reversible, looking backward (as I do in chapter 9). Better yet, our practice could sweep end to end from either direction, stopping wherever the action is: a serious indication of harm, a sign of freedom.

Age studies suggests that increasingly, discourses and practices and institutions address us as beings-who-age, rather than according to our other attributes. At any age, this has the "totalizing" effect from which "subordinated and disadvantaged identities" particularly suffer, in the words of philosopher Christine Overall.[21] Being reduced to our age is a process that is stigmatizing no matter what one's age, and some people avoid stigmas by closing their minds. As gendering and "race-ing" become less totalizing, can we keep "age-ing" from taking their place?

Beyond Slice-of-Life Studies

To accomplish its ends, age studies needs to clear a postdisciplinary space (like gender or race studies) that can encourage all the existing fields that "do" age critically to find ways to integrate. This breakthrough is not going to come through simple addition. Looked at one way, currently existing age studies, aside from life-span history and developmental studies, means gerontology plus childhood studies plus youth studies plus midlife studies. It's a slices-of-life field. So effectively are the slabs of the life course and the glaciations of historical time held apart that few people read up on other time zones. (For the scholars, they're not adjacent!) This is understandable. These fields developed in different eras and contexts, out of disparate methodologies, epistemologies, ethical and political interests, motives, passions. The literature is immense in some fields (like gerontology, which also has monster conferences and numerous journals) and little and uneven in others (like midlife studies, which is overwhelmed with pop psychology). Some disciplines are rich in social, feminist, literary, historical, and critical perspectives around age; in others, such approaches are marginalized. Each slice has its own blind side toward the construct of age.

The outcome is that in the very field—if age studies can yet be called a field—that should be deconstructing age, many practices inadvertently mimic decline ideology's divide-and-conquer strategy. We are often cheerily reminded that "everyone ages," but that pious fact will not by itself enable us to overcome the divisiveness of the new time machines. Age studies must certainly concern itself with representations of the "stages" and "cohorts," but warily, balancing its concern to note cultural differentiations with what Henry Giroux calls "the daunting fear of essentializing the category."[22] When I focus on the age curriculums of North American culture, I try to expose the particular age classes that are affected. Whether you and I will heed each new time machine as it is wheeled out depends not so much on how "old" we are chronologically as on whether its scope is trained on the age class we have come to identify with. Critics can work with more than one slice of life and blur the edges, as Susan M. Squier and Jennifer Hockey and Allison James do.[23] (Age culture can also make two stages seem alike, with consequences as unpleasant as when it constructs difference.) If in any given chapter, I start with a single age class, as I did in chapter 1, it is always to enable a comparative move—to discern, for instance, how threats, entitlements, and attributions (as well as actual losses and prizes) come to be distributed across the whole life.

Hope for the future integration of age studies comes from the exceptions to the rule of mimicry, by borrowing from the strengths of allied fields and by suggesting adaptations to them. Some of the most inventive critics are looking at self-writing and other narratives that construct life courses. They could attend to the age historians, whose focus on "local settings and particular populations moves the literature farther from the master narratives," as David Troyansky notes, while both could specify more exactly how the boss scripts function.[24] Critical feminist developmental psychology has much to contribute; so does family history, which deals with generations of real people in intimate connections and historical settings (rather than with named cohorts). Some researchers would need to concern themselves more with economics; others with representations of the life-course imaginaries. I will end part 2 by imagining in detail the merger of cultural studies (which ignores later ages) and critical/humanistic/feminist gerontology (which ignores earlier ages). That combo anticipates other postdisciplinary convergences that might be made for the sake of theorizing age better and analyzing the ideology to bits.

Integrating the Disciplines

Age studies is further divided by the disciplinary origins of those monitoring their special *tranche de vie*. Those studying childhood, for example, include literary and art critics, anthropologists, linguists, psychologists—cultural, narrative, and cognitive (Piagetian and other), psychoanalysts (Freudians, Jungians, Kohutians, feminists)—and so forth, not to mention researchers in pediatrics. Do they all recognize one another as fellows in childhood studies? Do any of them consider that they "do" age? Scholars and theorists who might collaborate are often in separate university departments. Each stage of life is like a large island approached by explorers coming from different directions. Sometimes divided by discipline *and* by their stage-of-life focus, explorers don't always meet cute. Some don't want to meet at all.

This is a preposterous situation, some readers may respond. Age studies, as anything more than my dreamy form of words, is like a lasso around an archipelago. But there are ways forward here too. Feminist cultural studies is an excellent model, although too often age is prominent by its absence. Two recent anthologies—*Figuring Age* (arising from a memorable feminist conference on age studies in the arts and humanities) and *The Handbook of the Humanities and Aging*, which includes social science perspectives—are impressive. Although both are fixed on what is called "later life," they demonstrate what the will-to-breadth can achieve in the right hands.[25]

The problem you set determines where you head for intellectual allies. All the hooks that the science museum exhibit sank into me—kids running away, damaging storytelling, parental anesthesia, technology's lies, biographical promises and life-course injustices, cultural crimes—led me to the necessary postdisciplinary future of age studies. Just to read that encounter through to the ideology that manufactured its components, assembled them, snuck the machine past the guards, and kicked it into action, I had to lasso together visual studies, narratology, socialization theory, history of time, life-course economics, the history of the emotions, ethical philosophy. I had to think childhood and the rest of life together.

My first question with any text, whether it has age written all over it or nowhere on it, is, "What *exactly* has age got to do with it?" Each time I would step out, hoping that feminist historians of acting, say—or theorists of the postcolonial body, or psychological anthropologists interested in development and social change, or critics of the novel—would have added age in just the way I needed or at least would be doing work finely textured enough for me to go forward. When I found good critics who ignored age as an analytic tool or used it perfunctorily, I fretted, "Why don't they try?" which led to, "What is left out?" Such mutters are the basso continuo of critique. I felt harsh at times toward those who naturalize trends that I think are contestable and merit a fight. The normative social scientists take for granted our malleability to the machine's behests. It's already a norm! End of story. Some postmodernists reinforce the cult of youth. It's uni-age? End of story. But this is not the place to be unwelcoming. When there's disappointment, that's also a cause of excitement: "Yes, age studies is needed here too."

This chapter is a first attempt to describe a reconfigured age studies. The rest of the book is my particular practice. I've been speculative at times. Speculation is the point of postdisciplinary fields—and the start-up risk they run. As age critics open up agendas at the borders of interdisciplines, "gaps" in our knowledge, methods, and theory may be defined differently by critics from the various fields that intersect ours, and may vary in importance to those critics. Practitioners could take to heart a warning of Stuart Hall's about an inherent problem: "If you work on culture . . . if culture happens to be what seizes hold of your soul, you have to recognize that you will always be working in an area of displacement. There's always something decentered about the medium of culture, about language, textuality, and signification, which always escapes and evades the attempt to link it, directly and immediately, with other structures."[26] What we can hope is that if we err or omit and someone objects, the field grows. Doing age work makes me feel both humble and exhilarated. For many, this state of affairs may be a lure.

$$\longleftrightarrow$$

Maybe few can practice age studies in its full eclecticism, yet our notions of what the field might gain from unifying can be comprehensive and utopian. Whatever our first disciplinary allegiances, we are likely to find that any advances in integration produce more complex, satisfying, and challenging accounts of culture and ideology, and guides to more successful resistance.

Age studies is and will be anthropological because the contents of a given age identity depend on individuals' positions within their heterogeneous cultures and communities and families. It is psychosocial and developmental because affects and stories depend on the relational, interactive, sometimes unconscious meanings of our ages, bodies, and named stages of life as these change and accumulate over time—and because age hierarchy can borrow from any bias toward accumulation. It is historical because it recognizes that age cultures change, sometimes rapidly, often unevenly, and with cause; and that people "write" their age autobiographies within the limits of particular conjunctions.

It is materialist in factoring in the economic sources of subjectivity, the structures that institutionalize the life course, and embodiment. It is above all humanistic (you see where *I* am coming from) because it emphasizes the language we use, the genres our stories get shaped into, our visual and verbal discourses. The most ambitious work would try to integrate the intrapsychic, the interpersonal, the communal, the economic, the literary and cultural, and the political, whether dealing with one stage or the whole life.

Becoming Articulate

Age critics must become more eloquent, coherent, and, to begin with, precise. Many of our most important experiences with age or aging—like those of the children in Boston and L.A.—pass with the wrong names or no names. Our unalphabetized lexicon of age-related concepts is puny. We are abandoned to ideology for lack of language. Age studies must struggle to bring misrecorded and unexamined experience into language. With aging narratives so covert, contradictory, and often invisible, it's time to define the sources of our storytelling about age and aging more inclusively, from the idiosyncratic to the conversational and interactive, and beyond to the local and national story forms. Building on the concept of telling single identities more completely over time, chapter 8 describes a critical form of age auto/biography that ends up in a richer version of selfhood. These are steps in the transformation of individual consciousness. Beyond this lies possible resistance to the dominant imaginaries— both progress and decline—and creativity in thinking age and aging beyond current social constructions.

Concepts are "always and only occasioned by problems," Elizabeth Grosz points out. Concepts for her are "temporary contraptions" whose function is to provoke "multiple responses, conceptual, perceptual, and affective." Vocabularies from one discipline can sometimes function well as "forms of mobilization" in others, "bringing together heterogeneous elements, creating new events, making the new real."[27] Publicizing concepts like the "premium on experience" and the "age/wage curve" reminds economists to consider age more often, and humanizing the terms through anecdotes engages noneconomists. "Timing"—another concept I borrowed from Tamara Hareven's life-span approach—when applied to cultural texts helped me think more exactly about speed-up and what was being contested in the war over the midlife.[28] My analysis here, with its new concepts, joins the struggle. Overall, I am trying to enlarge the ground "age" covers. Yes, I say to any age-workers who shy from the term "age." Yes, whether you "do" youth or you "do" old age or "the life course," you're on your way to age studies. To those in fields whose notions swim apart, I say, see what might happen when you net together odd fish, like "narrative" and "aging" and the "age/wage curve," "decline" and "childhood," the "stages" and "nonlinearity," "life-course imaginaries" and "life-course development." Into whatever debate is hot in your field (or beginning to cool off), try integrating age.

Doing age theory will change theory. Trying to integrate age into existing theory will raise perplexing questions, leading well beyond the confines of this book. To age critics looking at the contemporary world and its relation to past age cultures, age and aging are bound to become more puzzling at first. Perhaps that is my perception because of my temperament or the byways this book has led me, but I think estrangement is necessary to an emerging field. The children at the science museum were given a bad answer before they had posed a proper question. That's why they were bewildered and distressed. And so, but with deepening reflection, are we all. Age studies will pose the questions in response to perceived suffering and in response to its own internally produced curiosity. To put aging into the "tones" of theory (logical, comparative, wry, amazed, angry, utopian, whimsical, compassionate, interrogative, problematizing) is already to deprive decline of recourse to automatic features. May the contraptions we produce function well against the ever-new time machines.

Remaining Inclusive

Gender, race, class, sexuality, disability, nationality have each and interactively become more curious and interesting as critics exposed their cultural intricacies and historical origins. The same is happening with "age" and "aging" as they metamorphose into "being aged by culture." Most current age critics will, I hope, view themselves as part of the project even in these early days, before institutionalization into courses, journals, conferences, departments, centers. Some use the name "age studies" and know the eponymous book series and the Rockefeller Fellowships in Age Studies of 1996–1998.[29] In some disciplines, scholars will be glad to have respites from their age ghetto, where they get less consideration than they deserve, by moving into a postdiscipline where prestige accrues to those doing any part of this stimulating new work. Research projects that might have seemed arcane suddenly are linked to real concerns. Definitions matter.

Those who decide to participate in age work for the first time will probably—like current practitioners—want to reexamine their original discipline's presuppositions about age, determine fresh objects of study, try to elevate the level of age analysis in their own work, and devise more frequent joint agendas with age critics from other methodologies. Many theorists whose energies are necessary to the development of the field might suddenly join the project once it has the promise of being deconstructive, systematic, politically meaningful, and prestigious. Until now they have only paid lip service to age, as Kathleen Woodward points out more gently. "Along with race, gender and age are the most salient markers of social difference. Recent research in cultural studies has been virtually dominated by studies of difference. We have invented courses in colleges and universities that study gender, race, sexual orientation, ethnicity, and class. But not age."[30]

To enlarge its collective, age studies needs a critical pedagogy. Age could be mainstreamed in precisely those courses that pride themselves on teaching optimal resistance to propaganda. Such courses can be located in high schools, colleges, and programs for learning in retirement. Some people might teach age for its psychological benefits, to strengthen younger people against the decline forces colonizing their minds; heuristically, to strengthen ideology critique or explicate the construction of the emotions; or for political motives, like breaking down the difference that divides the body politic or organizing cross-generational alliances. New ideas about age will replace the simple formulas people spout if they have been driven by tabloid nightmares of "Geezer Takeover!" captive to visual terrorism and media scientism, or ashamed of declining so young and tempted by fantasies of *FountainofYouth.biz*. Some teachers and writers will seek to make themselves public intellectuals, eager to have "age critic" or "theorist" prefixed to their name if that will advance the project's objectives.

There's risk from another quarter. Age studies cries up "age" as indispensable—as a concept, a construct, a category. But age ideology also foregrounds age. It shouts, "Age is indispensable for thinking about society. Demography *means* age. Age matters more than any other difference." There are dangers inherent to the field likely to come from any successes we have. As I have shown, foregrounding age tends to minimize or obliterate other axes of difference. (The history of theories and movements that each for a time overemphasized their own category—woman, black—might also lead us to raise this issue.) The more we do our job as age critics, the more we might seem to reinforce the ideology, to listeners not ready to make distinctions. This is the salience problem in another guise.

Can we raise age consciousness without falling into such traps? Age studies has to place its warnings prominently.

←——→

If age culture is everywhere—if it is relevant at all ages, if the ideology is mystifying and threatening and its history still largely unknown, if the intellectual problems of age are challenging and constant and proliferate as soon as each commonsense certainty is discredited, if the theoretical issues are powerful and the political stakes are high, if knowledge about age changes people deeply—readers should sooner or later be moved to conclude, "Age *matters.*" Ever growing, the feeling "Age *really* matters, and we know how!" will sweep away many obstacles to engagement and pull others with us into its flow. And passionate insight is where all revolutions in thinking and behavior and action start.

Age Identity Revisited

What is this science which only holds good when its
subjects stand still?

—*Martin Nicolaus*[1]

Age and aging are absent from much of the theorizing that has made intellectual life so exciting in the past twenty years. Work done on topics like time, the body, narrative, socialization, identity, multiplicity of selves, and auto/biography (just to make a short manageable list), could usefully intersect with age or aging but often, disappointingly, does not. You don't have to call yourself an age critic to have noticed the problem. Charles Altieri, a decade ago, in "Temporality and the Necessity of Dialectic," broadly called age "the missing dimension of contemporary [postmodern] theory." Many feminists have said the same of feminist theory. Usually it's a lack of emphasis on *time* that gets noticed and explained: Frederic Jameson treated it as a neglect of modernist *durée;* Nancy Fraser explained it by observing how much of theory is written in spatial metaphors, which "bracket" the diachronic.[2] Even in theorizing that is explicitly diachronic, aging—an aspect of personal rather than historical time—is omitted. The idea that identity changes over time (a staple of researchers in development) remains stubbornly undeveloped in so-called high theory.

I want to relate this omission to a critical observation of Stuart Hall's: "The logic of the discourse of identity assumes a stable subject." This is an old problem: in Western culture since Locke, according to autobiography theorist Jens Brockmeier, identity is "that part . . . that remains unchanged."[3] But the problem has a contemporary source too. Some of the issues that have kept identity theory a compelling field over the past decade maintain a rigid unchangeability by focusing on imposed, internalized subject positions that (age theory would want to emphasize) we learn young. Constructionists in the tradition of ideology critique identified with Michel Foucault and Judith Butler are *this close* to treating having an identity as being in a permanent fix. Their constructed bodies (heterosexual, female, male, of color) are socialized in other ways but have no explicit age and experience temporality only as repetition.[4] (The anorexic body, by contrast, has an age because it comes from psychoanalytic and developmental theory.)

How can so much contemporary theorizing maintain a no-age subject and stubbornly neglect being aged by culture in an era of speed-up, premature superannuation, and named age cohorts, when the most cursory look at our age culture shows people (including immigrants from very different age cultures) internalizing a rigid new decline ideology not only in malleable childhood but in maturity? The present chapter contextualizes the newer fix identified in chapter 1: that Americans *must* change and "age" but also stay young forever.

I propose we start by taking more serious account of the *age-linked duration* that any narrative of time passing in a character's life represents. I think it's eye-opening to regard your selfhood as a set of narratives about aging, as required by aging within a given culture.[5] Examining lives-as-narrated in the United States generates new questions: not whether identities change but *when* narrators speak of change; not how hard it is to make liberating changes in general, but *why* in the case of aging, it is much harder. An age studies perspective produces a stronger critique of static notions of identity while not idealizing change. It takes a different step toward postidentity, and offers a more powerful way to protect oneself from decline ideology. I hope to get "age" and "identity" included whenever the topics of ideology or resistance arise. Age (specifically, aging-as-decline) can no longer be omitted from the lists of the great categorical oppressions.[6] By the end, more of us might recognize we have a great stake in the resistant projects of age studies—not only because we have bodies, but because we tell and retell our life stories.

IDENTITY IS A STORY OF AGING

Once you've lived long enough, an identity story is always a story of aging. In discussing identity formation, theorists tend to focus on change and stability.

(This brackets progress and decline, which I believe are always in play.) Emphasizing change or stability is also a narrative choice, and you don't make it the same way for every identity, or every time. In the practice of life storytelling, as Stuart Hall points out, "Most of us do recognize that our identities have changed over time." Pace Foucault, activists and critical theorists (feminist, multiculturalist, psychotherapeutic) argue that although it may be hard to shift, amend, or extirpate deeply internalized identities—"a more painful process than it sounds," Raymond Williams observed—some do manage it.[7] But even though some personal changes can be theorized as both possible and progressive, Hall suggests an empathetic political reason why theory has been static: "we've assumed that there is something which we can call our identity which, in a rapidly shifting world, has the great advantage of staying still."[8] "[B]elief in perpetual change, mobility, plasticity," comments Terry Eagleton, "is a fantasy largely in the service of the status quo."[9] It omits all the historical-strength coercions to feel altered and to speak of change. With these in mind, we understand why people—even survivors of genocides and exiles—may want to claim "I'm the same person I used to be." When it is a case of murders or expulsions, however, they can *name* the powers hostile to them. Not so for aging-in-culture.

"I'm the same person I used to be" is a verbal formula also deployed by people who have internalized that they are aging past youth, who feel an internal exile. (You don't say it on your tenth birthday.) It is intended as their way to still feel at home in the embodied self, but it feels weak and inconsistent because the same person then has to say, "Of course I've changed too."

In many sorrowful contexts, it is unclear whether an advantage lies on the side of emphasizing change or self-sameness. Adolescent native Canadians could be said to need *both:* their entire context must improve for them to remain valued persons in their traditional identity. Given workforce change, forced obsolescence, and the need to tell progress narrative, which is preferable: Should I say my identity is stable (to myself, for psychological reassurance) or should I say it's rapidly adaptable (to the demanding boss)? Which side is "progress" on? Clinging to change can be as repetitious, as coerced, as ideological, as telling a story of self-sameness. *Difference* from past selves is what global cosmopolitans increasingly harp on as the main meaning of the diachronic, while the excluded in all settings struggle for the means to make life changes equal progress.[10] *Change* as the meaning of aging needs as much historicized deconstruction as any other time machine in our robotic age vocabulary.

When the risks are high, our discursive decisions will be attempts to hold on to our worth. Disregard the etymology of "identity" from Latin *idem,* "same." It now refers just as plausibly to the self that we change or wish could change, because identity is really coming to mean "me-ness," and anything-for-progress might have to be my dominant story. Stillness and change can be simultaneously meaningful: true to the rules of culture, true to subjective feelings. Verbal choices representing the meaning of "aging" get made under pressure, in particular historical, geographical, economic, discursive, and chronological contexts.

I think we can end some of this fruitless oscillation and get other benefits as well by redefining the concept of "age identity." This term (or "aging identity") is widely used by humanistic gerontologists, but no one I've read has felt the need to define it. It usually seems to mean the "age lore" or pretheorized "age consciousness" of a person or imagined character who turns out to be no longer young, and whose ideas and feelings are cued to "aging" in standard ageist parlance ("Under *Sexuality,* see *Loss of libido, Viagra*"; "Under *Health,* see *Menopause; Alzheimer's*"). Most people's "age identity" appears to be heavy on the declining body and product placement, light on culture.

In my view, however, this turns age identity into a grim card catalog with an erroneous index. It might be good for the catalog to have a name (*Livre des idées réçues,* perhaps?), but not this one. It is, to begin with, misleading to skip over the young when identity stories can begin so early. It is dehumanizing to ignore the diverse ways we experience "aging" and our deep resistances to imposed declines. (Without these resistances, we would all be robots produced by the freaky time machines, and age studies would be run by a College of Cosmetic Surgeons.) It is illogical and damaging to keep "aging" in artificial conceptual isolation from our multiple identities. These identities could all be told better as stories of aging, properly defined. Indeed, in telling our life-course stories even in a naive way, we are carrying on an activity with latent subversive potential.

AGE IDENTITY AS AN ACHIEVEMENT

The days are gone, but are never to be emptied.

—*Penelope Lively*[11]

In my redefinition, age identity is an achievement of storytelling about whatever has come to us through aging. Anyone can produce such stories, starting fairly young. It takes only the slightest uptick of reflectiveness for people to observe that they may already do so, and to realize that, with not much effort, by underlining the interpretive element of "aging," they could do so more benignly, with more self-awareness, knowledge, and agency.

Age identity is a special subset of autobiography—which I understand broadly, as a narrative that anyone can tell about one's self, to self and others, whether informally in conversation or written for archival purposes. No particular level of education is required. Age identity is special because its focus is on the meaning of long time, although it can highlight one-time events or short periods as epiphanies. It's what I report when I stand back to survey where my "historic" trail has led me.[12] From observation and self-report, I think that identity over time can be seen as a sense of an achieved portmanteau "me"—made up, for each subject, of all its changeable and continuing selves to-gether—connected in different ways, or intermittently, but sometimes barely at all, to a sensuously material body.

This partially conscious, partially unselfconscious, agglomeration includes private, self-defined traits, relationships, heartbreaks, and desires: the secret my father told me when I was eleven; the one I told my son when he was twenty-one; stuff I'll never confide about early sex, ambitions relinquished, dreams maintained against the odds. Memories of this kind feel authentic, and if they are not, nothing is. Bharati Mukherjee, in her novel *The Holder of the World*, imagines a team collecting "the thousand most relevant facts, the thousand things that make me me, you you—to construct a kind of personality ge-nome."[13] Atop my thousand and one, I am the rich continuing heir of my past as well as the owner of the current last word. I believe in theory that all my age identities are tinged with culture and that I am the manipulative teller, but adding to my secret history feels different: exciting, sobering, serendipitous, endless.

Most of the rest of our age identities are personal versions of how the culture has seen us from childhood on. They start off socially constructed in a much more outer-directed way by coming with public labels like daughter, and cul-tural identities like girl and Jew and American, to mention only a few of my own earliest.[14] Body-based co-identities—gender, race, sexuality—can sometimes serve as examples of telling a story of change in age identity. Even though our families of descent may give some attributes of femaleness or nonwhiteness or homosexuality a good vibe, it doesn't take much aging for those of us with non-dominant identities to discover that these attributes have degrading sides and to possibly feel ourselves trapped in them. There may have been miserable early periods of wishing-to-have-another-body (or passing), that is, of trying to get out of the fix by changing oneself rather than the culture. But by reimposing our own meanings on these disgraced "identities," we can privately experience them as real, positive, necessary, even cherished possessions. As June Jordan says, "I am reaching for words to describe the difference between a common identity that has been imposed and the individual identity any one of us will choose, once she gains that chance."[15] The sociology of knowledge distin-guishes between socially ascribed and private meanings for identity.[16] Volun-tarily discarding "identities" that have become unwanted or altering their meanings can also be part of the process of forming an age identity. Aging can give us proofs that we have some narrative agency, some way of squeezing out from under subjections.

In how many ways has "woman," for example, changed its meaning for me? Over time, I learned how to extirpate those elements of female identity that made me hate myself (as the not-male, the intellectual inferior, she-who-decays-more-rapidly). Over decades of adulthood I have gained a more private, more valuable gendered identity: "Woman" began to mean, for example, women-identified, child-rearing, resourceful, career-oriented, politically active, and a good deal more. (What "causes" such developments—history, maturational processes, initiative, premiums for experience, sheer luck, the power of narrative forms?—is a separate issue for the next chapter. Here I just call it "aging.") Each identity—parent, activist, writer—could also be told separately, through its own thematic narrative. "White" became a conscious identity with a history. In remaking/retelling selfhood, I was helped mostly by female friends of different ages and racial/ethnic origins who were getting out of similar fixes. Backed by feminism, many of us tried to enhance the dominant public definitions of "female," "black," "Asian." Continuity lies in the label I choose to hold on to ("woman"), change in the subjective contents of the named category.

In other words, as Stuart Hall helpfully suggests, "We have now to reconceptualize [age] identity as a *process* of *identification*." [17] In contrast to *conferred* identity, psychologist James Marcia says, "identity begins to be [willingly] constructed when the individual starts to make decisions about who to be, with what group to affiliate, what beliefs to adopt." [18] Presumably this starts after childhood and goes on with increasing authority throughout life. Black and Latino empowerment, transgendered pride, anti-anti-Semitism, postcolonialism—there are many models for discarding "imposed" attributes and developing acceptable ones with difficulty, relief, or exultation. Sandra Lee Bartky describes the "dialectic" of her "hyphenated consciousness" as a Jewish American over many decades and many contexts. William S. Wilkerson gives a wonderfully clear example of "transformation" from his "pre-gay" situation, when in some sense he didn't know who he was, to gay identity. The new knowledge he gained altered his prior "experience." [19]

I'm most interested in the ideological changes reported as new truths and freedom. But every thread of selfhood that requires the Before and After of aging can be turned into a story of identity. When did you pick up a certain skill or overcome a painful ignorance? The telling need not be in the form of a progress narrative: how you came to be an alcoholic, lost your wife, or earned your peak wage at forty-three can make just as engaging a story. Who is utterly lacking in age identities? Who does not have at least one to bore the public with? Who does not gnaw a somewhat different version of the same one, privately? Any self we can identify has a potential story line, potentially rich in detail and value, deeply imbricated in time, and made possible by aging.

Theorists rightly propose that we possess multiple selves. But so far that means only synchronic, simultaneous selves bumping hips. These multiples look pretty static from the point of view of age studies. We can be multiple not just simultaneously but—crucial to any complete accounts of selfhood or of historical changes like speed-up—*sequentially.* I learned this first from Proust, who early in *A la recherche du temps perdu* named the Marcel who had formerly loved his girlfriend Gilberte a dead self. The person "who remembers [her or] his past has not been for a long time the same being, the child or adolescent [or, I add, midlife person or elder] who lived that past," Georges Gusdorf says.[20] I too sometimes call my past selves "her" rather than "me."[21] But age identity's "community of selves" is panoptic enough to incorporate such ghosts. I also recognize some of those "hers" as me, particularly when I recall sentences said by my much loved dead or when I perform activities I started long ago.

When I use "multiple selves," I mean to emphasize the diachronic side of each identity (while remembering that sequence too is a story). Leigh Gilmore speaks of "the profound shakiness caused by the motion of all these *Is.*"[22] Temporally, there are more kinds of shaking going on. When I think of co-identities aging together, I observe another novelty. Multiculturalists say our co-identities can't be separated, that they blend. This is sometimes true. Some intertwine in effects—say, activism against racism, against sexism, and against decline, fortifying one another. But at times, one co-identity rises in importance: being "a parent" of an adult son in wartime, being "a woman" in a new marriage, being "no-longer-young" in a new workplace where everyone is half your age, being "independent" when newly unemployed. At such a time, the explosive dominance of that identity becomes one's major new story. Or—back to the poetics and politics of continuity—your major story could be defying people who want you to change an identity and hugging onto it, maybe even as it becomes anachronistic: considering oneself a "youthful" rebel when one is in fact an effective midlife activist.

If, in telling our state-of-being, we find some co-identities disliked but admitted; some discarded or defunct; some unchanged; some improving; some in flux of new importance; some about loss and some about gain—all in all, the storied identities feel like possessions. Mine. Achievements of my telling and of my aging. Such achievements deeply and rightly matter to people.

Freely Holding On

We may be able to estimate how much our storied identities matter, if we can tease out why people might resist the idea of having an important identity stripped from them. Although as a first-year student in college I wrote a paper titled "I Wish I Were a Man" and meant it, I would now be shocked to wake up one morning in a parallel universe in a male body-mind. I would fight to get back my lifelong, self-defined female aspect even if I had to relinquish some thrilling male privilege to do so. I would fight the same way if I woke up in the mind-body of another woman.

I would fight the same way if I woke up recognizably "myself" but appreciably younger. As an experiment, an alluring trip in a time machine, this has a momentary appeal. A brief visit could be a memory refresher, a chance to visit with my dead, avoid that back injury. But if it had to be a life sentence to start over again at thirty-three or forty-seven, the prospect quickly becomes dismaying, a guarantee of losses. I don't want to know less, have felt less. I would not want to skip back into the past with the certainty of losing the later practices and stories—even the failings—I have acquired. Together, they make me. "I" am a package, I discover, of achieved selfhood. When I have been thinking deeply in this vein, my body-mind has less surface upon which decline is writing, more that is etched from within by experience. (This is relevant to acting age, discussed in chapter 9.) If I couldn't be the same embodied self, I cannot wish to have an earlier bodily surface. Although decline assures me that at a later age I will inevitably wish just that, I want to go on record as stating that, short of chronic pain or terminal illness (and who knows, perhaps even then), I plan with the help of age studies to defeat that prophecy.

In short, if I felt that *any* of my important identities could be threatened by a switch, I'd fight. I discover through this experiment that I want my identities, public and private, to be relatively stable—not inert but within my control, changeable primarily at *my* will, narratable first of all and most authoritatively by me. I need to wake up every day securely still "me." My native mind-body— as is, keeping my smells, my quirky pinky, my laugh lines, my swath of gray, my prior "hers"—I find works for me here as a sign of continuity, wholeness, and change: whatever I currently know as me-ness. In fact, age identity must have some healthy narcissism attached to it because I find the word "unique" rising in a wicked and irrepressible way. No objection known to me quite squelches it.

I imagine most people who have lived in their adult selves for decades would find some level of similar resistance to such proposed switches. They do not have to be certified age critics who have read essays on counternarratives and age activism. They do not have to like every aspect of their "me" to value their age identity, follow my argument, or do age studies. In fact, the people likely to gain most are those who dislike parts of their "body-based" selves—the parts they label "aging." They can try to make concentrating on the rich history of their identities as customary as a tic, as necessary as exercise. By practicing this storytelling on a lot of identities marked as "achievements" rather than declines (some of them, like race and gender, body-based), they may build up their sense of the overall value of time passing—just as they learned to do as children—and see whether this habit changes the ratio for them.

Aging is what matters in these accounts: "long-known" if not "decades" has been a necessary term, and "acquisition"—of story and identity and sometimes agency—has been a latent idea. This is no irritating abstract "temporality." Acquiring secrets, deciding whom to become, affiliating, adopting beliefs, "verifying" a new identity—this takes life time.[23] Or, if we hold that a particular identity is static, it is because we have proved our commitment to it. Either process requires evidence over time. Seen from within, identities are personal and recognizable outcomes, confirmed by aging. Some of mine started in childhood. The back story of "the Brain," "the finally befriended": I could have told these when I was fifteen. One or two didn't have a usable narrative shape until I was forty, and that shape has probably changed since. Some skip periods or whole "age stages" when nothing much happened to that particular identity, as the students found through Jo Spence's phototherapy groups. It doesn't require much life time to acquire an age identity or two; but presumably the more aging, the bigger the range of our identities that have acquired stories around them and the fuller and more shapely the stories.

Achieved identity—intimate, rarely spoken, feeling long-lived-in whether it is or not—constitutes our sense of coming into being. Aging involves a narrative. Aging *is* a set of narratives. I have been praising aging aslant, but it's good to make our appreciation explicit before we ask how much these tellings are under our own control.

←——→

Through a fragment of autobiography and a mental travelogue, I have made a start at adding an intimate narrative of aging to the account of self-fashioning. Literary, cultural, and social theory need this. Doesn't selfhood in a postmodern era need a slowed-down, fuller account of the fourth dimension? Each story and the accumulated, comprehensive self could be called, without confusion, "age identity." I would prefer a term with a gerund, the "-ing" of ongoingness. "Aging identity" would be less static. But at the present time "aging" is so crowded toward later life, it's problematic. The term "aging identity" might keep a reader of twenty-five from asking herself whether she has a story to tell that comes from aging-past-childhood and thus getting the cultural protection of starting this verbal practice young. But in the coinage "age identity," aging is the *ground of possibility* of developing any identities at all.

AGE IDENTITY AND IDENTITY STRIPPING

It is important to adjust our view of selfhood to recognize that we feel loyalty toward what, on reflection, can certainly be called "aging," because there *is* one actual and fearfully powerful public project that undoes our age identity for us: decline ideology. An invisible producer of economic differences, an omnipresent regulator of age-inflected discourses, a constant pressure on our sense of life time, its master narrative needs to be revealed in all its workings. The dominant European-American model gives shape and meaning to what sociologist Marlis Buchmann has called the "public life course." [24] But, using a body-based story in a divided society, the master narrative of aging comes in specific differentiated "versions" (told by or about men, women, various classes, races, sexualities, ethnicities). You tailor it to yourself, fitting together uniquely personal, group, and universal elements.

The master narrative starts, as we have seen, as a story of progress and becomes a peak-and-(early)-decline story. The peak now occurs long before death or old age, heading backward toward an idealized early midlife or young adulthood. [25] Even if it were possible for one period of life to be consistently better on most measures than all other periods, as youth is supposed to be, no one stays long in the good "stages." Chronological aging—one of the most interesting inventions of civilization—and the drift encoded in the stages might all by themselves assure "change," but not that change is read as primarily loss or exile. [26] Even "the Xers" (so recently a synonym for youth) are told they are "aging," the social name for bad alterations. According to the prevailing script, even if we also make progress, we are supposed to internalize decline as our dominant private age identity.

I think we could usefully call this process "identity stripping," because it is a story of losing what we had. [27] What American youth *has* includes a personal share of such valued traits as attractiveness, health, creativity, brains, charm, articulateness, efficacy, sensitivity, and, best of all, promise. "Promise" means not just stable possession of such cultural capital, but accumulation. During the long midlife, people telling age identities might therefore be expected to rank their "self" same or higher on many measures—at least when speaking to self in honesty or to pollsters hoping to quantify positive aging. As I noted earlier, many do.

But the situations are innumerable when they don't or can't access this treasure; or when their continued telling of progress stories feels subtly faked—Main Street showiness, a partial lie. Personal traits (in contrast to socially given ones like "male" or "Japanese-American") can seem to the possessor more fragile, subjective, less solid. For some, drops in socioeconomic status drag their valued traits down. The children in the science museum were hit with the loss of facial attractiveness, the first item on my list. With remarkable regularity, when decline offers a cue, adults' autobiographical accounts draw on its scripts.

Many decline narratives appear too shameful to tell: the losses are too devastating or permanent. But one fragment that many speakers have been taught to consider obligatory is a "Scene of Confession" when a speaker admits ranking lower on allegedly age-related items.

"Welcome to middle age!" I was thirty-three years old at the time, and I had just injured my lower back on a squash court. "Welcome to middle age!" my squash partner remarked as he observed me unable to stand up straight. It was the very first time I had been invited to think of myself as middle aged and I did not welcome the comment. . . . As I told [others] about my life-stage transition on the squash court that afternoon they shared with me their remedies for countering or at least slowing, the drift into middle age.[28]

The man telling this story is a professor of anthropology, an expert on old age in India who goes on to call the Euro-American midlife a cultural fiction with real consequences: in other words, he's an age critic. But by beginning his excellent anthology with an anecdote about his "life-stage transition" into worse health at thirty-three (health was the second item on my list of valued traits), and by not challenging his interlocutors' reliance on "remedies" for "slowing the drift," he implies that there is no way anyone can critically resist dominant age ideology. But aging was not what happened first in his body. It was an injury. If he had been a college athlete, it would have been treated with a non-age-graded antispasmodic rather than a joke.

The repertory teaches the "naturalness" of an abrupt "Entry into Midlife Aging." This tale, set on another court, is also told by a man and a professor:

A few years ago, in my late thirties, I began to play basketball with undergraduates at Boston College. After a few months I became a "regular" on the court and imagined that I was just "one of the guys." One day as I was walking off the court, feeling particularly good about a well-played game, a teammate turned to me and said, "Nice game, *sir.*" That one communication disabused me of the "one of the guys'" self-image. Everyone experiences similar moments during which age-related self-conceptions are called into question.[29]

The exchange he describes has nothing to do with his traits, or any necessary loss. It's about a remnant of polite age hierarchy that the older man dislikes. The author, a professor of sociology, concludes this anecdote in a rational, confiding tone, with a static social-science reminder that "everyone experiences similar moments," as if experience were obligatory and had no cultural component.[30] He calls his essay "Changing Age Consciousness," but he's no agent of change. His mind was changed for him. This anecdote is not told in a tone of pain; it's only rueful. But it teaches the lesson of passive resignation all the better.

Such scenes of confession and sudden entry into precocious midlife aging used to be thought of as women's stories; now more often they are also told by men. This suggests how much male privilege at midlife has been eroding. Here is further proof that middle-class white men (including tenured professors) are being more firmly joined to women in the devalued category of the "middle aged," at ages in their mid and late thirties. (The serious unisex effects—his-and-her face lifts, male biological clocks as well as female—have nothing to do with midlife gender "convergence," psychology's name for voluntary changes in which men become more affective and women more efficacious, crossing a gender border that operates more strongly on youth.) If midlife decline is the current "human" reality, men too must repeat fragments of it. And women who are feminists may find a renaturalized discourse of the "human" harder to fight. It will require a new mind set.

When well-educated and sensitive people overlook problems, it is often because an Other is in question. But these fragments show how we can dutifully apply decline metaphors to our own selves: even practiced trope-users do. (The two men whose stories I quote don't appear to accept decline's most desolating conclusions, but others—including the children in the science museum—might.) Decline does not make us feel more at home in our body-mind. Whatever an "I" is richly fashioning inwardly as an age identity, the tight script begs us to confess that "I am *really* losing—and *must* lose." We may fall deeper into naive positivism and discouragement with every passing day.

In circumstances like these, the need emerges "to protect the mature imagination from hostile and fragmenting conceptions of the life course," as social gerontologist Simon Biggs puts it.[31] Why is it so hard, even being young, to fend off the master narrative of decline?

Telling the Master Narrative of Decline Pertinaciously

Decline's power over our narratives is overdetermined, as I showed in part 1 through mounting evidence from various venues, including pop culture (toothpaste containers, fashion photos, horror movies), medical visits, personnel offices, discrimination law. Decline's "knowledge" circulates in daily cliches ("You're only as old as you feel") and goes all the way up to the most elaborated age anecdote of all, the realist novel. Decline's discourses are simple, thorough, vastly diffused, sly, and all-explanatory. But I've said that saturation doesn't explain why some apply them personally and others don't. Even having one's age class directly targeted by the messages doesn't explain enough.

Here I want to emphasize the more general, invasive operations of decline's repertory. What we call "experience" is always mediated; it is an interpretive moment although it may not be felt as such. When the experience is pain, or a loss, or a potential loss, it may come already marked as "age-linked." This may or may not have any scientific accuracy (and the science, as the HRT debacle of 2002 showed, is always changing). If you decide that the source is physiological decline rather than something that is *not* age-linked, or if you believe that decline points to a pure body without cultural admixture, this may have serious adverse consequences. Decline shapes cognition, worldview, feelings. "There is no subject whose identity and desires have not been shaped to some degree" by dominant fictions, as Kaja Silverman says. Powerful mediations, as William Wilkerson remarks, affect "both what we attend to and what we might infer from our experience." [32] Decline blocks alternative focuses and happier conclusions, more optimistic planning, more mixed emotions.

With culture wiped off the blackboard, decline teaches us to be minutely and excruciatingly attentive to designated parts. When Clov in Samuel Beckett's *Endgame* says, "There's no more nature," Hamm rants, "But we breathe, we change! We lose our hair, our teeth! Our bloom! Our ideals!" [33] Each confession makes us one more instance of universal decline. Thus we treat our singular body-mind as just one among others. Paul Ricoeur calls this "impersonal description." [34] Decline drags a chain of "inevitability" however young we are when forced to say we feel it, making us forget the odds that we may keep our jobs and enjoy later-life health and longevity. Losing a tooth or forgetting a name,[35] waking up in a sweat or not reaching an orgasm, if decline owns the narrative, become "symptoms" that sweep us forward on the slick rails of the ideologized life course from "age-related" to "death." Men and women learn to resent the "body" that lets them down, rather than blaming the forces that structure feelings of decline and that link "age" to the body in knotted chains of signifiers. Your pain, the *same* pain, once it is considered "age-related," may entail *more* suffering. It is to counter this that I try to wrench the signifer "aging" conceptually farther away from later life and closer to narrative, and use "identity *stripping*" even though it could be argued that decline builds an oversized new identity on the basis of body parts.

Acceptance of decline has powerful effects—even, paradoxically, benefits. Sandra Bartky has explained that disciplinary practices that turn a "female" body into a "feminine" one can be conceived of as skills. To acquire a "sense of mastery" and "secure sense of identity," I imagine that some girls might play smaller, dumber; boys, tougher, colder.[36] Becoming an older body under the sign of decline involves masochistic internalizations that run all the way to self-hatred, but skillful learners of the narrative also acquire a thorough explanatory system. By reinforcing the "realism" and human universality of the supposedly all-biological process, decline lore confers astringent Emersonian wisdom on those who repeat it: "I know the script! I accept life! (What choice do I have?)" This counters whatever might gripe us if we let ourselves feel the idiocy of having to repeat the scripts, be the butt of jokes, find a smiling face for every defect another person is allowed to notice, on and off the squash court. How can the professor rebut? "I'm thirty-three, you yo-yo!"? "Don't project your middle-ageism on me"? "Fuck 'life-stage-transition' language"? And how can we deflect the pity if our disability is worse than having your back go out on the squash court? Age theory has no sound bites yet. Every invention is a tongue twister. But any lame thing will do to break the automaticity.

Decline, on its side, has slick answers to every critical objection. "Vanity" dismisses anti-ageism. Countering aging is simply self-interest; how could that be a collective concern? (If you overlooked an early mention of my age, have you been trying to decide how old—or young—I am? How old must I be, in your opinion, to care about my age identity and call losing bits of it "identity stripping"?) Anti-ageism is also circumvented by the current definition of "resistance." In the general population, which includes, of course, the academic world, resistance often amounts to little more than mouthing—signing discreetly, in as many ways as possible—"*I'm* not aging" or "*I'm* not middle-aged." Decline provides a regime of knowledge in which decline is "truth" and resistance is called (borrowing from psychoanalysis at its most hegemonic) "denial." When "acceptance" is structured as the opposite of "denial," this constitutes aging as a biological "truth" (only truths can be "denied"); builds in failure (you confess your aging faults, laugh at ageist jokes, groan at the mention of birthdays), and structures consumption of anti-aging goods, practices, and medications as the only egress.

As Raymond Williams remarked (not in connection with age, unfortunately), "A structure of feeling as deep as this enacts a world, as well as interpreting it, so that we learn it from experience as well as from ideology." [37] When unopposed, age ideology can make us experience aging as if decline were, at one and the same time, (1) the *only* process of time, (2) a merely *personal* process (an effect that ignores both the universalizing features of the master narrative and its supple constructions of difference), and (3) a *universal* biological process (an effect that erases economics, other group vulnerabilities, and one's latent power to describe one's own age identities differently). Against all that, continuity or progress could seem a harmless sweet fable.

Presumably the next stage after a person accepts decline in the body-mind, in a culture where the loudspeakers blare out positive aging, is to figure out how to live with it. Is the answer a pseudophilosophical "ambiguity": both are true, a little progress, a little decline? Or does one try to decide that one or the other is *more* true, if only for oneself? Some people practicing positive aging make decline come true by diving into anti-aging practices. Yet even deciding to work out a few hours longer a week refers to a competitive contrast with a past self and can lead to nostalgia. Dyeing one's hair—surely quite harmless to others, even if it lets down the side—reminds one frequently that one is passing for younger, a drip-drip of demoralization.

Very little evidence of decline is accepted as proof that decline is stronger than progress (a single word like "sir" can do it). As long as nature dominates the nature/nurture framework, it will take enormous, continuous, Sisyphean, evidences of progress to counter this. Absent age theory, decline can often win hands down, as we undeniably grow older *and* the media and the economy produce more evidence of decline occurring younger. This simultaneity can have a bewildering, confounding effect even on age critics.

To the degree that we learn to tell the script of change-as-decline feelingly, each of us loses power doubly—to create our own unfolding narrative of age identity and to share it publicly. Decline narrative used to make me helpless. Now that I see it as narrative (backed up by economics), it offends me. The sorrow that some people direct at "aging" would be better directed into anger at the culture that produces daily doses of indoctrination and decline "experience."

REBUTTING THE SCRIPTS/TELLING
AUTOBIOGRAPHY RESISTANTLY

There is a way out if one recognizes that decline is an ideology, learns more about its techniques, and invents resistances. As someone who has been slowly teaching myself a critical age-conscious perspective over many years, I think that once we begin to resist, age work will be psychologically liberating, intellectually energizing, politically empowering. Here and in chapter 8, I stick with selfhood and strengthening the self through analysis, rebuttal, and life storytelling. To begin with, age studies needs little more than educated sensitivity to decline cues and a quick tongue. (To the squash partner from hell, I would like to say, "And *you* get the Ponce de Leon Prize for Early Ageism.")[38] As we undo our internalizations, our ripostes will come more quickly.

The basketball court anecdote can also be reframed resistantly. Everything about that miniature narrative hid its social construction. The professor's maleness and occupational superiority need to be pointed out. Settings like colleges, gyms, certain parts of cities, work places, and vacation spots over the past thirty years have come to be youth-oriented, provoking the spiteful age gaze and generation-gap discourses. Narratively, the professor was not untutored and unprepared. Expecting such a scene, young as he was, he in fact constructed a perverse rite in which, on a sacred site—the basketball court—he expelled himself from guyness by interpreting a single syllable as an expulsion order from the entire status-superior group. Perhaps the younger teammates had been waiting for him to say, "Call me Dave," while the professor deferred, enjoying a pleasant sense of age hierarchy. Privileged attributes may also be *lost* on becoming merely one of the guys. The professor might have told a more interesting story had he reported that he had some share in producing as well as interpreting this exchange. He could have wondered whether regretting seniority serves his and our purposes. If only for their readers' sake, anyone who thinks the world needs another edition of the "Entry into Midlife Aging" should stop and ask what pressures have led them to such self-conceptions.

Say that next, building on success, we refuse to confess. I want to repudiate the official story entitled "Your Desperately Failing Memory" and stage a "Scene of Not Confessing." Here's one replacement for the standard script:

Possessing my precious age identity, when I need to quickly sum up the quality of my mind (in private), I expect a positive balance. As I slowly overcame the sexist infantilization of graduate school, I accepted that I have a good-enough brain. But suppose one day self-judgment is anxiously cued by a new strip stratagem. "My memory loss!" At that panicky moment, feminist age studies reminds me that I have no reason to speak that script of self-estrangement automatically. My trouble is having caught a very nasty virus from our toxic age culture. My task should be to discover the virulent strain that lowered my defenses.

Midlife memory loss as a profound decline became a dangerous and unavoidable theme in the 1990s. Conversations, print, "information" essays, and advertising taught Americans how "natural" it was. A fiftyish friend sent a birthday card about forgetfulness and wrote, "I'm trying to remember to take gingko, BUT . . ." Steve Martin got an entire page in the *New Yorker* to tell the same joke, under the title "Changes in the Memory after Fifty." Martin cleverly parodied the midlife self-help books that construct a titanic defect in order to offer their supposedly simple solution: "Sometimes it's fun to sit in your garden and try to remember your dog's name. Here's how: simply watch the dog's ears while calling out pet names at random." *USA Weekend* had a long article called "Are You Losing Your Mind?" which asserted that "age-associated memory impairment" can begin "in the 30s but usually becomes noticeable in the mid-40s to early 50s. . . . Even a slight decrease in memory seems like a tragedy," the author editorialized, instructing us how to feel.[39] As products appeared, the media made Alzheimer's into an epidemic among the elderly, a nightmare for Boomers.

Only middle-ageism explains why memory problems are suddenly being popularly associated with the early midlife. Decades of research show that memory loss is not accurately associated even with old ages, and that if "source memory" weakens, aging brings compensatory mental gains.[40] We know that children have trouble memorizing answers to test questions, and teenagers have problems recalling errands, yet age-associated memory loss is not associated with the young. If stress produces cortisol-controlled degeneration (one theory that accepts the hypothesis of age-graded loss), why not blame stress agents, like your ex, 24/7, the distractions of multitasking, your lack of health insurance? Most research on memory only compares college students to subjects over seventy. Memory at midlife has never been thought different enough to need study.

All of this contrasts vividly with a remark made by my late father-in-law in the 1960s. George was a brilliant raconteur, handsome, white-haired since thirty, a college professor. He once said to the assembled young, "I've forgotten more than you'll ever know." David and I repeated the witticism with relish, as a promise that we too would have his huge capacity for knowledge by the time we came to be his age. Thirty years ago, within the vastness of midlife competencies, forgetfulness was not a devastating portent. Age hierarchy was unwounded.

The shock that leads people to age theory may come from seeing that they actually have a *choice* of narratives—between the dominant one that wars against their own best interests and an as-yet-to-be-written one that serves them.[41] If we have children, we cannot prevent them from learning the narrative norms, but we can protect them through counternarratives. "How I Developed My Most Important Age Identity" could be a dinner table round-robin, along with "My Earliest Experiences of Ageism." To develop age consciousness, a parent could say, "You already have an age identity as a mentor/amateur entomologist/reader of chapter books," or observe, "Oh, that's a decline story, isn't it?"

Startling changes might come from taking aging seriously as meaningful discourse. How can we ever have thought we aged by nature alone? As age studies radical hypothesis leads it to enlarge the domain of the cultural, let's enjoy the pleasure of being undeceived. As age studies diminishes the realm of the natural, let's rejoice each time resignation becomes unnecessary. As the Serenity Prayer suggests, wisdom is learning to know the difference.

In this chapter, I have treated naivete in the writing of age identities not as a problem but as a resource. In the chapter 8, lack of true age consciousness is the problem I begin with. Because age identity is always already another narrative, it can become more conscious of its own workings. The "Scene of Not Confessing" is an example of writing about being aged by culture *critically*. Age-wise autobiographies will pit explicit analysis against insinuations, getting us beyond existing ideology critiques. Thinking aging through this thicker kind of life writing is a step in the transformation of consciousness. Hasn't "aging" already come to seem far more complex? It looks better in quotation marks, more unnatural.

GETTING ON WITH AGE THEORY

There is invigorating, complicated work ahead, even as a dismaying conclusion emerges: Americans are now probably more vulnerable to cultural aging than to any other known cultural assault. But I am sometimes sanguine. Movements based on other deconstructions have made headway in the decades since Foucault's despondency about whether subordinated identities could change. I count on anger, hope, curiosity, and a dawning sense that bit by bit we can sub-due some of decline's cohorts, gleaming in scarlet and gold. On our side we have narcissism, the need for continuity, the habit of progress narrative from child-hood, the adult practice of telling more complex age identities, remnants of age hierarchy. Many people have these native resources. Some might find them-selves motivated to transfer their existing ideology critique—the respect, sen-sitivity, skills, and urgency that go into analyzing gender, class, race/ethnicity, sexual identity, nation, or place—to this new field of power and contest, age.

As we further inventory the multiple sources of decline ideology, many people who wouldn't (yet) fight the power of globalization, the wage race-to-the-bottom, or seniority-busting head on may choose cultural combat at some point because this script feels too tight. What is "undeniable" is fixed too nar-rowly: the genres too few, the tones of voice delimited, the plot outlined. We are made to be "story poor." That our children may also come to suffer such "nar-rative deprivation" might give this mission another motive.[42] Once we can dis-tinguish between the culture's master narrative of aging and our own versions, we may conclude that its threats to being and becoming are resistible.

At best, as life storytellers we will be recovering ageists for a very long time. But people have much to gain, even on their lonely own. One by one we can mock the harmful banalities that injure us. If as a result of my repudiating the "Scene of Shocked Forgetting," the other confessions and entries, other people were to bite their tongues before launching into similar decline stories and then feel wickedly liberated and go on to badmouth another compulsory practice, a larger community would already be alive. And as a collective forms, bold en-deavors no longer seem impossible.

Unlearning the master narrative of decline may be as painful and prolonged as extirpating internalized racism and sexism. We'll need self-love to get through the process. We'll need tolerance—or do I mean impatience—as people go on dinning the dominant narrative into our ears. We'll need aggres-sion to finger the commerce in aging. We'll need power to reveal the age effects of transnational capitalism, to change the practices that are backing decline down the life course.

Perhaps selfhood in a postmodern era will *not*, after all, have four dimen-sions in the current way. The modern self in twentieth-century America has been like those blow-up toys that fall over from their low center of gravity. In-sofar as "temporality" was implicitly reduced to one dominant narrative of the life course (the oppressive, biologized/positivist, universal decline story), the material body loomed lopsided, body-heavy, with grotesquely age-graded fea-tures. But if, in a gigantic cultural shift, we begin to redescribe life time through innumerable age-conscious narratives, the culture might finally find itself mov-ing toward a different kind of "body-mind." This one would be weighted with culture at all ages. Aging would be a constitutive aspect of all identities, and identities would be an achievement of aging. Once "age" joined "race" and "gender" and "disability," as a trouble sign of imposed difference, many "body" references would make no sense unless put within scare quotes. The body, less the victim of the hypercritical age gaze, would feel less spectacularly "specular." In more and friendlier contexts—as I detail in chapter 9—the self could perform its body as a highly present, individuated, interesting, expressive, favored partner. Subjectively, to its owner, the body-mind would retain its valuable narcissism much longer in the life course. If we decline less, we might not need to say we "age less."

Perhaps when "the body" intersects with age, our stories cannot ever be entirely free of cultural impositions. But even now we can imagine a good deal more freedom and pleasure and hopefulness in having an age identity than many of us currently experience—a better chance at those values that the master narratives deny.

From Life Storytelling to Age Autobiography

> But to get access to what one possesses within, apparently
> the most natural thing in the world, is actually the most difficult.
>
> — *Gabrielle Roy*[1]

THE EMBODIED PSYCHE IN CULTURE, OVER TIME

The embodied psyche in culture, over time: I would offer that this formulation of selfhood is the true Grail of the human sciences. This is what writers dream of representing, what theorists yearn to understand. There is a subtle war going on within the disciplines about what others omit. Anthropologists believe that what gets left out of nonethnographic accounts of the life course is "culture," the unregarded atmosphere.[2] Psychotherapists claim that the severest neglect is of "psyche": neither ethnography, biography, nor surveys can reach deep enough into each particular interior self or into the family matrix that cuts mental pathways for the temporal journey. Developmentalists believe that they alone get beyond child-centeredness to the whole life. Psychological anthropologists, material-feminist psychoanalysts, and interactionist philosophers all think it is their field in particular that bridges the inner and outer divide, best integrating intersubjectivity, or the body-mind. Historians retort that then the likeliest omission is *long time:* Anticipating majority or menopause in the America of 1860 was different from doing so in 1960. All rely on their privileged form of narrative, now that "the narrative turn" that has been the beat of the humanities has started to have profound effects on social studies.

Age critics seek the same Grail, and they counter that "over life time" is now the dimension of culture that (in contrast to "psyche" or even "embodiment") most needs to be unfolded and expanded. Putting aside the great achievement of learning to tell age identities, where age is concerned the last thing the self seems to understand are the circumstances that have beat on its tellings. It knows all too well its age "troubles" (to borrow a distinction from C. Wright Mills) but not its age "issues." [3]

One issue gets us to the heart of the matter. How do the subjects of a particular culture come up with their comprehensive narratives of what they call "aging"—those stories, prospective or retrospective, about moving through long swaths of their particular course of life? Such stories have intensely personal aspects, but they are comprehensible because they are tied to shared (dominant) models of "the way aging really goes." I have been calling these naturalized mega-narratives the "life-course imaginaries." I use the plural because those of China or Samoa, for example, presumably are—or once were—different from those of the United States and because even here there are many. I use "imaginary" to emphasize their constructedness; "life-course" because the imaginaries influence us not just toward the end, not just at the beginning, but lifelong, from early childhood on. Progress and decline structure them all, and relate what might otherwise seem like fragments. (The "Xers" and "Boomers" were united, for example, by an implied decline imaginary trying to make the Boomers' traditional progress seem unfair.) Development, ordered in linear fashion as childhood then youth then maturity then old age, may make a "whole life" at some other level, but it doesn't account for the influence of these imaginaries on ordinary life storytelling. To go on with that accounting, I need in this chapter to move from spontaneous telling to self-reflective writing (with the understanding that, as age consciousness gets deepened by the reflectiveness of writing, it can work its way into richer oral forms).

Autobiography is winning the life-writing sweepstakes, becoming the most important evidence of the human. Critics recognize this with the term "memoir envy." Ordinary people write their life stories or family memoirs, sometimes in courses, sometimes in secret. The past decade has seen much rich theorizing of self-writing, paralleled by the astounding production and retrieval of diaries, autobiographical fictions, confessions, apologies, testimonies, autoethnographies, thanatographies, oral histories. Despite their doubt that the self has good access to its past, postmodern narratologists can accept that it nevertheless has the best access there is. (Next to it, biography is at best inspired guessing;

ethnography, at worst, putting words in somebody else's mouth.) Against stories written *about* a self from outside, only self—constituted so profoundly by its own word—gets the authoritative last word.

Whatever aspect of "age" or "aging" we want to look at starts from a first-person declaration about that lifelong process, whether readers consider that report "truth" or the best-blessed fiction. But autobiographers, and life storytelling as a whole, could become far more acutely aware of the ways through which people are aged by culture. The theory of "age identity" adds temporality to static identity theory by helping us accept aging as an integral part of our sub-identities. But aging-as-narrative is not the full story of being aged by culture. By showing that progress is as much a life-course imaginary as decline, by showing how subtly or brazenly the war goes on between the two, and by re-analyzing aging-in-culture, I arrive at "critical age autobiography." Writing this introspective, historical genre might give us a better method for understanding the embodied psyche in culture, over time. For the disciplines, the next interesting moves might emerge from those working on autobiography who can think their problems through the critical perspectives of age studies.

THE AMERICAN DREAM AS A LIFE-COURSE NARRATIVE

Narratives may have most power over us when they are most invisible, that is, infinitely repeatable in ordinary life but unnoticed and unanalyzed. The "American Dream" is actually—whatever else it may be—such a narrative. It flourishes in the half-lit, semiconscious realm of conversation and writing, where all the other master narratives once dwelt. It is an example of a life-course imaginary told by people in their everyday lives, over time, about work and its consequences: first to themselves prospectively, then in medias res, and finally, retrospectively.

Usually there's a motive or a pressure to tell a particular Dream narrative to others. I first heard one told by my mother, spontaneously, as she was sitting at the dinette table doing her lesson plans for her first-grade class. I must have been in mid-adolescence, so she was then in her early forties. She'd been teaching maybe four years. For me, this is a vivid memory; I would swear to it under oath:

> Well, there was the base pay that I started with, $—— [giving the dollar amount of the first salary she had earned]; then there was an increase of 3.2 percent the first year; the second year an increase of [she gave the percent increase each year since], so that's $——; plus the extra for the in-service courses, plus the extra for the extra degree [she had an M.A.], so that makes $——.

Every year the numbers got bigger, and the implication was that they always would. (They did, thanks to the American Federation of Teachers.) My mother loved the litany.[4] She also loved children and teaching in itself; later, training apprentice teachers; the friends it made her—it was all John Dewey, conviviality, and mission. Talk about narrative pleasure! I have heard many self-delighting talkers in my time and judge their solid satisfaction by this oft-told version of an incremental progress tale anchored to a rising age/wage curve.

My father, by contrast, when pressed, told economic stories that featured exciting and puzzling events—running booze to Trenton for a bootlegger during the Depression, working for a "haberdasher"—as well as an episode of failure (six months of unemployment, mentioned once and never again). He had a daily story, certainly: up and out at six in all weathers, home late, hard work. He was a small businessman who went during those years from installing oil burners to co-owning a landscape nursery, delivering beverages from his own truck, running his own parking lot. There was accumulation, there was saving; I knew he made the mortgage payments. But he told no long-line economic story; he lacked a plot with narrative unity. What he earned was never mentioned. I assumed it veered up and down from year to year. This was frustrating and unsatisfying. I wanted my parents to have matched narratives; I wanted yet another happy progress story as a model and portent. His was incomplete. Or he didn't have one.

Frank Lentricchia talks about unpublished anecdotes that "stand in for a bigger story, a socially pivotal and pervasive biography."[5] My parents' storytelling inducted me young, as must happen to children, into what may be the biggest of those stories. What hers matched and his did not, I can finally see, was the cultural archetype of success, with its nifty graphic shape (exhilarated storytelling in the kitchen, shopping expeditions made possible by the annual surpluses) and its personally applicable telos (my future going-to-college, leading toward some unknown career curving above theirs into empyreans of the elite). It was a family life-course story involving even more than two generations, because my mother felt that her success was owed to her immigrant father, who during the Depression had used his earnings as the owner of a window-washing firm to put her through college. My father rarely mentioned his parents as earners: they had owned a precarious butter-and-egg store in Philadelphia. He had joined the labor force as a part-time furniture mover's assistant when he was ten years old.

My mother's autobiography had idiosyncratic elements, of course, but because she was permanently hooked into a seniority system it was also a story of the good worklife that many Americans wanted to tell about themselves, and would still like to be able to tell. (The local gender oddity was that my mother had the perfect story; my father the ad hoc, shapeless, deprived one. This gave me at first odd ideas about men, and later, a deep relationship to feminism but an unorthodox one, which readers of Carolyn Steedman's *Landscape for a Good Woman* might recognize. If my father had not dropped his crumbs of biography, I might never have followed his sort of working-class meander with empathy in later life. I might even have missed such clues in my childhood, even though I was living inside a struggling family. I could have been wholly embedded in smoother, middle-class storytelling.)

Whether as spur, delusion, or reward, the so-called American Dream is a model national biography that shapes subjectivity and life storytelling. It's the *Pilgrim's Progress* of our secular, capitalist world. Working Americans of all hyphenations strive in some relationship to it. It seems purely personal or domestic because it is so often focused on owning a "home," but it is an economic life-course story that can only be realized through the opportunity structures of a particular material world in historical time—the business cycle, the lead ceiling, the export of occupations, the lack of adult retraining, the delusive premium on youth—in relation to such individual factors as our differential access to education, unionization, legal remedies. My mother's relative whiteness made some of these benefits possible (Jews were not yet white-white in the 1950s, but they were whiter than people of color). The Dream requires extrinsic measures like steady employment, decent salary, security, and of course a rising age/wage curve and no pressure to superannuate oneself prematurely. But this material infrastructure, as well as the number, ages, and qualities of those who "fail," is concealed under an innocuous patriotic label that is also apparently ahistorical.

My mother's story introduced me to this basic progress narrative in the most imposing way: as a prospective story that could be mine. My early identifications with her, my disidentifications with my father—this original slight bent in my character, self-concept, and narrative wistfulness was confirmed over many years by my shooting up through the public education system in Brooklyn, going to Radcliffe, getting an M.A. I seemed to be on my way to joining the elite. In my particular case, the actual progress as opposed to the imagined narrative was thwarted by the academic depression of 1975, the year I received my Ph.D., a year after my father died. But remember the me who didn't relinquish progress when the scars on her knee hadn't disappeared by the time she married? My 1975 self held tight to her/her mother's/our national narrative of progress, gulped down the anguish of missed vocation, found another kind of university job, and by 1988—but by now with some degree of detachment—published a book about the "invention" of the progress novel of the middle years.

Over the years, I discovered yet more reason to be sensitive to aging narratives, whether progress or decline. My father's disconcerting counterexample acted as an irritant and stimulant. For a long time, my understanding of him was hampered—empathetically obstructed—by the lack of fit between his work history and the requirements of the dominant narrative. For most of my adult life, I continued to believe that he was stoically telling himself a decline story about his trajectory. I admired his fortitude, but for a long time I couldn't understand why he didn't just *change his story.*

Over time his watchful daughter reinterpreted his situation and came closer to him. I came to see that in his later versions, he had many selves, not all of which were ruled by decline. In terms of his financial age identity, he actually wound up quite prosperous by his 1930s young-adult standard. Retirement—late retirement, at about sixty-seven—made an enormous positive difference to him. He came to visit us, built us a shop in the basement and stocked it with his own tools, played tennis with his grandson, argued less fiercely at family political discussions. Getting out of competitive and exploitative capitalism was one secret of such later-life happiness as he acquired. Maybe he changed his overall story then: he certainly looked sunnier. But I think, on balance, that history loomed too large. He was a political animal and his side, the side of the oppressed around the world, appeared to be losing. I don't know for sure.

On the other hand, I saw the efforts my mother had to make to maintain her favorite narrative. For her, too, secure income was nowhere near the whole story. She had extraordinary temperamental resilience. But (as it will) the rising age/wage curve cushioned some of life's shocking drops into the pit.

Through these biographical retellings and the readings they led me to, I came to see both the limitations and the power of this narrative called the American Dream. As an economic life-course story, it privileges only the part of the life-course that coincides with workforce participation: "life" from the first paycheck—perhaps from part-time hourly work as early as twelve or sixteen—until exit, early or late, voluntary or forced. An economic life-course story also has a reflux effect on the earlier and later ages that appear to "surround" the working life, childhood and old age. They are both cast as unproductive and dependent; at their best, sites of idle consumerism. Old age, in particular, can be treated as a shard of life detached from the main site, an archaeological fragment that ought to be lovely in itself but is more likely to drift into basement neglect. And the comfort (or misery) of old age depends in part on earlier acquisitions—a house, pension, Social Security, savings—tied into your economic history. My father did not feel inconsequential financially because he made his triumphant escape into retirement with a pool of savings from his years of thirteen-hour days.

Both of my parents' stories, and my own, showed me how central our *economic* possibilities are to age auto/biography. The so-called American Dream narrative, the drive for "progress," and its violent twin, the fact and fear of midlife decline, cannot absolutely determine but certainly interactively affect any meaningful life story we tell during our working years and beyond about selfhood and development, the fate of the family life course, friendship, community, avocations.

Having been exposed to such intimate vicissitudes in the two warring master narratives made me in the long run suspicious of their claims and cautious in their vicinity. As long as I live, perhaps, every one of my later selves will have something new to add about its relation to these dominant American narratives—and about their relation to each other, a weird symbiosis. Latterly, at times, I know I am sounding like my disillusioned and stoic father.

So far, despite mounting wariness, I must confess that in answer to the question, "Which narrative had the greatest effect on you?" I still find myself trying to write my "experience" as a progress story. I feel the power of the dominant genre every time I close my mouth to wonder, "How can I make this *not* sound like a decline story?" Or every time I open my mouth to utter a prospective narrative and find myself sounding like my good mother. So, if the identity theorists want a history of change in relation to storytelling, it's there. And if they want a history of continuity, it's there too.

Cultural studies as is could deal with my father's worklife and his politics and with my mother's seniority system and aspirations. But it cannot deal with everything: not with the pressures exerted (differently on each of the three of us) by the preexisting imaginaries, nor with the adjustments we each kept having to make to our particular narratives as our life courses proceeded. For this we need age autobiography. My progress narrative can be smarter than a plain storytelling because it knows it must find a place for the influence of my parents' stories, and give history and culture and adversity their due.

Age autobiography can also deal with my strange oscillations over midlife in my professional relation to the dominant narratives. I started by looking for progress everywhere (like my mother) and then had to learn to deal with decline (like my father), and now try to fit them together (like a good daughter of both). Put more abstractly: I needed, and we all need, a feminist, materialist, critical/cultural, historically minded, cross-disciplinary age studies with one foot planted in the humanities before we can have a fuller notion of "temporality" that foregrounds narrative-as-life-history. And before we can see even our own unique storytellings as tie-dyed by the life-course imaginaries of our time.

But this is enough, I think, about my secrets and those of others, given that I lend us as personae solely to exemplify the move from life storytelling to age autobiography. Now I can explain some obstacles to understanding the genre, and, after that, some methods and theories that might make it more easily writable, and thus better known and more influential.

INTRODUCING A MAGUS IN A THEORY HAT

For the sake of brevity and detachment, I'm going to summon up a spokeswoman I call the Age Autobiographer. She has the same dream, the same yearning set out at the beginning of this chapter: to encompass the embodied psyche in culture, over time, through new autobiographical writing. We hear her voice before we see her: a well-modulated voice, but with edges. She says tartly, "A *whole-life* perspective for starters, please. Margaret's tale started in adolescence, but it goes on and on, discreet as she is about those twists. Aren't most of you kind of fixated on the early years? Calling twenty-something 'the coming of age'! Chained by Freud, literary romance, and the cult of youth? Still distracted by the male model? 'Age autobiography'—*my* genre!—is comprehensive. To get to it, keep everything in motion, life keeps going until the end."

Turning to academic teachers of biography (fictional and nonfictional), she frowns, "With your curriculum so fixed on classics of youth, aren't you hooking the young narcissistically on first love, first trek, first encounter with otherness—as if there were no landmark events later in life? Speaking just for the moment on behalf of the majority of students in higher education who are older than twenty-two, I'll tell you plainly that however vivid the prose, I'm bored with youthful errors, and youthful sorrows don't shake me. You boast that you're not afraid of Others. But the midlife, whose voice the younger hear whenever phoning Mom or Dad, *that* you don't teach. (Isn't it time to reread young-adult romances—from *Pride and Prejudice* to the latest date movies— looking at how midlife parents deal with their adult offspring's troublesome trip to the altar and the condition of their own love life?) The old are a fortiori neglected, women even more than men. Except for a few oral historians, continuing-education teachers, lesbian activists, literary gerontologists, feminists, and age critics, all that is *too* Other.

"Do you still want to say," she queries the analyzed, "that the infant or adolescent individuation from parents is more fascinating than the final individuation in midlife or after, where the orphan self discovers its survival skills and tells truly untold material?" To autobiographers she pleads, "Tell the rest of us stories that don't only star you young. The whole culture doesn't have to *love* aging-into-old-age for more of you to change your ways. Write the later-life masterpieces the professors would have to teach."

She acknowledges the historians of the present, as cultural critics sometimes call themselves.[6] "True, we need to know the economic structures and discursive attitudes that affect the young. But grow up and describe the ones that impinge on middle and late life as well. Will you be ruled by the current laws of cool forever? Where is the progressive narrative of development that considers political identification an identity that enables us in later life to continue to resist hostile ideologies, or even to start to resist them then?[7] You can't help save Social Security until you see how the rightwing media, afraid to attack the respected or pitied elderly, are constructing the pseudobiography of 'Boomers' as 'greedy' and 'self-righteous' people who *deserve* to have to work until seventy. Feminists, my good allies, it's time to recognize how often now dominant culture tries to make age so fraught, even for men, that it can override gender, race, class—every other social category and subjectively wrought identity—and how often it succeeds!"

To the humanistic gerontologists, she says, "Friends, your good work is a mainstay of existing age studies. But think harder about the narratives *you* privilege. The 'life review' is well and good, but loosen up on your preferred protagonist. It's not just the elderly who reminisce, and even happy people have memories of their earlier life forms. In our accelerated capitalist conditions, you must see that people at ever younger ages can feel driven to defend their record, combat helpless nostalgia, and limit their expectations of the future. Like sacks of garbage being tossed down flights of stairs, the alleged losses of 'old age' are crashing down the ladder of years, rung by rung. Age studies won't forget the elderly. Could we tentatively agree, as a gesture toward life-course solidarity, that age autobiography can potentially be written by any subject old enough to have seen a prior self fade and a new one emerge and to know why? And, for the sake of intensity and the oddball, that age autobiography needn't limit itself to 'common themes' from 'everyday life'?" [8]

She stops herself reflectively. "People have to realize they're not automatically savvy about 'being aged by culture' simply by having lived long enough to call what clobbers them 'aging,' any more than women understood what being 'gendered' was before feminism. Surviving midlife by dint of health and wealth isn't enough of a watershed to justify a 'single-experience autobiography.' [9] Passively traversing so-called transitions and stages does not expertise make. Mouthing your era's cliches about 'the big Five-Oh' or describing your eighties (welcome as that might be as an 'authentic' insider account) doesn't raise age consciousness in the right ways. [10] We must revise the telling of both regular life stories and age identities to do that."

Here, our Age Autobiographer begins to resemble one of those "special goddesses" for people in trouble drawn by cartoonist Nicole Hollander. She gently lowers onto her head a fanciful cap, adorned with cutout gilded stars and luminous crescent moon. "My theory hat," she says. "Age autobiography is made possible by the idea that people can work with their own naive autobiographies to discover more about how they were and are aged by their culture or subcultures. 'We routinely under*tell* the text of our lives,' as Gary M. Kenyon and William L. Randall note. [11] Where age is concerned, this must be true even of the most garrulous and of those with magically detailed memories. But now at last we can begin to produce life writing acutely aware of what specific age forces, among them the life-course imaginaries, have engaged us, and how much learning, internalizing, and rejecting has been going on. What feminist autobiography is to being sexed and gendered, and antiracist autobiography is to being racialized, age autobiography will be to being aged by culture—the revealer of the conditions of discourse.

"This gives us an augmented theory of 'autobiography as cultural criticism.'[12] I add to Nancy K. Miller's important feminist concept of 1991 something missing: age. Not rawly experienced 'aging' but reflections on being aged by culture. How does any subject get from unconsciousness to insight, about a process that has been kept so ahistorical, biological, falsely overpersonalized, essentialized, passive, and mystified?" Here, with graceful and respectful gesture she unveils a tiny bookcase. "New as it is, age studies will help us produce this more flexible, analytic, exciting genre of memoir. Arising from the humanities and social sciences, age studies is creating an archive that links age research and arguments across the disciplinary borders. Age autobiography will not need to relinquish any of the turbulence and monotony and mixed emotions of living, or any of the esthetic pleasures of structure and rhetoric, just because it becomes smarter and wiser about the long term, the imaginaries, and the other contexts in which 'time' passing, passed, and to come—a.k.a., aging—gets its meanings."

Our Age Autobiographer points to herself. "For my disruptive appearance today I come forward as Magus and Muse of one privileged literary form, scolding ideologue, well-digger, stargazer, . . . My 'I' comprehends all my 'core' and 'subidentities' and my 'traits' and their interactions.[13] As cultural anthropologist Unni Wikan says, a 'conceptual "I"' helps to 'hold all the others together and provides a roughly coherent account of ourselves.'[14] As an age critic, I call this 'I' the Latest, or rather the Oldest, Self.

"Like any autobiography but more self-consciously, age autobiography starts with the Oldest Self's strong present feelings about its past selves. Emotion recollected, and probably not in tranquillity, because so often a current burning need drives one's *recherche du temps perdu*.[15] Revision, theorists currently seem to agree, is 'the primary act of memory.'[16] But age autobiography cares less about querying the Oldest Self's 'truth'—that quaint positivist concern of the 1990s[17]—and more about how it uses its immense power over the past. It's time to assert (subversively) that the primary basis of revision is *remembering*: this is the connection that an 'I' of today would swear to under oath, the sensation Proust recovered that gave him so intense a happiness, or if you prefer, the neuronal accumulation that warrants that we are continuous beings, permanent containers of our pasts. Over memory, an honest Latest Self controls mainly 'the retrospective invention of causes.' 'We can't know the reasons why we do what we do,' says William Todd Schultz, 'but we are free to make them up.'[18]

"What is the motive when, like Interpol after the most wanted, an 'I' of today passionately chases down a particular 'I' of yesterday? Normal autobiography often handles temporal shakiness by stopping off *without comment* at an earlier self in the series. Two plain points of comparison (with *some* time between to measure change or development) are the minimum that narrative needs to produce a plot in which age and aging are implicated. Choosing the two points is never random, as Margaret said about selecting the particular juvenile self who so admired her fortyish mother: she was showing you how alluring confident progress was to an adolescent. The Oldest Self's choices have consequences as well as motives: Margaret's admiration may have obliquely reinforced our belief in age hierarchy. Discovering the conditions of our implicit narrative choices can lead us to other secret biases of our presentation of aging.

"But the demands of plot can't take all the blame for why the past is so often presented in storytelling as difference from our current self. The most puzzling quality of the much-memoried 'I' may be its constitutive habit of *othering* past selves as strangers while holding tight onto its right to say what they felt and how they relate.[19] Is that a description of autobiography, or even a definition? Only a theory that includes being aged by culture could handle that paradox of desire and constraint! In the milieu of American age ideology, sped-up as it is, which often requires us to change or to speak as if changed (or consider ourselves failed), continuity can become a precious possession, and memory can be seen as an achievement of continuity. A character in a Mary Gordon novella 'sees that she has before her an important task': to find in her life a 'wick' of selfhood.[20]

"Today's 'I' interrogates those cherished perpetrators of yesteryear, those actors of past dramas, imagines their answers, narrates their 'experience.' Even when it chooses to tell a decline story that privileges youth—'I knew more about love at forty than I do now'—the Oldest Self rules. It, after all, has loftily decided what is finally worth knowing about love. Even when it screams, 'I can't remember enough!' or denies its power or its own best qualities, it does not, and cannot, relinquish possession of the last word. Therefore age autobiography's method is to make the Latest Self explicitly present, because this is the narrator who gives meanings to time and change and who can explain where the meanings come from. How and at what age and in what circumstances did the 'I' learn (for instance) when in the life course we must change, what counts as difference and what continuity is considered 'authentic,' whether only the passive changes are called 'aging,' who can change at will. One way to focus is by reworking our narratives of age identity.

"Take my Author. Since her Latest Self clings to the identification 'woman' as one of her primary selves, I note how pityingly she regards the seventeen-year-old who used the term tentatively for herself in 1958, and how much more proudly and firmly she says 'woman' as an older person. She was one of those who were urged in the 1980s to ask for recognition as heroic, self-fashioning, world-historical gendered beings. Since I am *her* Age Autobiographer, the observer half of our participant-observer team, I happen to know that she wanted to speak in terms of change because there was a gripping movement promoting it. They called it "solidarity," and recognizing her need for this, she wept. Like others, she had to recognize her envy of male power and obtain an increment of power herself (the economy abetting) before she could tell a more 'responsible counterstory'—Hilde Nelson's term—less binary, less savage.[21] Nowadays, 'woman' actually plays a smaller role in Margaret's core, because her 1950s and 1980s gender essentialism has eroded, but it nevertheless has a sizable role in her IDentikit as a coalition builder and activist. Margaret on her sequential age identities could just as easily spin you a mini-history of the once-shy self that now speaks in public, and she can't wait for you to ask how she came to feel postmaternal! And after she finished, I could elaborate a richer commentary on every single tale.

"The willing subject can do this for herself, of course—even though storytelling often starts as a current pulling the proudest rower helplessly down a furious stream. Raymond Williams wrote, in a kindly way, 'Because really to have understood the social pressures on our own thinking, or when we come to that wonderful although at first terrible realisation that what we are thinking is what a lot of other people have thought . . . that is an extraordinary experience.' He called the outcome a 'very high kind of freedom.' Part of that freedom is to 'understand the possibilities of writing.'[22] Age autobiography is a complex life-course narrative plus an age-wise critical commentary about being aged by culture.

"We come to this state by asking, of each personal legend recalled, one simple, insinuating, never finally answerable question: 'Why do I say what I say? What are my sources?' At this early stage, I won't slaver after too much analytic rigor. The point is that the Latest Self may speak with autocratic, meaning-making power about itself, its past selves, and the temporal in-between, but it can, albeit with difficulty, critique its own storytelling as well."

With a sweep of her arm, the Age Autobiographer displays a huge bookcase that goes from Augustine to Zsa-Zsa. "In currently existing autobiographies, aging is often cliched. When people tell a life-course plot, they may drop some evidence of *how* selves are aged by culture. But 'not all of it is analyzable in the sense of yielding potentially valuable information about aging and the self,' as Harry J. Berman has observed.[23] One road to autobiography critique is to show what's missing in the writing of others, as I began to do on Margaret's story of being a woman over time. I didn't do this to prove her 'wrong,' only to show how much more context she could have given.

"Better life writing about age elevates subtextual matters into explicitness and contextualizes their spotty evidence. It scrutinizes the major age effects produced by the narrating 'I.' Too often, 'change' means either progress or decline, treated in dramatically binary fashion, as befits the war between the imaginaries. Take George Orwell, who vividly focused on the horrors of his childhood boarding school in his essay 'Such, Such were the Joys.' Yet in the very last line, he asserts that if he went back to Crossgates he should feel only 'what one invariably feels . . . "How small everything has grown, and how terrible is the deterioration in myself!"' In one sentence he produced a sharp reversal in the meaning of time passed, lifted from *Decline Manual 101:* Omit causes, imply that 'deterioration' is natural—happens to everyone. Being Orwell, he added a twist to the *Manual:* that the obvious improvements of adult vision—getting the proportions right, consciously condemning tyranny—were not compensation enough for this vague but massive loss.

"No question, the Latest Self has the power to use any early self that attracts it, draw any moral, without the irritating interference of biographical denial. (What could be sillier than a biographer declaring that little Eric Blair cannot have been *that* unhappy.) But what are these deteriorations, which Orwell hasn't mentioned? After escaping so much early sorrow simply by becoming an adult, why did he choose to end on a nostalgic note as oppressive as if he had finally loved mud, beatings, hierarchy, and stupidity more than the rest of life itself? So canny about class and racialization, how did he fall into the trap of decline? No age critic can answer such questions definitively, however steeped in Orwell's biography. But it's possible that he favored that particular antecedent age *in order* to finish in a minor key. Whatever else is divulged, imperatives like 'Accept personal decline as the dominant' can become so powerful by being submerged that, as many other accounts of childhood beside Orwell's show, nostalgia propels the genre. 'Accept personal progress as the dominant'—the mantra of positive aging—may be equally submerged. Neither of these life-course imaginaries wants to make its sources explicit.

"If Orwell were now writing critical age autobiography rather than plain autobiography, he would want to explain. Might the deterioration that he located in himself be a displacement from Cold War history? From the economic or sexual construction of the male midlife in Britain in 1950? An effect of reading too much late at night in *High-Art Decline Fiction 202?* Did he ever believe in life-course progress (which can sometimes be confused with historical progress and then rejected as an illusion)? There's intricate painful history to be told about one's selves having struggled under the crossed weights of these imaginaries, perhaps not just once but over time. (Margaret only sketched such conflicts.) If age autobiography is a *critical* story of the relationship between at least two temporal selves, we want to read the one created by the most self-scrutinizing of the Latest Selves."

The Age Autobiographer pauses and looks at me. "Your turn," she says suddenly. "How are you going to anatomize this enlightened scrutiny?" With that, she blithely tips her gaudy hat, and, hat and all, vanishes. You may imagine me standing next to the bookcase. I would like to lean on it, if it were not so low. Well, then.

She called me her Author, but the challenge is to become *her*. After writing fragments of my autobiography, which reveal what my Oldest Self believes

about my aging-in-culture, I have to be willing to stand up as a critical age autobiographer to that self too, seeking in the crevices of my own intimate prose
what remains to be conceptualized. Okay. "Naive insiders" *become* freer experts
by writing this form. And we must do it movingly and entertainingly, because
people fear the "boredom" of age critique, superstitiously anticipating discomfort rather than liberation from thinking aging! As soon as many people produce age autobiography and are known to be doing it, age studies can have a
transforming effect on the age-naive life storytelling that people offer in conversation or, even when they're distinguished writers, in auto/biographies.

DEVELOPING AGE CONSCIOUSNESS

Through patiently disinterring and deciphering our age-related sources, any of
us can bit by bit discover how being aged by culture, in discursive and historical senses still largely to be determined, has affected each and all of our multiple
identities and come to be narrated by the Latest Self.

Discovering your sources has a pedigree. An African American writer in one
of Ruth Ray's life-writing courses asked her peers, "Are you making any effort
to look at your past and examine what's been fed into you and see, is that appropriate [now]?"[24] She meant racialized difference. We have to recall what was
fed into us, starting young and unawares, as "knowledge" about age, or more
particularly, as in the dinette or the Boston Museum of Science, aging. Much of
this information is semiconscious, but it is latently available. "Many elements
extremely important to the social actor (among them consciousness of age . . .)
are in both psychological theory and the mind of the actor removed from the
boundary of the construction called the self," John W. Meyer has said.[25] Who
would have anticipated, reading my mother's happy little speech, calculating
her rising income, that listening to it would have anything to do with my sense
of aging (let alone hers)? Yet it was foundational. And it is particularly useful as
an instance of a midlife parent teaching an aging narrative because it had nothing at all to do with my mother as a specular body, either in her forties or later,
when she chose to retire with a tidy pension.

True age consciousness puts into the minds of actors concepts that we might
be willing to connect with self and recognize as "being aged by culture." If I had
not stumbled upon the concept of the "age/wage curve," I might never have
connected my mother's storytelling in the dinette with aging. And if I hadn't
been a narratologist first and finally an age critic, I might never have recognized
the American Dream I held on to so tenaciously as a life-course narrative, and,
like all the others, a guide. It took a lot to lift the fog.

The result of developing one's age consciousness in this step-by-step way,
rising above simplicity and mystification, is different from the touchy con-

sciousness of "being young," or "no-longer-young," or "old." Such pretheorized, prehistoricized formulas stock the mental rolodex. I think of the often-repeated statement, "I'm still young." I heard this recently from a Brandeis student, aged twenty, when we were discussing the way senior men seek out first-year women instead of juniors like herself. As a counterassertion, does this help her? The children in the booth could have said it. Would it have helped them?

Defensiveness ignores decline ideology, now clamped over the life course at age twenty, like a kink in a hose. Even the carrot of the American Dream can be seen as a decline cue. Any progress narrative must beware of establishing an arc of ideal age-graded accomplishment that disregards context. Capitalism, patriarchy, age ideology: invisible hands drastically twitch our possibilities for progressing or declining. People sense that this is not "the body" at work. But lacking vocabulary to understand these contingencies (or perhaps, lacking the means to fight them), they fall back helplessly on a solipsistic claim. "I'm still young" can be said by ninety-year-olds and be neither less true nor more absurd. It can sound wistful ("It shouldn't be this way"), defiant ("Of course I'm young!"), anxious, disappointed, buoyant, dismissive. But any response like this that automatically foregrounds age makes it harder to retort, "Any of us can be superannuated. The forces outside of us that shift the age peaks could continue to do so if every American lived to one hundred in perfect health."

"Age consciousness" is the term now used for statements—like "I'm still young"—that foreground age and aging naively. But this is an obstacle to true age consciousness. As long as we remain uncritically oblivious to context, we let ourselves become *too* conscious of age. If only the children at the museum had been taught enough to be able to say, "This hoax has nothing to do with my aging. This is what 'being aged by culture' means!" That shock of recognition needs to circulate. Then we could keep the term "age consciousness" but dignify it with a new meaning, parallel to "race consciousness."

Living as we do *before* age studies, recovering the social lore and narratives about age, aging, and the life course that we learned as children and adolescents and young adults and relearned later, will require a cumulative effort of adult recall. Over thirty years, many autobiographies and novels have added to the store of ideas about how women in various subject positions were treated as "older" women, and how they felt. But there's much less detail about men, or about how differently situated women and men learned age (including what they read)—not just the attributes of people at older ages but the life-course imaginaries. There's not enough imagination about resisting decline. May the plaintive echo of "I don't want to grow older!" inspire recollections.

The history of my telling progress narrative confirms that even children hold "implicit theories of the life course," as William M. Runyan believes. It would be valuable to investigate "the processes through which these theories are constructed and revised." [26] Another way might be to reanalyze the biographies we tell of other, older people, especially our parents. As theorist Laura Marcus writes, "Recounting one's own life almost inevitably entails writing the life of an other." [27] Autobiography is often (as suggested by the subtitle of Carolyn Steedman's memoir about her mother and herself) "the story of two lives." It may be helpful to see how our parents are aged by culture—telling their ongoing age narratives and perhaps revising their implicit theories—in order to compare their stories with our own and to recognize cultural aging in our own lives.

There are many insidious cultural and psychological obstacles to writing a more critical kind of age auto/biography. It's all too common for younger people to have no imagination, no concept, of anyone older than they having an intense self-projected life course like their own. In *Speak, Memory,* the memoir Vladimir Nabokov wrote when he was almost fifty, he well describes his "queer shock" when he learned that his drawing master, "whose age I used to synchronize with that of granduncles," had married a young woman: "It was as if life had impinged upon my creative rights by wriggling on beyond the subjective limits so elegantly and economically set by childhood memories that I thought I had signed and sealed." [28] Even when a writer discovers into how tightly cramped a package he has stuffed the life of an elder, the discovery may be used not to expand his age consciousness but to prove how wise he has become by aging. Nabokov's metaphor of "signing and sealing" childhood memories implies that only the young misuse their lordly biographical rights, and only over insignificant elders. But at fifty, he too—so rhapsodic about his mother when she was his, and young, and doting on him—neglected to tell the reader what happened to her *afterward.* He had settled on a divine elegiac mode, and her émigré life in Prague didn't fit. Likewise, Steedman's dazzling bitter graph of her mother's decline couldn't accommodate Edna's activities, friendships, or sense of self between forty-three and death, a long span. What is almost entirely missing from Steedman's joint auto/biography is her mother's midlife. There are fifty ways to lose our midlife mother, and perhaps therefore, our own later selves. [29]

If such obliterations are in part the result of the careless middle-ageism that adult children are exposed to, then at least some is recuperable. I kept watching my father, that man of silences, and listening to him, as old as he got, waiting to see what would happen. Curiosity can undo indifference, probably even dislike. The data and stories—and (even an antipositivist might want to call them) lies—that we learned in our credulous youth are not necessarily expunged. Rather, many have been repressed through naturalization, half-forgotten through being undervalued, or misread because we lack the right theoretical lenses.

←——→

We close in first on one embodied psyche in culture over time: our own. If enough of us, starting young enough, develop our highly conscientious egoism to that end, we could collectively enrich our understanding of narrativized development and generalize beyond the self.

Once we are no longer so distracted by the naturalized body, we may be able to apply textual sensitivity to our own life writing. In order not to get our thoughts "entangled in metaphors, and act fatally on the strength of them" (a warning from George Eliot),[30] we may ask, What are our most precious metaphors for aging, our favorite age myths? For my part, I am writing a political family memoir about becoming a Nicaraguan activist in my late forties, to be called *There Is a World Elsewhere.* I know my metaphor used to be travel. If Europe was my first obsession, then "how not to be a tourist" was my next. Once I was fairly apolitical and guilty. Now I raise funds for women's literacy, gender, law, and health programs in San Juan del Sur, my Sister City, and return to Nicaragua annually to build schools.[31] How do we choose our metaphors or myths? If being ruled by them limits us, does learning how they work free us? When we write age autobiography, how do we decide between daily diary or purely retrospective form, languages of teleology or process, stasis or continuity? How do we use age location (cohort, chronological age, generation) more cautiously? Does breaking the progress/decline binary have any effect on the change/continuity binary? How else do our life-course imaginaries work for and against us? Etcetera. That "etcetera" means we have no good inventory yet of what exactly to watch for.

With more material, we might be able to discriminate among the ways we possess to say *how* people are aged through culture. How would you or I decide whether a life story we tell is *more* influenced by one source or another? Is it primarily temperament that aligns someone with a life-course imaginary, or is it upbringing, intersubjectivity, maturational processes? Or is it income, business cycles, and timing? Or physico/medico/commercial/specular forces (just to start with these)? The disciplines might plump for the particular forces they tend to work with, but having numbers of diverse age autobiographies might put the weight differently. Until we learn how to interrelate all this age-related material, no one can "tell fully." Once we begin, "telling fully" will be redefined.

It would really be more exact to call this goal "cultural criticism *through* age autobiography" or "autobiography *for* age critique." We are merely at the beginnings of the expertise needed.

To many memoirists, all this may seem too strenuous a charge. They like to set it down just as it seems to come to them, allegedly "raw" and "authentic." Like Nathalie Sarraute, they say, "I want to . . . caress this immutable image, to cover it with words, but not too thickly, I'm so afraid of spoiling it."[32] Activists and theorists can respond, "Not to worry. We spoiled nothing by teaching ourselves more complete and responsible versions of 'gender' and 'race' and 'sexuality.'" The same can come true for age. At all ages, the process of age autobiography can be as flush with excitement as any self-query that we turn into illumination and more meaningful prose. Understanding age serves the kind of adult development that can come "through narrative challenge," as Ruth Ray shows.[33] In my forties and fifties and now my sixties, in conversation as in writing, I have taken on the task of making my being aged by culture visible, to bolster not myself alone but others against the sucking undertow of nonbeing. Women, experiencing this earlier than same-age men; men, now also facing the tidal wave of contemporary decline, could write age autobiography for the thrill of narrative freedom.

There is no world elsewhere, in which we few, we happy few, could live in a bubble of perfectible age consciousness. Longing for justice for the life course must drive our writing. I've critiqued positive aging, the American Dream, all the fairy tales that are blind to context. But progress is a grand narrative with a difference: it supports hope, development, family unity, respect for aging, and, once reconceptualized, progressive political agendas that conservatives can work for too. How could we make progress narrative so gravely self-aware, compelling, and fair that living up to it would become a rightful claim on society, on behalf of the life course? These are high, new, persistent questions.

Age autobiographies in quantity, with their better understanding of the embodied psyche in culture over time, are going to be more valuable than existing self-reflective life writing in transforming age consciousness. Those who write beautiful and interesting ones will be waking up a nation that ignores being aged by culture at the very time when age is becoming the difference that makes a difference. Ultimately, transforming ordinary life storytelling will be the best way to comprehend our troubled world and a sign that we are changing it profoundly.

Acting Age on Stage

Age-Appropriate Casting, the Default Body, and Valuing the Property of Having an Age

> Without flesh
> there is the constant worry
> of flight.
>
> —*Afaa Michael Weaver*[1]

THE DEFAULT BODY

We know that gender is a performance because we can see it feigned so well. About age as a performance, we need to start the arguments.

In the history of Euro-American cross-dressing since actual women were first permitted on the stage—"breeches" parts, Victorian *grandes dames* in tights, female impersonators, drag kings—gender probably didn't need to be feigned well.[2] Now that it does, unintentional parodies, not to mention camp, remind audiences that the actor is not someone who learned that particular gendered behavior from childhood. From time to time a subtle portrayal across the still-persistent binary convinces you that a nonnative gender can be imitated utterly without strain. Adrien Lester, a six-foot Afro-British man born in 1970, was a convincing and charming Rosalind in the acclaimed all-male Cheek by Jowl production of *As You Like It* at the Brooklyn Academy of Music in 1994.

He established Rosalind in the first scenes as a long-boned adolescent tomboy not yet beguiled by femininity, naturally willowy but awkward out of modesty.

Gender always has an age too, although theorists rarely notice this. Let's put life time into gender and gender into life time. Lester's triumph at playing *younger* might be applauded more than his success at playing female if they were not inextricably combined. He and director Declan Donnellan chose for Rosalind a vivid turning-point of female adolescence: this was a girl pushing her way toward authority, easing herself into sexuality and love through the testing of Orlando in the Forest of Arden. She grew years in the forest. As Orlando's mock mentor, she developed a more assertive stance than the girlish droop and slight fidget forced on her by her initial passive circumstances; it gave her scope for wit, teasing, and self-mockery. Rosalind has been played—for the gag—as if she fell in love at first sight and dropped into static "deep womanly tenderness."[3] The aging angle makes the part more nuanced line by line and the play more suspenseful.

The body's expressions are partly derived from socialization, as the body-mechanics experts realized first. Moshe Feldenkrais wrote, "The posture, attitudes, and facial expressions are acquired features fitting the environment, and therefore come under the heading of learning."[4] Gender in real time has a performance history, which can become part of our life story if we learn how to tell it. Acting one's gender begins in early childhood. When you learn cultural attitudes and habits that early, they become second nature, "native." As Judith Butler points out, you can't fall out of character even performing them day after day, all day. Adolescents consolidate a first adult gender style somewhere between hypermasculinity and hyperfemininity, after observing elements from their culture's spectrum as performed by peers and people older than they are.

These consolidations of habit are not fixed and final. It would be wrong to assume, interactionist philosopher Shannon Sullivan says, "that prevailing custom molds one once and then never influences one again, as if the self's store of plasticity were somehow exhausted by its initial formation."[5] During an individual's life course, people can opt for new bodily attitudes, habits, and self-descriptions. How many women raised in a prefeminist era learned later, as I did, to harden their voices in public, to drop the questioning intonation at the end of a sentence, to stop punctuating utterances with giggles, to smile less and compose their faces a bit more sternly, signaling, "No longer a babe, an easy mark—no longer *that* young"?

Feminism didn't determine the specifics, only a broad goal. Perhaps encouraged by my vocal successes, I just as consciously changed my walk. I reduced the swivel, stretched the line, sped up the tempo. I did this after taking a job in an almost all-male administrative hierarchy at Harvard when I was thirty-five. The walk too, conveying the impression that I was always busily efficient, made me look older. My more mature voice and walk had physiological/subjective effects, making me feel more vital and authoritative and safer from being hit on. (Call such effects "physiomental," to break down one area of Cartesian dualism.) Seeing all this as if I were applauding a successful actor, I embraced "older." I cut my long hair. My first faint wrinkles came to seem a positive part of my age effect. I thought they helped me look more like the men in suits.

Some of the performance effects were intended; others no doubt were unwitting. Either way, our behaviors have associations with age because of the incessant automatic functioning of the age gaze. It would be stupidly arbitrary for someone to say, of my steadier walk, "That's pure gender!" or "That's an age cue only" when the new signals blended (along with my whiteness, my ethnicity, my stature, etc.) into a coherent whole: me. Age studies cannot think of bodies apart from the history of the signs of age.

At first people who make such changes are merely sampling, but in time, if public opprobrium is not oppressive, they acquire a new native body that now feels permanent. They aren't "acting" anymore. For feminists, the earlier degree of femininity they had discarded would be the act. They would feel as ridiculous as Dolly Parton wannabes. The new embodiment has become their new default—a package of habits. (I use "default" in the word-processing sense, where you can decide a part of what will appear on your screen automatically.) My default body is the current visible manifestation of my selfhood, my embodied psyche in culture over time.

This example of people forming partially new native bodies over time suggests how a "meaningfully different performance can be enacted," as Sullivan puts it.[6] "Age on the body," which is what is usually meant by "aging," has traditionally been considered a continuum in which visible change is driven by *involuntary* mechanisms, such as biochemical processes or external stress, trauma, accident. This view makes us passive victims of "aging processes." But age studies emphasizes the active side of interactive performances. Building on my example of Margaret-in-University-Hall, we can disrupt the alleged passivity of age appearances—occasionally, as needed—by the idea of intentional changes of behavior. A body, like an identity, is better thought of as a series of try-ons and reaffirmed performances: new consolidations. Age on the body can involve both passive accretions and will.

This kind of agency should not be confused with the willful practices of cosmetic surgery. Changing the default, for feminists, relied on each of us finely personalizing a way of feeling and moving. The mixed signals that resulted offered an alternative to racist/sexist/ageist visual culture, "the system of power relations that constructs the meaning of what we see," in the words of Amy Robinson.[7] The men and women who get facelifts or liposuction, by contrast, try on a crude appliance to pass for "younger" to stereotyped eyes. Whatever else is wrong with this, it's like stuffing in falsies or a pair of socks to represent gender. It's both bad acting and a misreading of culture. They are treating "age"—or in this case "youth"—as a wholly separable identity. Obliterating a few of the obvious signals that everyone knows come solely from the age code, like "wrinkles" or "love handles," they try to forget that in our culture the hypercritical age gaze notices all the more obsessively their other decline-linked signals.

Since Anthony Giddens considers similar practices "reflexive projects" of the self, my last example of changing the age-look of the default body comes from *unconscious* intentions.[8] A friend told me decades ago an angry story about how his midlife father had prematurely started shuffling and making his shoulders sag. Nothing had happened to his health. He *wanted* to appear "old"—old enough to avoid responsibility for remedying his failures, according to his son. His foot-dragging and frail stance made him feel justified in giving up painful effort. He too was treating age as a separate, easily actable identity. The store of habits that he borrowed from was just as banal as the one the surgery patients use, but in his case it came from the shelf filled with decline prostheses. He had to cut out running with his dog—snip away all the spontaneous inconsistencies of his native body. He too was a bad actor (in his son's eyes), but he easily convinced the sort of onlookers who expect only decline.

Using these three willful examples from everyday life, we can now understand a little better how, where age is concerned, we both *have* a body and (for ourselves at times, if only briefly, and for others always) *perform* our body.

So what do I look like deep backstage—as sociologist Erving Goffman might ask—years later, say, walking in the park alone? Living from the inside out, I can't often catch myself. But I know that in the park I can't look one uniform age. Sometimes I squat like a kid, maybe even drop a giggle; sometimes I march like that 1980s administrator. When I'm utterly absorbed by a thought I know I fall into a slower meditative pace. Bits of past behavior survive, accumulated from stages of my life course to date. Our default bodies, always at work whether we are conscious of them or not, produce diverse age effects (and effects of other kinds). This variety is normal, not inconsistent but rather, as long as we are not feeling watched, integrated into a whole. Like movie stars, eventually we each have our distinguishing, unduplicatable gestalt. All we need is an audience trained to notice. This chapter helps to create all of us as just that audience.

ACTING AGE ON STAGE

To think further about age as a performance in normal life, it would be useful to think about how well or badly age can be feigned by professionals. The stage rather than film is the right venue for testing this: there actors are live (as we are), without retakes or lens filters, in a place where the entire body can be seen from most angles. Traditional realist productions more than experimental ones are where the risk is highest.[9] There you can't have a character without project-ing an age. Time passes, feigning has duration: dropping out of character be-comes a hideous possibility. There on stage the "meatiness" of bodies is in-escapably vivid.

These are fascinating bodies from whom we cannot avert our eyes. On the stage, of course, no age is a priori worse than another. (Jessica Tandy in her eighties was more vivid than the dewiest starlet.) When the curtain goes up, all are potentially subjects worthy of our gaze, potentially suspenseful, lives in be-ing. However you define "presence," they've got it.[10] *There* is our ideal life world. Being able to forget the body, which some think a good deal for "older" people, would not seem ideal if our bodies at all ages could be present in such compelling ways.[11] And while I'm in the theater, I do feel my own body-mind is thrillingly present and significant, like that of the actors I identify with. The empathy I feel with their movements and words makes the experience of going to a play psychosomatically intense.

Perhaps from this situation, age studies can draw wisdom for real life. Many theorists have treated bodies as if they had as little meat as puppets, subject to history and discourse even in sexuality, illness, and pain. I argued earlier that over our whole life course, visual culture has tremendous power, setting the ways we can regard our own bodies and those of others (call this the historical side of "age specularity"). Theorist John Rouse rightly says that "[a]ll the signi-fying systems used by theater and drama are always already part of other cul-tural texts"—especially the text of the actor's body.[12] Thus our ageist ideology may infiltrate representation and interpretation by the audience. And yet . . . there in the theater are those peremptory bodies—of all ages. How do they, with our connivance, resist the decline gaze?

In turning to those bodies, I am trying to figure out another way to make the existing power relations around age work better for our whole life course. Ear-lier, I said that at our desire life-course narratives could be written to give us *less* body. But another criterion for a good theory of bodies in age studies is that it finds—or imagines the preconditions for—greater value in the always aging bodies we own and shape. I've said how I discovered more freedom and con-trol in performing my body live in the office. Perhaps the stagecraft of bodies can next rescue me—and possibly current theory and ageist culture—from the bodiless overemphasis on the plasticity of bodies, from the neglect of age as a construct, and, where older bodies are concerned (especially female, racialized, or disabled), from knee-jerk devaluation and the lure of the "posthuman."

Is age a performance in every theatrical case? In playing younger and in play-ing older, by definition it must be. (It doesn't follow that either can be feigned well, or equally well.) Is age also being performed when, say, an actor plays an age within her *own* chronological age range? Remember an actor too has a de-fault body constantly present, in innumerable ways itself, liable to peek out of his performance. Such curious questions could be precisely the tangential new angle needed for approaching the vexed issues of bodies in culture and culture in bodies.

Age theorists are able to address the specularity of age in visual media (helped by interactionists and phenomenologists even if they still omit age). And age critics can begin to dialogue with theater and performance studies about playing age on stage. In the next three sections ("Acting Younger," "Acting Older," "Acting our Age"), I want first to sharpen the difference between *having* an age and *performing* an age on stage.

Acting Younger

Recent plays by Athol Fugard, Paula Vogel, and Pamela Gien raise interesting questions about casting and age (and aging) because they are written in a form that is becoming more frequent on stage as the empire of autobiography spreads: the "memoir" in which an older self recalls a much younger self. In novels and other written forms that describe multiple temporal selves, the body that in life would accompany these changes is absent unless elements of it are proactively described. There's no ever-present default.

In visual representations of auto/biography, however, the body comes to the fore. Presenting a self aging over long periods of life time has its conventions. In movies, the most common naturalistic convention is to cast two actors of appropriate ages: young-adult Pip routinely replaces child Pip in *Great Expectations.* The casting director provides a sequential shorthand for aging; the costume designer handles history. But, we may object, offering two different people for one selfhood denies an important subjective experience of temporality: as adults, we don't feel or say that we have had two or more bodies. Only one, a grounding in sameness. In fact, without that palpable tie, the concept of multiple sequential selves might not have the foil it needs to seem like an interesting idea.

But when an age auto/biography is put on stage and two or more selves are played by *one* actor, as in our own subjectivity, representing age difference becomes more problematic. In Paula Vogel's *How I Learned to Drive,* a fortyish woman (Debra Winger in the American Repertory Theater production I saw) played her midlife character and its younger selves, with many stops between eleven and eighteen. In *The Syringa Tree,* author Pamela Gien played her current self and other selves starting all the way back at six. In Athol Fugard's *The Captain's Tiger* (subtitled *A Memoir for the Stage*), Fugard, who was close to seventy, played his Latest Self and his twenty-year-old self.[13]

In all these instances, the actor before our eyes had passed so far beyond the younger self's age stage that the ability to play younger was immediately in question. (This was not forty-three playing thirty, or sixty-three playing forty-five, or eighty-one playing sixty-five, which can often be read as "the same stage.") All the actors conveyed the body language and voice of youth or childhood convincingly, and in Gien's case brilliantly. She played twenty-seven other characters without a change of costume. Playing herself at six, this woman of forty chose a high-pitched voice with hyperperfect enunciation.[14] In one establishing scene, she amazingly made her arms seem short as a child's. She was touching each fingernail of her left hand with the pointer nail of her right, holding the fingers stiff (the antithesis of pubertal languor) as in a demonstration that must be done ritually right. That careful voice repeated a magic prophecy about the future. "Grandpa George says you can *tell* how lucky you're going to be if you look at those litt-ul white spots on your nails. White spots on your thumb means *gifts*. White spots on your index finger, you will have *friends*. White spots on your middle finger, you will have *foes*." Holding her fingers close to her bent head would have played as myopic if she hadn't already had us reading her as a child. Little Pam's faith in prospective narrative was also childlike.

Performing a younger self doesn't try to hide the presence of the actual, older person. (Anne Basting, an age critic in performance studies, describes the *butoh* artist Kazuo Ohno dancing everything from a baby to a flirty young woman with his own nearly naked eighty-six-year-old body plainly visible.)[15] When actors play *younger*, we are willing to see double. In Western realist autobiographical drama, make-up, hairstyle, and clothes are chosen to be suitable to the older body-self. Building a younger character then starts with the dialogue that is right for that particular child or adolescent. Gien's child felt so densely multilayered that one thought of Stanislavski's decree that "even the little toe on his right foot should belong to the character."[16]

But that's not true. What isn't said is that the little toe and everything else you *don't* work on come from your default body. Playing a younger age does not require the actor to work very much off the default. The illusion is simplified by statements about age, above all. Vogel's play is full of statements casually indicating how old the girl is in each scene; without them the audience would be lost. When *The Captain's Tiger* opens, Fugard's current remembering self has a poetic monologue about the past that ends by *saying* he was twenty. Fugard then made the switch to the younger self by simply grabbing and buoyantly sitting on a box, enthusiastically writing a letter out loud: "SS Graigaur, Somewhere in the Red Sea. Dear Mom, I sincerely hope you didn't faint when you read [this] address."[17] The boyish letter-from-camp style and the ingenuous relationship to a mother sufficiently indicate his youth. If an imitation of youth or childhood doesn't attain an Actor's Studio ideal of mimicry, it can be effective without that.

"The stage actor has an audience trained to contribute a great deal to the dramatic illusion," Lionel Barrymore once observed, "The film audience is not so trained."[18] In staged memoir, we accept a sketchy age-likeness that depends on simple age-associated cues. Individual as Gien's six-year-old was, she also pitched her voice higher, stood on a swing, skipped. Signals of "childhood" are so well marked that every spectator will get them.[19] An actor can select two or three of the following: voice (intonation, volume, breath, or "timing"), face (nuances of expression, musculature), movement (gesture, stance, stride, posture), and forget the rest.

Specifically, what makes playing younger so readily credible (compared with playing older) can only be our culture's unconscious shared understandings of the default body's development. First, Gien *has been* younger psychologically and physiologically: she could draw on sense memories from her own childhood as well as observation. Dana Ivey has said that her performances depend on "taking on characters that I've exhibited since I was a child." [20] Anne Basting calls the stylizations of Kazuo Ohno across the life course "an exercise in seeing in depth"; "time is *produced by [his] body*." [21] This works in dramatized memoir because viewers accept a few good big moves as deep, privileged access to the character's past.

The illusion depends on our not noticing how much an actor relies on the default body of his older self to fill in sameness as well as change. Phenomenologist Bert O. States notices that even when a character "changes with every scene . . . the eye and ear get the notion that something called character is iterating itself." [22] He asks why. The answer must lie in the default body, which unconsciously projects elements that the audience must unconsciously read as samenesses across the character's life. Putting his arms akimbo didn't confer on Fugard any particular age. The little toe doesn't change. Much default behavior, picked up over many years of life, has *no special, fixed age associations.* As Joan Williams says about reading gender from kids' behavior, "gender-appropriate traits are attributed to gender, whereas [other] traits are attributed to personality, birth order, or some other explanatory system." [23] Age performances are policed, but not as sternly as gender. One proof is that only in fragments does age behavior work through drastic oppositional codes (skipping signals "youth" and looks "funny" for doing "old age"). If a few elements are coded as exclusively "age," many unnamed age effects swim alongside, also produced by the default body.

Casting an older actor for a two-self autobiography relies on one of these cloudy age effects: that where there is age difference, the older self is superior. The use of an older actor as a framing device jumpstarts the assumption that older comprehends younger in memory, judges its experience, has authority, possesses the last word. The presence of an older self thus implies that the life course involves some progress. The progress narrative—I discover, a bit to my shock—is deeply embedded in casting age appropriately for the Oldest Self. Fugard's play, it turns out, is a *Künstlerroman*, a story about his discovering his artistic vocation, as well as a psychological thriller, about the way loving your mother and hating your father and repressing these feelings get in the way. All this Tiger had discovered by twenty; Fugard didn't need a sixty-seven-year-old narrator for that. So perhaps they could have cast a young man for Tiger at twenty, who would play older to do Fugard at sixty-seven?

That would have deprived us of Fugard at sixty-seven playing Tiger at the time he left home and went to sea as a slight, timid virgin. For those youthful characteristics, Fugard's own frailty was not a bad stand-in. Shrinkingly cupping his hands over his privates, he parodied a boy's fear of emasculating heterosexuality. Fugard also conveyed an attitude to that fear appropriate to his later age: that it was recollected truthfully, that it had been excessive, that he was not making fun of it. Fugard did this by using technique (cupped hands) against the wreckage of his native face; kind tones of voice against the ironies on the page. How could an undisguisably young actor *play* an older body playing a younger body with loving detachment, as Fugard did so easily?

The default body is so powerful that it can also inadvertently undermine a play's message. In *How I Learned to Drive,* L'il Bit's Oldest Self is telling about a juvenile relationship with her uncle that turned incestuous. Debra Winger appeared first as a fortyish L'il Bit, looking slouchy, a little hunched over, maybe worn or shy. Winger also played herself at the prepubertal age when her uncle is no more to her than the most compatible member of her dysfunctional family, and then at the adolescent age when uncle can take niece out alone with the excuse of teaching her how to drive, and she moved on to the college-age self who lies in bed in a hotel room with him and at once ends the confusing and anguished relationship. The uncle was played—another consequential decision—by a man who looked the same age as Winger: in real life, her husband, Arliss Howard. He had the mien Vogel wants: the fatherly Gregory Peck type from *To Kill a Mockingbird.* The problem of casting Uncle Peck no older than L'il Bit worsens as the level of incestuous abuse rises. Despite Winger's ability to play younger/hurt/innocent, the bedroom scene appeared to be between midlife consenting adults. Casting a child actor as the younger self would have been undesirable on several levels, as pedophilia and because the question at issue—as in Gien's play—is whether adults can repair the living harms of their past.[24] But Winger's midlife body got in the way of Vogel's script, which is clearer about the long-term irreversible damage of abuse.

When playing younger is not about memoir, many instances are linked to a star's need to go on working and an audience's desire to see her do so. Bernhardt in midlife played *Hamlet:* the audience wanted to see their icon. In 1995, Carol Channing reprised herself as she had been in *Dolly* in 1964, three decades past being the midlife widow of Westchester. It wasn't exactly "passing" in the street (as white, or of a higher class, or younger), where the goal is to get viewers not to look twice. Everyone could seek the signs of her being "old for the role." But many in the audience—especially spectators closer to Channing's age—

wanted the charisma to succeed; they admired the likeness more if they noted a disparity because they'd been taught that Channing's imitation of youth was the sauciest female retort to ageism.[25] There's more leeway for stars. Hired to show "some aspect of herself that the audience finds identifiable," the star is given more slack than "the character actor [who] is hired to seem to *be* the character" (as Kathleen Chalfant nicely puts it).[26] But Marcello Mastroianni, nothing if not a star, saw the limits of age appropriateness as narrower; and although film gives immense leeway to aging men to play young, he applied the limits to himself. "The important thing is to know what season of your life you are living, and not to try to be something on the screen which is ridiculous. Maybe that is the only planning I ever did: not to take on parts that were outside of my ability, both physical and psychological."[27]

Acting Older

> [S]tereotype exists where the body is absent.
>
> —*Barbara Kruger*[28]

Playing an older character in realist theater is much harder than playing one younger. At every moment this is a question of "passing," where if the audience has to look twice the game is up. A younger actor dare not relax control; relying unconsciously on the default body will only reveal its unwanted youth. There was an era when playing much older was admired as art. In the eighteenth century certain actors could start as young as twenty playing "old men"—that was their line of business. Goethe mentions one who created "the most perfect illusion," and adds what I said about playing younger, "we can also remember the double pleasure the actor gave us."[29] Today's twenty-year-olds would no longer dare (or care) to specialize that way.

Hiding the younger default body as thoroughly as possible is now necessary to the illusion of playing older. In Tony Kushner's *Angels in America* in New York City, the talented Kathleen Chalfant played (among other characters) a rabbi of eighty-six. When she played a male doctor her own age, she felt she had to work hard, for example, on such nuances of "gender" as the exact shade of aggression some midlife men have acquired. As the rabbi, her disguise built the character: the brevity of the part, a floor-length gabardine, a beard and sidelocks, a marked accent, plus a New York audience appreciating the shtick.[30] This was sufficient for Kushner: had he auditioned fourteen eighty-year-old rabbis and Chalfant, he might still have chosen her.

The opposite of this, you might say, was French film director Emmanuel Finkiel's decision to cast a feature film using actual Yiddish-speaking immigrants to France who were also required to be between the ages of sixty-five and ninety-five and to have Ashkenazi rather than Sephardic accents. He auditioned four hundred nonactors over nearly a year. *Casting* (2001), based on the extraordinary footage saved from the auditions, shines philosophical light on meticulous documentary realism. When six women (who in group identity appear to have everything in common) say a single line, what is salient is their astonishing variety. First, hard as it may be to credit, in their accents; then, in the age cues they emitted. In many cases, I could not tell their ages within the defined thirty-year span—the problem posed by the Paris exhibit Un Siècle as well—but the ambiguity was even more striking because in *Casting* they move and speak. Finkiel acquired a faithful record of each in comparison to all—a rebuke to those who think "old age" has a simple set of codes any actor can quote.[31]

Actors and acting schools have a vested interest in believing that the body of the actor is an empty vessel, fillable with whatever otherness the director pours into it. Directors, casting directors, and rehearsal spectators know better. Casting is "the first reduction . . . from what may also be imagined," Herbert Blau says; "the actors who are not cast are always telling you that."[32]

And actors too can be modest—humble specifically about the ability to play older. Matthew Sussman, who understudied Ron Leibman for the part of Roy Cohn in *Angels in America*, says, "Roy Cohn . . . was a twenty-five year stretch and a very different temperament than my own." There's a scene between Cohn and Joe, a young Mormon who's just coming out. Sussman says that as Leibman conceived it, "[i]t's a scene about being older, about fathers and sons. Ron does that scene great, but I couldn't bring the weight of age to it." He used a gray wig but otherwise did not play for age, emphasizing instead "unbroken physical contact . . . a human-scale seduction."[33]

Since playing the midlife is impossible for most younger actors, playing *much* older—"carrying a cane" (as if in answer to the riddle "What has three legs in the evening?")—becomes an ever-present temptation. The older relatives in L'il Bit's family were cast using students from the A.R.T.'s training program, the Institute. Vogel's notes suggest that the mother and aunt be played by women "between thirty and fifty" and the grandfather by a man "thirty to forty." The family is not meant to be realistic; they don't age along with the child. But the Institute twenty-somethings were left to grimace, hee-haw, and jiggle. Grandma fled from sex like a cartoon virgin; Grandpa bent out his knees like a cardboard geezer. (I couldn't help but think of the man who became my husband stroking his beardless chin at age six.) The pastiche of age awakened in the audience "that still latent feeling that [according to Fredric Jameson] there exists something *normal* compared to which what is being imitated is rather comic."[34] The effects—as the uncle and niece advance toward incest before the students' unseeing greasepaint-wrinkled eyes—were grotesque.

One reason for having quite young people play older is financial. The head of a regional company believes that "he has an obligation to assign minor parts to deserving National Theatre Conservatory students—each of whom represents a $30,000 per year investment by the Denver Center—even though [older] local actors might be qualified to play those roles."[35] As job offers disappear (not for this reason alone), older actors abandon the career, leaving fewer available.

The practical critic's objection to this kind of age-blind casting is that it so often looks amateurish. Insufficiently corporeal twenty-year-olds play midlife parents to their same-age "children"; as Cleopatra nearly anticipated, undergrads girl her greatness. Some students do manage to look older than their peers because of native body-shape, physiognomy, girth, or beards—in nothing do people differ more than in their age, even at twenty-five. But when thespians cannot natively pass for older, they're rarely adept enough for the immense continuous effort it takes to simulate an older age well. "Acting is more like juggling," Hollis Huston says.[36] Many things on stage must be done "as it were unconsciously, leaving the intelligence free to grapple with the intellectual and emotional requirements of the part": this was the general rule promulgated by actor John McCullough in 1882.[37] More specifically, when playing older, younger actors lack the default body-mind, its vast range of sense memories, the psychological relation to the past. (Likewise, while elderly subjects in a test see in themselves traits considered both young and elderly, young adults mostly see themselves in the far more limited terms of youthfully named traits.)[38] An excellent midlife actor playing Miss Daisy copied her grandmother's voice, used her own Southern accent, recalled her sensations when relearning to walk, and still discovered "that I was getting too old too soon." As Ann Basting says, "This forward imagining is tricky territory."[39]

Surely I am not the only spectator who notices that younger actors often feign older ages badly. Some liberatory evolutions seem to be raising the standard of "realism" with regard to age. In film, it wasn't just close-ups and high resolution that ended the hegemonic practice of putting white actors in blackface or having them speak pidgin for "Oriental" roles. That occurred because a historical movement made whites ashamed of stereotypes and hiring exclusions. When Native Americans or Latinos are cast for roles written for them, we don't use "realism" as a slur meaning "essentialist," "timid," or "reactionary." That has become a norm for roles from categories we are truly watching. (For a Russian, let's say, we're not watching so hard.) Movements for "representation" in performance and politics have power over our eyes.

If an age studies movement had similar power, what would it ideally want of theatrical casting, in order to change visual culture? We have many more old people than in Goethe's day: Can we use their presences to teach ourselves to watch representations of old age as connoisseurs—with eyes more like

Finkiel's, say? Why should we be forced, by an only 90 percent–successful stage illusion, to notice the stubborn material of the default body? Omit performance art, which has its own criteria. On the mainstream stage, perhaps—except in the two-self memoir or the rare life-course exhibition (Cicely Tyson playing Miss Jane Pittman, Gielgud playing the Ages of Life)—we will not want to see age feigned at all.

What problematizes my discussion of performing "age" on stage is that I haven't said what "age" is, visually or behaviorally. Indeed, believing that it is usually not best treated as a separate performable identity, I've tried to make it harder to define. We recognize race by color and ethnicity by accent and gender by femininity or masculinity. But there's no prompt book for doing "the midlife," and little more than a tattered anachronistic copy for caricaturing old age. You earn age effects—on life as on the stage—by living a certain length of time.

Age-appropriate casting is a way of advancing into these complex unfamiliar issues. Is it, by itself, the solution? There is a difference yet to be formulated between *embodying* one's native age in a default way and *playing* a character of one's own stage of life in a play in which age matters.

Playing Your Age

The real has "the ease of identity."

—*Peggy Phelan*[40]

In 1997, Vanessa Redgrave mounted an *Antony and Cleopatra* at the Public Theater in New York and played Cleopatra herself. I was eagerly awaiting the performance. Cleopatra can be played as a midlife woman, as we would say now: she had Caesar in her youth, these are no longer her "salad days / When I was green in judgment, cold in blood" (I.v.73–74). Redgrave was close to the top of the age range plausible for Cleopatra. She made her first appearance moving swiftly on bare feet. Her punk-cut red hair swayed in a mass above her forehead, "like quills upon the fretful porpentine." She twirled; she twisted her neck alertly; energy flowed out of her wrists, her knees, her chin. The problem was that she was *playing* at youth and youth alone. She did Cleopatra as a Baby Boomer afraid of going over the hill. She started too high, as if the queen were often aware of needing to hop through a public market.

I didn't like the concept; indeed, I grieved over the concept. Anachronistically reading this into Shakespeare's lines is now all too easy; it's a sad symptom of the sexist middle-ageism of current Anglo-American culture. Yet disliking the anxious concept is from my larger point of view irrelevant. I left just as convinced that except in period productions using boys, Cleopatra should be acted by women in their middle years—the age that Shakespeare's text broadly indicates, transposed to our era. Not every midlife actress can play Cleopatra, but anyone who is right must have the range of behaviors that goes with having a long memory and an older look. Only an age-appropriate actor finds that some of the age-effects she or he needs to convey will be expressed even without knowing what they are.

Remember my walk in the park, spotted with inconsistencies no ordinary observer would notice? I want to make more of the curiously underacknowledged fact that having an age consists of no uniform set of age-associated behaviors. Stephen Spinella applied this general truth to acting when he said of his character Prior that "when he's charming and clever he has a queen's [fluid/young female] body, and when he's serious or angry . . . he has the body of his father." [41] One reason we nonactors too can't fall out of character with reference to our native age is because having an age contains so much variability. Complexity and even contradiction in character are crucial to all great acting and dramatic development. An actor finds it easier to play *against* or *around* type when it takes less effort to maintain. Let me give one example of using this range.

The Captain in Strindberg's *Dance of Death* is supposed to be married twenty-five years and is ten years older than his wife, Alice. Ian McKellen, playing him in New York City, used a stiff carriage and an ability to caper to establish the Captain's bodily norm, his self-presentation to his wife, played by Helen Mirren, and his soldiers. [42] McKellen as the histrionic Edgar evinces more vitality than the considerably younger David Strathairn, as Alice's cousin Kurt. But two or three times, McKellen sketched "elderly" mannerisms: the "heehee" of an actor doing old age as a cackle, the slight shuffle that could also convey fatigue or depression. In the audience, swept along by the multiple intentions of this intelligent production, I noticed these effects without stopping. After the Captain collapses, however, sitting in bed out of uniform with his bare arms stringy, his gray hair wilder, Edgar looked innately vulnerable. This was no facile cliche but the actor going slack, doing the bare forked creature that his real age made visible and plausible. Yet the Captain's late-midlife robustness became prominent again in the next act when he came back from the doctor's, boasting spitefully to his wife that he will live another twenty years. He is lying: he is dying. Playing only his "own" age (unlike Gien, Winger, Fugard), McKellen relied on having his body operate appropriately without intention. But—witness those stringy arms—he and the director also deployed some of its wide range of age-appearances with savvy about our age codes. The value of the default lies not just in the younger parts of the spectrum, but in *all of them.* "This whole psychophysical spectrum is mine!" we could all declare. [43]

An age can be feigned—backward down the life course much more easily than forward—but once so much can be lost, why bother?

Age Hierarchy

There's another reason why age works best as an unconscious ground of being, on stage and in life. This involves age hierarchies.[44] Age-inappropriate casting risks evading the substantial differences in knowledge, self-control, power, and moral responsibility that separate younger and older people in our ideal cultural imaginary of age and in many of our real human relations. Plays mostly stage relationships between people at different phases of the life course, where the actor's stage of life is a proxy: innocence for childhood; judgment for middle-age. Age hierarchy or its abominable alternatives suffuse dramatic representation, as *How I Learned to Drive* suggests. If the people in question are parents and their children, this difference is no shallow or discardable proxy.

At the climax of Shakespeare's *Coriolanus,* the great general's great mother pleads with him not to destroy their native city, Rome. To save Rome she requires him to defy his only allies, the Volscians, who will inevitably kill him. I followed this implacable postmaternal decree at the Brooklyn Academy of Music, watching—from high up in the gods—Ralph Fiennes as Coriolanus and Barbara Jefford as his mother, Volumnia. Finding her arguments met with silence, the mother stood in the center of the stage, ready to scornfully turn her back on her son forever.

Chalk-white, Ralph Fiennes took so slight a beat that it could not even register as a deferral. He fell over his mother's hand in a collapse as immense and slow and inevitable as if a snow-top had cracked from its base and toppled sideways in one piece before an adjacent iceberg. The movement had the grandeur of the nineteenth-century theater of gesture. And yet it was not a tableau held for the sake of our visual pleasure. It asked no pity, and yet it said, "You have no pity for me: you do not put me in the balance even as a feather." The son fell before his mother's monstrous decision without protest, accepting the nullification of his life. It was the tragic fulcrum of the play, a gesture Shakespeare did not write but to which all his means tended. It was an "inarguable" moment of theater, as Herbert Blau describes such moments.[45]

> Oh mother, mother!
> What have you done? Behold, the heavens do ope,
> The gods look down, and this unnatural scene
> They laugh at.
>
> (V.iii.182–85)

Fiennes is notable for his posture, rigid almost beyond the perpendicular. As Coriolanus, he had up to this point reared back out of contempt for the world. No other actor could have made bending forward such a capitulation. But to what inexorability did the stiff-backed Fiennes as Coriolanus bow?

The moment of tragic geste worked because of the Volumnia to whom Barbara Jefford brought her full seventy years. The power that was in her, like a god or a fate, depended on the hierarchy between mother and son. Only a woman could make credible that she was once a mother of an infant, who now boasts, as Coppélia Kahn says, of "her achievement in transcending affection to invest, as it were, in government bonds—in the honor he wins in a 'cruel war.'" [46] By getting him to sacrifice himself, *she* will save Rome. Only a woman of that age can have envied her son his martial manhood as long and as hideously. The history of that relationship was symbolized by the age difference between their bodies. His slender rigidity and quick determined gait had been counterposed throughout the play to Volumnia's mountainous solidity, energetic heavy-footed pace, and dour inflexibility of maternal ownership. Her body was voluminous: Shakespeare punningly led the costumer to its form. Her expanse of matriarchal chest seemed as remote as possible from breast milk, a carapace better adapted to display the medals a male general of her years and mettle would have worn. Jefford added to this gender ambiguity a fixity of feature that was like a mask: habit overlaying monomania as if worn daily over the course of actual years. An actor who understood "seventy" as confinement, reduced physiomental energy, or diminution in size, could not play this Volumnia. Jefford wielded her default body for its gravitas: the weight of time, familial history, authority.

But for all this to move us, the mother's dominance also had to be recognized on our side of the fourth wall. It had to be conferred by us. Yet in contemporary culture, postmaternal authority has been much attenuated, even in visual symbolism: many women who are no longer girls aim at the almost anorexic form and youthful gesture that abjure power. These days some midlife mothers are weakened vis-à-vis their adult children by "empty-nest syndrome." Others are detached from the traditional pattern of "living through their children" by feminist egalitarianism, alternative work, and postmaternal friendship with adult offspring. Many adult sons have a record of indifference to maternal opinion. Yet men's anger at postmaternal control survives such changes and probably feeds revivals of *Coriolanus*. [47] It is amazing that age hierarchy as a traditional structure of feeling has not yet disappeared from the avant-garde halls of BAM.

One counterargument to age-appropriate casting is that age is not always the most salient feature of a character. Herbert Blau told me that he once directed a twenty-eight-year-old who was extraordinary as Lear. Michael O'Sullivan played the misogynistic and sexually embittered sides of the king with powerful ferocity. In the storm scene, he created a gesture of someone tearing off his genitals. Blau wanted that rage then. O'Sullivan wore a long-haired white wig and a long uneven white beard, a floor-length feathery smock that hid his native body. Blau says now that he was "hallucinatorily older than anybody, of whatever age, I've ever seen in the role." O'Sullivan's age was "a matter of presence. His just being there, regal, knowing, with a sort of seductive wit, conveyed what you couldn't conceivably have unless you'd lived a long time." But, Blau said to me, "I was only twenty-seven then myself." [48]

Most actors lacking an older default body would have a hard time dealing with Lear's vast arc. Lear needs credible strength to start with—at what might be called his continuing age/wage peak—because his unjust power must awaken in the audience anxious, needy, rebellious, infant, and adolescent feelings. A director can also lose the arc by casting Lear too old—too frail, or senile—for that moment of (his) arbitrariness and (our) resentment. In the scenes with his other daughters he needs to be strong enough to resist being stripped of his long-held identities as king and father. Only when carrying the dead Cordelia, after hours of real time being battered, does he finally describe himself with an age, the mythic/ironic "four-score and upward, not an hour more or less" (IV.vii.60). This declaration should not be read backward into the beginning of the play as if it were a literal fact.

Without age hierarchy, subversions of it in the nontraditional theater would also fail. [49] (In Tina Howe's *Birth and After Birth*, for example, the four-year-old child is supposed to be played by an adult. "The children are monstrously knowing and controlling, while grown-ups cultivate infantile behavior.") [50] If we lose the relative privilege and modest authority of midlife, if age hierarchy were to erode further, this loss could also steal away the intelligibility—and the poignance, tragedy, and irony—of much literature and performance.

BEYOND "AGE-BLIND" CASTING

Age-appropriate casting arises as a topic for age studies at a particularly interesting moment in theater history and critical theory, because in precisely the same decades in which racially and ethnically appropriate casting has become a norm, "crossing" or "transgressing" traditional bodily categories has become the avant-garde rage.

So I am bringing up some of the issues of representing the-body-in-time and the-body-over-time on stage at a moment when the simplest way to respond might be to retort, "Age too shouldn't matter." Since King Lear has been played by a much younger man, by age-appropriate women white and black—why not a younger woman? Or, to take an intriguing triple-cross: Why couldn't Beckett's Didi and Gogo be played by talented twenty-year-old women of color, performing the exhausted, irritated, or stoic hopelessness of some ghetto youth? The change from old men to Boricuas would reveal that for Beckett a decline version of "old age" was made to stand in for *all* the sorrowful human conditions. Bodily decrepitude in old age has been a powerful metaphor for loss in Western culture since Sophocles' *Oedipus at Colonus*. We saw that majesty reduced to pathos in Strindberg's Edgar sitting up bare-armed in bed. Once we know to look, the geste of decline is everywhere in contemporary plays. It is now ripe for conscious critique.

Up to this point I have argued on behalf of the dominant mainstream performance practice of age-appropriate casting, as not just esthetically right (and deeply satisfying when well acted), but as powerfully countercultural, a force for sustaining threatened bodies and age relations. But I can also advocate revisionism in age casting (e.g., those twenty-year-old Puerto Rican women) when this would advance an anti-ageist agenda by making startling theater. Such choices wouldn't be "age-blind" even when they chose to be "age-inappropriate"; they would be wise to culture, refusing to strengthen our own overfed belief in decline. This could have the resistant alienation effect that Bertolt Brecht described as essential "to underline the historical aspect of a specific social condition" or to show up "the dominant viewpoint as the viewpoint of the dominators." [51] Will performance-theater regard age-wise casting as one of its missions? How will it transcend its potential life-course blindness?

CONCLUSIONS OFFSTAGE AND ON

Ideally, our culture needs a robust and profound general conviction that (barring exceptions that a director would feel the need to justify) age-appropriate casting is powerful and "right." But my main point is really quite different. The long march through age-inappropriate casting has been a ploy to get readers to think about the manifestations of age on the body in the dazzlingly bright light of *presence*. I have tried to show that age—*having an age*—is already unconsciously treated in some venues as a valuable "property" whose value grows over time.[52] Thematizing bodies often reinforces dysfunction, critics worry.[53] But not in this case, where the whole psychophysical spectrum is in play, in ordinary life as it is on stage—wherever much of what is called "character" is conveyed by age apparent on a default body.

In going to the theater, I found a bigger hole in age ideology's cult of youth than I expected. The notion that there might be more value to having an "older" age already exists in many people's minds, but in limited ways: defensively on the part of the beleaguered ("We're still able"), piously on the part of gerontologists, the positive-aging movement, and the allegedly favored young. American age activism needs more radical kinds of help. Loving both acting and many properties of aging, I had an instinct that seeing bodies with age *as if they were on stage* would give this now utopian idea—of aging as cultural capital, increasing over time—more kick and more sincerity.

With the public or specular bodies that age studies deals with here, an individual's culture and psyche and age are indelibly, uniquely, preciously embodied. Such body-minds are much less vulnerable to "the spectres of Cartesian dualism, biological reductionism, and essentialism" that some critics worry about. These are likelier to haunt the static bodies or bodiless minds that theory so often addresses.[54] From an age studies perspective, the concept of "the default body" responds to these spectres in some interesting ways. It signifies. Even when from the neck down the body is lost in urns, or the actor paraplegic, signification emerges. On the street or in the park too, the physiomental equipment of "the actor" is not dual, genetically determined, or fixed. Expressivity is an ontological property that grows over time, visibly, through our default bodies. This is not a property of its owner in isolation but is read through the social (the spectator's perception in relation to our symbolic age codes and the actors' ability to play with the codes).

Recognizing our exhilaration in the theater can lead to looking at all "actors" who are no longer young with intense witnessing of the age effects of their bodies and a fine learned appreciation of the value of our accumulated acquisitions. Don't start this experiment with people decades older than yourself. Start with you and me, in living motion. Using the connotations of the default body, how can individuals reconceive *themselves* as bodies with watchable presence?[55] There's a touch of the magic wand here, but these applications may stir your imaginations and eventually purify the age gaze of the crowd.

My final worries concern the extent to which the theater, as both art and business, can let itself be run by decline values. One issue is whether an actor can do age on stage over a whole working life. A talented twenty-five-year-old actress thinks something like, "Ideally, Ophelia now, Cleopatra in ten-fifteen-twenty years, Volumnia later yet." Her male counterpart thinks, "Hamlet now, Othello in ten-twenty years, then Lear." That idea of age sequencing seems right. If professional directors do more age-blind casting, they will almost certainly hire younger actors to play parts that are scripted for older people, not the other way around. Unchecked, the theater might move imperceptibly toward the condition of the movies, where hiring young has become a general practice, severely reducing work for people over forty (who make up only one-third of those working; 73 percent of them are men).[56] Scriptwriters aren't asked to write as many older parts. The result of this vicious cycle is that film is a youth-ghetto in which few actors survive past their own native youth. Hiring young is sexist—because in our visual culture women appear to "age" sooner than men—

as well as middle-ageist and ageist. Hiring young because it is cheaper, which corporate America is trying to make acceptable in other lines of work, should be scorned in the professional theater.

A culture needs to see people of all ages on the stage of the world, rather than the increasing *disappearance of older default bodies* that results from the cult of youth, marketing to youth, midlife downsizing, age segregation in housing, and so on. As it is, these practices confirm younger people in their culturally cultivated inability to imagine older people as viable centers of self, or to imagine themselves older as still specularly fascinating. In midlife and old people the absence of same-age bodies in visual culture constantly reinforces decline feelings, to the point where terrifying nonbeing is a risk. Or it leaves the edge of irritation that comes from helpless knowledge. It would be harmful if the professional realist theater too failed to live up to one of its unstated missions: representing a complete bodily life world with all our ages in it.

Life-course blindness is as real as other kinds (racialized, gendered, homophobic). To ignore it in the theater—or on life's other stages—is wrong, not just on the legal grounds of job discrimination, but on esthetic, ethical, developmental, cultural, and democratic grounds: that it lessens the value of aging as a rightful growing property, which each of us could enjoy in others and accrue for ourselves.

Age Studies as Cultural Studies

Beyond Slice-of-Life

> [B]ut the human mind no the human mind has
> nothing to do with age. As I say so, tears come into my eyes.
>
> — *Gertrude Stein, 1936 (aged sixty-two)*[1]

"STAGING" THE LIFE COURSE

Over the past century in the United States, as age has become increasingly dominant as a category slicer and determinant of subjectivities, the life "stage" has become more prominent and does more of that emphatic work. Begin with the imperious trend toward sundering the continuous life into imaginary parts, reified by naming. My analysis of the contrived war between "the Xers" and "the Boomers" points to that trend. The West had long managed to make do with fewer categories (childhood, youth, adulthood, old age), blurrier boundaries between them, and vaguer pigs in each poke. Starting around 1880, however, we witness in rapid succession the rewriting of old age as a medical problem, the inventions of retirement, "pediatrics," "gerontology," "geriatrics," "adolescence," the middle years, the relocation of a male climacteric from age sixty-three to the midlife, "flapper," "Lost Generation," "postgraduate mother," "empty nest." All this had occurred by the mid-1930s in the United

States. Thereafter we mark the appearance of "teenagers" in the 1940s, "aging Baby Boomers" in the 1980s, and "Generations X and Y" in the 1990s.[2] "Gray" and "golden" are not colors but age designations. The new characters come with pseudobiographies. On top of these, there are the "young old" and the "old old." Gerontologists themselves have subdivided old age. Quite a syllabus of stagey fictions.

Now people born late enough to be vulnerable bear not only an age class but often a named "cohort" on top of a "generation." Blurry categories (called "stages" without quotation marks by those who refuse to regard them as inventions of culture) are reified by normative social science, while journalists trot out their labels. These are identities that can in certain contexts trump all others. Being "old" probably was the first age category to suffer that deindividualizing, demeaning power.[3] But this late entree to objectification has spread back down the life course. By now, being "fifty" or "an Xer" can seem *more* significant in some contexts than being, say, a woman, Chicano, or gay, not only in the dominant imaginary of the life course but to the person in question. Belonging to an age category is now supposed to predict attributes, styles (or even more sharply, "cultures"), group interests, values, even feelings. Some people adjust almost instantaneously to match, or say they match, the latest descriptions of their designated age group. Your age in itself, neutral as a fact, can work like aging-as-decline to strip away other personal, idiosyncratic identities. You can add age—not only old age, but other age stages—as another identity that, lacking consciousness-raising (through cultural critique, age autobiography, an antidecline movement) can feel totalizing. Age class or stage or named cohort or generation is not of course experienced as inflexibly uppermost by every individual at all times. As Glenda Laws mercifully observed, "Age is intermittent." Culture still harps on gender, class, sexual orientation, and race. Age-class attributions change over time for some (like the Xers); there's some give within some designations. "Midlife" has no distinct borders: it's perilously malleable. All the borders are messy: having no objective reality, they must be. People age out of one age class into the next but not out of named cohorts (Ys don't become Xers). We fall in and out of *feeling* aged by culture.

Difference marked by age is another of the "essentialist boundaries" that can be used to divide the body politic and the labor force to make coalition politics difficult.[4] It creates apparent consensus that certain age classes are hostile to each other, as chapter 3 showed. Between the two currently prominent segments, young adulthood and the middle years, the advantages of power are increasingly said to be in contest—over who deserves to get employment, Social Security, a future. "Youth" and "childhood" are wielded against the elderly. The latter—many still helplessly poor—are often represented as "greedy geezers" possessed of world-historical riches. In the century in which old age before mortality has become a norm, miracles of public health and pharmacology do not prevent longevity from being rendered problematic to its possessors.[5]

However well many elderly people are doing, the adjective "old" has become a problem because it's a devastatingly intractable simile. "Old age" is so unsayable it needs a euphemism; "aging" was and still is used in its place, so "aging" too has come implicitly to signify decline and can be used even of the young, as in "aging Xers." "Young" and "old" are often simply ways of saying intrinsically good and bad. The trope circulates in discourses about everything from biotechnology to pop music, from "young" cities to "sunset" industries, from the "old" Cold War to the globalized "New" Economy.[6] When a government maintains ships badly, the press obligingly hides fault by calling them "aging fleets"; neglected urban homes become "aging housing units." When gerontologists first invented "young old" and "old old," they were merely rough chronological divisions. Then the terms became evaluative. You're not really "old old" unless you're both old and sick. But if you're eighty-eight and healthy, and running a small nonprofit part-time, like my mother, can you deny you're "old old"?

Every stage after the preoedipal has been problematized. Childhood is being seen as increasingly at risk, whether from loss of innocence or loss of autonomy is arguable. Children are also considered dangerous. One proof is supposed to be grade-school homicides, although they show a steep, three-decade decline.[7] Although "youth" is the object of a cult, it too is viewed as a set of crises (drugs, crime, suicide, unemployment) for some young people. Youth is still or always a "dangerous age," as 1950s bad boys, bad girls, and Beats are transubstantiated into '68ers, Yuppies, '80s rappers, and '90s slackers, lifers, sluts, and teen mothers. In the 1990s, the press invented "juvenile superpredators," even though most violent crime is committed by adults.[8] Even though health and money burnish the stereotype of the wealthy as they age past youth, middle-ageism lowers its sights so that the state of being not-young can be dreaded—remarked upon, joked about—much earlier. "Old age" is becoming a fire alarm.

The negatives linked to having an age or stage have spread across the life course. Age lore has multiplied—the adages and the jokes, the insertions of age into common topics (health, food, exercise). There's a lot more to say if you want to keep up and many more occasions when references to age (often with its disadvantages patent) are expected. Everyone who tells autobiographical memories pays more attention to age, at earlier ages, than they would have in the past. I notice this in conversation, and it is both boring and terrifying. Although only the midlife has the term "crisis" regularly attached to it, and only "old age" can't be courteously mentioned by name, the past century's reconstructions have effectively posed every marked age of life as a crisis. Every age is problematic, or rather, *having* an age is the danger.

Even in summary, these constitute extraordinary modern and postmodern shifts in this particular aspect of age, life-course *dismemberment:* more age categories and emphasis on divisions between them, more stereotyping by age, and thus ever more cues to speak and think age. What might more formally be called the "sequential-crisis model" of the ages is taking its place inside the decline narrative and alongside the coercion to change perpetually without ever aging. Age as a system gets more totalizing while the habit of thinking of age as natural becomes more deeply entrenched. We don't yet know the full range of effects. But Gertrude Stein's tears responded, I believe, to the first barbs of change.[9] For Stein and her peers, scientistic decline narrative caused pain by asserting that creativity helplessly wanes with hormones. As poet and philosopher, she was able to deny the tears and admit the tears in the same compressed breath. She didn't have to make a happy face. Perhaps there was less positive-aging censorship then. No individual exposed to dominant acculturations today can be entirely unaffected by current age lore and aging narratives—in their intimate self-assessments, judgments of others, autobiographical practices, plausible expectations, tendencies to nostalgia.[10] Potentially, all of us, whatever our chronological age, may recognize that we have a stake in age studies. Its goal cannot be to make age irrelevant—it's long been too late for that—but to understand how and why age is being insistently foregrounded.

←——→

Age studies is here, ideally, to do this general work. But on the question of studying dismembered "stages" it is blindsided, as I have suggested, by the inherent slice-of-life approaches of its subdisciplines. Here, as a way of strengthening the emerging field, I want to argue for the necessity of a convergence between critical gerontology and cultural studies.[11] Other approaches whose life-course imaginaries are more continuous—like auto/biography theory, field anthropology, social history, or developmental psychology—could perhaps also merge with cultural studies to focus critically on the staging of the life course. I hope they will. But my two current points of departure have symbolic significance.

To converge, critical gerontologists would have to expand beyond their subjects of expertise, old age and the elderly. They would have to deal with the fact that they often unconsciously tuck in the midlife. (Even feminists writing about women use forty or fifty years of "later life" as the Other to youth without comment.) Reconceptualizing, gerontologists would find themselves exploding what Christoph Conrad has called "this artificial unity" on which gerontology's "self-defined competence" has been based.[12] When cultural critics, whose relation to age is mostly buried in unconsciousness, turn to "age" now, most enjoy a form of youthism. "The young" (most often urban men) take the place of the proletariat as their vanguard class; *their* tastes re-enchant the phenomena of pop culture. As *the* sexy resistant subject in criticism or an endangered species, youth displaces other Others. Cultural critics would have to become as alert to "age" as they have proved to be to other categories of difference.

Critical gerontology and cultural studies share ideas and values that fit them to understand age ideology, and they supply complementary tools for confronting it. Influenced by feminist, poststructuralist, multicultural, and left theories, both fields share a commitment to examining cultural practices, economic conditions, and public policy from the point of view of their involvements with power. History-minded though both are, their involvement in the fluctuating contemporary world makes both alertly, not to say nervously, "presentist." Practitioners of both are committed to enabling people to become and remain active—to be *agents.* Harry Moody describes critical gerontology as focused on "problems of social justice . . . interpreting the meaning of human experience . . . understanding cultural tendencies." Stuart Hall, the charismatic former director of the Centre for Contemporary Cultural Studies in Birmingham, England, would use similar language. Both approaches know that culture deals out life or death literally—the rationing of health care alone proves it.[13]

Finally, some gerontologists could be considered "organic intellectuals" in ways that age critics—who know the term comes from Antonio Gramsci— might emulate. These public intellectuals, many of them feminists, speak about, on behalf of, to, and *from* the group they study. I am thinking of Barbara Mac-Donald, Baba Copper, Maggie Kuhn, Bernice Neugarten, Betty Friedan, the Rileys, among others. Their efforts have enrolled people in a self-conscious movement (with organizations attached, like the Gray Panthers), beating a drum for progressive public policy. People who do not themselves know the meaning of "age grading" call their congressional representatives when the rights of elderly people are threatened. They make it harder for the media to spin these threats into nothing. Age studies too needs to create its own vast constituency of the concerned. No easy feat. Who speaks for the life course? How would we learn to do it?

A joint transfusion of keywords could be one means and measure of interchange. *Keywords in Sociocultural Gerontology* is the title that Andrew Achenbaum, Steven Weiland, and Carole Haber borrowed, as they declare in their preface, from one of the founders of cultural studies, Raymond Williams.[14] Deciding exactly what concepts should be community property could be—I'd like it to be—a chewy philosophical issue. Here I propose only a short list, to try to provoke fuller inventories without raising the discomfort level prematurely. Age studies should be as ready to utilize "representation" as "age stratification," "historical conjuncture" as "ageism," "hegemony" as "age consciousness."[15]

Age studies should be as quick to deal with "the life-course imaginaries" as "the youth imaginaries" or the "old age imaginaries." Age studies should be like the other socially informed humanities and narratively informed social sciences in being historical and materialist as well as textually skillful, and as attuned as feminist theory to scientific discourse. An ideal field.

But age studies is a "field" that scarcely exists, that was named only in 1993. True, but not necessarily discouraging. Cultural studies itself, dating only from the 1960s and called by some of its practitioners "impossible," has provoked immense cognitive reorientations. Of course, rapprochement will not be stressless. Age studies makes an offer that both cultural criticism and critical gerontology—with notable exceptions from their humanist/feminist wings—have rather consistently refused: to wit, to study narratives, because they coauthor the life course. Cultural critics are notoriously sensitive to the stories inherent in mass culture (texts like newspaper polls, interviews, cable TV, book clubs, pop music, the romance, and practices like fashion, bodybuilding, and karaoke), putting them on a par with such other signs and instruments of consciousness as diaries, poetry, fiction, film, the psychotherapeutic case, the sermon. But most cultural critics lack the nose for narrative. In age studies, conjunctural analysis needs to be sensitive to the ways historical "troubles and issues" permeate life stories. Age and aging as we evolve is a personal residue—of stories we have heard, received or rejected, renegotiated and retold. Age analysis ties all these ideological vehicles, when possible, to their rhetorics and politics of age and aging. Speculation is the tensile strength—power and risk—of all cultural studies. Like a bridge linking an archipelago, whose piers must be set on many islands, age studies must reach in all directions for explanatory breadth.

It is impossible here and premature to try to survey the whole field on which these two bulky players approach each other. Instead, three "cases" follow, involving recent studies critically focused on, respectively, ageism, middle-ageism, and a crisis of youth. (I go backward, pursuing my experimental method.) They were chosen *as cases,* to enable me to note the likeliest directions age studies might go in, name particular problems that might hinder its effectiveness, and demonstrate that working toward this new intersection is already exciting and productive. Indeed, the challenges of age studies make it *the* place to do the next work.

Case 1: Against Ageism and Gerontophobia

In her critique of "the fundamentally ageist ideology of twentieth-century western culture," Kathleen Woodward's landmark book, *Aging and Its Discontents,* focuses on Freudian psychoanalysis and canonical modern literature. With her subtle readings of photographs, correspondence, fiction, theory; her mix of

challenge and respect for her influential sources; her sense of the stubborn refusal of many persons in old or sick bodies to be rewritten positively, and her
own mostly positive experiential writing, Woodward made old age textually *interesting*. Although she does not accept the idea of old age as "an empty signifier," she hollows out many a gerontophobic panic and ageist representation.[16] The book gave impetus to interrogating ageism (and by extension,
middle-ageism, the cult of youth, etc.) in the highest places of culture.

Key to her argument is that the ageism within Freudian psychoanalysis
(which she rightly calls "preeminently a theory of childhood") arises from
Freud's own midlife autobiography. He was forty when his father died; in
the son's opinion, after "his life had [long] been over." "It is the middle-aged
who . . . are apprehensive about old age," Woodward observes. Freud was also
aged by his culture in interpreting his own experience. Perhaps influenced by
the same contemporary babble about hormonal decline that caused Gertrude
Stein's tears, he believed he experienced a climacteric at fifty. Once having
crusted midlife with decline associations, he noted his declines into older age
more minutely. "Freud found aging more threatening than death itself," and
"he displaced his fear of old age onto death." Because he had based transference
on sexualized cathexis, he concluded that the very foundation of analysis was
denied to him when old because, as he said in frustration to the poet H.D., "You
do not think it worth your while to love me."[17] He constructed a "theory" of
psychical rigidity advancing with age, not only for women over thirty, as is well
known, but for men. Teresa Brennan comments, "Later analysts will take him
seriously, and advise against analysis for those over forty, on the grounds that
the psyche is too set in its paths."[18]

Woodward builds anti-ageist theory in ways that invite development. Her
Freud chapter led Brennan to meditate on the causes of "rigidity" that are *not*
linked to old age, exemplified by "Iris Murdoch's 'mother of a very large family' . . . often worn out before her time" or people who have reason to be "too
rigid" by forty. In an essay in the important collection *Figuring Age,* Brennan
provides a theory of ego development that makes learning lessons, establishing
"fixed points" for selfhood, and following "pathways" interactively necessary
starting in infancy. In the process, the ego must "bind" the "freely mobile energy that was so abundant in its youth." The downside (in Freud energy is
finite) is that this reduces energy for other projects. In the longer run, Brennan
asserts, "The more we see things from our own fixed point, the stronger the ego;
. . . the more *sedimented* [*our pathways,*] . . . *the more we age, and the closer we
come to death.*"[19]

Unwilling to see this psychic journey as ahistorical, ungendered, uniform, or
irreversible, Brennan brilliantly reminds us of social causes. It is because a
stronger "masculine party" seeks to "stave off aging" and reduce anxiety from
threats of change that he (it is usually a man) draws parasitically on the nurtur-

ing energies of another; he projects "that which is anxiety-ridden and confusing" onto "the feminine party," who absorbs them. Likewise, as we age, men and women alike must deal not only with our own sedimentation, but with "the refuse" flung off by the strivings of powerful younger Others.[20] Cultural images, in Brennan's theory of permeable selves, have "energetic" effects. When negative, they mount up on vulnerable subalterns as a kind of anaerobic waste.

Yet Brennan finds many practices that counter rigidity: viewing a play, meditating, lucking into a "sunny retirement." Presumably, also joining the age studies movement. Many practices "cathect to that refreshing consciousness which is free of the self."[21]

I read Brennan's essay as drawing ego psychology toward cultural politics. In her theory, although ego-supportive path building begins very early in life and is cumulative, its negative component can be accelerated or ameliorated at any age. It may be possible to unlink psychocognitive rigidity even further from her earthy, dirty metaphors of "sedimentation," "refuse," and "crusting": they seem to me to tie decline to age (and, irrationally, to death) despite Brennan's deconstructive aim. We might note that even in an ego-centered phase of life like adolescence, the crust can be broken by falling in love or encountering the intensities of higher education. If anxiety binds energy and escalates interpersonal cruelty, age critics could publish growing inventories of socially constructed sources of anxiety: capitalism's obsessive profit-motivated need for change, the exhaustions of child care or parent care, overwork. Answers to the biosocial syndrome formed by anxiety/projection/parasitism/bound pathways would then come unhesitatingly from politics (with no stop at anti-aging products): more raises and power as people in disadvantaged classes age, more talk about the relation between the weekend (brought to you by America's labor unions) and happy sexuality, more worker control over conditions of employment—in short, the "family values" agenda described at the end of chapter 5, with Brennan's additional emphasis on psychic and ethical benefits.

More fundamentally, we might query the link between "free mobile energy" and infant beings who cannot crawl or speak. The *use* of creative energy, as opposed to the potential, usually comes (to those with class freedom) only with adult agency. That freedom may last even after disease weakens the organism: one thinks of Flannery O'Connor writing despite lupus. Or, because work can be so demanding, freedom for creativity may come only after retirement—as it has for many "outsider" artists. Inertia need not be a correlate of increasing age. Even in less than optimal circumstances, we can become more energetic by finding reciprocal love or engaging work. We could reconceive the older pathways that we have "lovingly crafted" as identity *landmarks,* while recognizing that we have also started stimulating new paths elsewhere. Who is to say that "sedimentation" is the human default? As doubly multiple selves, can we not experience some good fixedness, some unnecessary fixedness, some good mobility, and some excessive mobility simultaneously at any age? Can we learn to notice that the percentages change irregularly over the life course? All this material could become part of our age autobiographies.

Perhaps the deconstruction of gerontophobia also requires severing many sutures between metaphors of generic aging-into-old-age (like borrowed energy and weighty sediments), and "the drive toward death" that Freud posited. Woodward says, "to completely rewrite the ideology of the aging body in the West, we would have to rewrite the meaning of death. And this we are not likely to do easily." [22] Yet she herself begins the severing in many ways. Freud's own stoic despair in fact had little to do with old age per se: as Woodward points out, over sixteen years he had many surgeries for cancer.

If we start not from psychoanalysis but from critical sociology, history, or anti-ageist memoir, "death" becomes rather more easily distinguished from old age. As David Sudnow argued years ago, after having witnessed 250 deaths in hospitals, "procedural definitions" (that conceal the moment of a person's death from other patients) treat "dying" as disjunct even from severe illness. Helping care for my terminally ill father years ago, I was shocked when, suddenly comatose, he was treated by a doctor as "essentially a corpse." With tremendous energy, my father had fought his terminal illness even past the point of paralysis. Those who watched him resist could never again associate dying with inertia. Stricken at sixty-eight, he died before he had a chance to grow old. In an anti-ageist culture, confusing being ill or being old with dying would be condemned as the premature imposition of "social death" and confusing being ill with being old would be frowned upon as a cruel category error.[23]

Case 2: Against Middle-Ageism

The invention of "the middle years" is proof positive of the drastic secular change in "aging." Now that so many fight over the meaning of the age class, it would be preposterous for anyone raised within mainstream culture to deny its existence. Once an unlabeled high plateau against which other age classes were implicitly measured, now the midlife is just another special interest, like childhood or old age, except that it lacks a lobby. Writing about this ever-changing invention has been one of my projects since the early 1980s. I think of it under the title *Midlife Fictions*. (It will become clear why my own work is one of my cases.)

The problems I posed kept expanding. In the work that became *Declining to Decline,* the first question was how to prove my intuition that, in recent decades in the United States, the cultural category "middle years" had gained firmer ontological status as part of being human.[24] The book took a major step in disaggregating the cacophany of Discourseland by marshaling evidence about the social construction of *male* decline. Cartoons, anecdotes, and novels about "entering" midlife, articles about male plastic surgery in the newspapers—all worked to suggest that midlife men, a group previously protected by the double standard of aging, were being exposed to a "structure of feeling" rather new to them: decline. Women were absorbing from the feminist movement and fiction a complex sense of "progress" at midlife. Yet they too were being targeted by a pervasive, interlocking system promoting midlife decline. It was the addition of men that most naturalized the age class. Universalizing the midlife undoes the work of "positive aging" even as its proponents work tirelessly to strengthen intrapsychic resistance. Aging became a unisex complaint with a childhood or adolescent exposure and a midlife onset. I redefined my task as explaining the increasing power of middle-ageism.

While my evidentiary field expanded, age remained a neglected analytic tool in most theory workshops. Yet I found certain developments (critical, socialist, feminist, poststructuralist) useful if reconceived with sufficient single-mindedness. I pick here only a few instances. Pro-feminist men's studies encouraged me to examine the supposedly privileged gender in its supposedly supreme moment, the middle years; while the feminist left enabled me to distinguish Father-Right from capitalism, which nerved me to reread patriarchy as being humbled by globalization. Antipositivism meant that I didn't have to answer the question, "When do the middle years begin?" with a chronological number, as many social scientists still do. I could ask instead, "In what context? For which subject? At what level of employment or consumption?" and that refusal helped me toward the concept of the life-course imaginaries. Foucault led me to Sandra Bartky's analysis of how power constructs emotions like feminine shame.[25] The sociology and history of the emotions enabled me to write about the construction of *midlife* emotions and other age-related feelings. Like this book, *Declining to Decline* opens with a scene of age anxiety.

My historical research had already shown me that people in their middle years have never been homogeneous in privilege. Before 1900, when a "gerontocratic economy" ruled, what good did age hierarchy do middle-aged men who were slaves or factory workers, or women past childbearing age? Those who study "fathers" and "mothers" historically or in film and fiction should be aware that parenting babies or middle-aged children are quite different matters. Fortunately, subdominant midlife narratives are beginning to appear: cultural anthropologists Katherine Newman and Thomas Weisner are doing very interesting work.[26] As it becomes harder to ignore the full range of midlife conditions, the class skews of positive aging will seem more egregious.

With midlife contexts so heterogeneous, I moved rapidly beyond thinking of my evidence as solely literary or "high," in order to comprehend all the artifacts of age ideology. How does a midlife imaginary get formulated so that so many listeners understand what "the big Five-Oh" means, know what tones are possible in response and what rebuttals are not? How do age ideas circulate from a cartoon to conversation, or twist from data into fiction? How do circumstances outside text also press human subjects toward more harmful beliefs and feelings about aging into another age of life?

Feminist political economy urged me not to ignore economic data: I found a few economists who disaggregated unemployment statistics in order to discover serious midlife job loss after around fifty. The pieces that an age critic ideally needs—discourses, practices, and material conditions—came together. I had a story with historical salience and psychological urgency. The story already had a name—"midlife crisis"—but that name was misleading: it implied that what is happening is only personal, intrapsychic, trivial, and occasional, when middle-ageism is a danger for the nation and the life course. The missing piece was resistance: imagining a political agenda, a plausible collective to realize it, a more resistant self to join the collective.

To encourage that self, I developed the traveling portmanteau genre I call "age autobiography." If history refuses to reveal "the shaping force of the writer's *current* situation," as Carolyn Steedman argues, feminist auto/biography and anthropology have shown ways to bring that situation alive.[27] My mixed form permitted me to be a current witness, and in some ways required it. I wrote about being dragged along by history, about learning how to tell my own tiny hopeful progress narrative as a child reading under the cold drenching of the Cold War, and about feeling coerced by shopping and HRT into applying decline narrative to my midlife self. I wrote about my son and my mother, as I do here too. They don't object to my telling these private histories, because writing *against* specific impositions might free all our generations.

Because I started from indelible moments of cultural confrontation each time, I was darting around my life and theirs; I wasn't privileging one slice of life consistently. I was aware that I had not been Xer-ized when I was my son's age, and that I did not enjoy the midlife security, both bodily and financial, that my mother had had at the same age. Through the swoops of such comparative practice, I found another, historically justifiable way to break out of slice-of-life studies. We are aged by culture throughout life. I'd love to have people explain how they came to this insight. Some, like Brennan meditating on the ups and downs of energy exchanges, or me rambling around in my son's and mother's age biographies, simply find ourselves in a fresh critical place beyond stage-obsession. We become age critics who suddenly have entire life-course imaginaries to reckon with in addition to (rather than instead of) disjunct parts. This changes the object of study. I return to the new problematic this constructs after my third case.

Case 3: Against "Youth in Crisis"

Youth "is present only when its presence is a problem, or is regarded as a problem," according to Dick Hebdige, who helped found subcultural studies of youth in Britain. Cultural critic Lawrence Grossberg considers youth "an empty signifier." [28] Charles Acland's impressive book, *Youth, Murder, Spectacle*, demonstrates how one signifying figure of youth—"youth gone wild"—has been filled to create a sense of crisis in the United States. Deviant youth—"and this is doubly true of African-American and Hispanic-American youth—is increasingly symbolically central, . . . defined as a threat to the stability of the social order." Acland warns that the crisis described in his book "is not about 'real' youth." On the contrary, he maintains, it's about "a discursive construct" that often imagines a "white upwardly mobile youth standing in for the U.S. as a whole." Like most cultural critics, he believes that such fictions have "profound effects upon the imaginary formation of youth as well as the real lives of the young." [29]

Acland's subject is the representation of youth crime in the 1980s, and the debates constructed around it. He singles out one white male-on-female murder in the upper middle class (Robert Chambers's 1986 strangling of Jennifer Levin in New York, the so-called Preppy Murder), and follows its textual permutations through news reports, criminal confession, photos, editorials, TV movies, talk shows. With each medium he shows how the discourse about the crime worked: first, how the two main characters were narrated and how the legal system participated in the narration; then how the discourse worked to maintain traditional sex and gender relations and racial stereotypes; and finally, how the crisis expanded.

His details are riveting. The press picked Levin's murder instead of a simultaneous rape and murder that was witnessed by police officers who did nothing to stop it. The dead woman was framed as a kinky seducer, as if she had the "male role of rapist," while the male murderer was given the part of the "not-too-bright bimbo" who went along as she ordered until things got out of control. Chambers's confession appeared to speak "the truth of female adolescent sexuality" rather than the truth of his misogyny or male sexual hysteria. "As the initial crime is being left far behind," Acland argues, "a general crisis of youth is being established" through "the intractable activity of sounding alarms." [30]

How could all this happen? Acland gives clues: "The next generation as a rhetorical concept has carried the impression of vision and hope," yet now the young "cannot expect even the same quality of life as their parents." [31] As age studies urges, he is trying to determine the exact economics and politics of using an age-class for crisis building. In the mid-1980s, did too many parents and adult children already anticipate a declining future for "the young"? We saw what that led to in the first Bush recession: the "slacker" stereotype. Then there were years spent recharacterizing "the Xers" as valuable workaholics, advancing the Boomer syndrome, obscuring the crisis of midlife economics.

Age studies also proposes that a close look at a single age class be accompanied (to start with) by an inquiry into how other age classes are affected. Acland notes that the rhetoric of youth in crisis points an accusing finger at "negligent parents," especially working mothers, and that all the age wars have a conservative bias. "'Generation' has no fundamental essence except as a problem," he says early on.[32] Many constructions of difference aggravate problems for two or three generations, and, as he shows, for gendered and racialized groups as well.

But Acland himself intensifies a generational difference when he invents "the disciplinary gaze of the adult" in film and decides it has a "patriarchal function as it attempts to replicate the qualities of the economic social."[33] Presumably this "adult gaze" is modeled on the "male gaze," a concept of theorist Laura Mulvey that brought film criticism out of its universalizing fog by gendering it. "The disciplinary gaze of the adult" could certainly serve analysis in many fields. But Acland's use constructs a monolith of homogeneously censorious "adults." "Patriarchal gaze" might be a more fruitful term; at least it admits that power is unevenly distributed between adult men and women. He ignores the gender of filmmakers (still mostly male) and their chronological ages and psychological motives. Many turn their backs on their notion of "adult" perspectives because the viewers they envision are mainly between twelve and twenty-eight, or fifteen and twenty-four, or they themselves are young men, or because even though they're older they continue to identify with a particular junior self or with the young in general.

The tendency to homogenize "older" age groups arises from a deep problem in cultural studies: its "long love affair with masculinist youth culture, romanticizing the tough rebelliousness of working-class boys": here Leerom Medevoi is paraphrasing Angela McRobbie.[34] Adding (young) women, as Angela McRobbie did, was an important move, but it still leaves only the young endowed with intracohort variability and compelling individuality. Indeed, adding the once neglected gendered or racialized or sexualized Other often simply fortifies an age class. There's some bias against maturity per se. To many cultural critics, it would be considered condescending to suggest that young people's values or points of view might improve as they "mature." "Youth culture contains all the appeal of that contentious time *outside* the adult," Acland says oddly. He misconceives development as "the easy flow toward the adult."[35] Nor does it occur to him that actors playing parents sometimes model something other than the "economically productive" or the utterly failed. (Kevin Klein in *Life as a House* and Meryl Streep in *One True Thing* come to mind. Apparently reconciliation between parents and nearly adult children is easier for filmmakers to imagine if the parents are dying.) In youth studies, aging-into-adulthood often seems to be unimagined; the midlife, through some flawed fall from grace, a repressive inexpressive "parent culture"; intergenerational relations inherently adversarial.

Insidiously socialized by decline ideology, critics may be hard put to recall that intracohort differences are also constructs, or to recognize that capitalism's subtle war on the midlife is bad news even for the young. They don't notice that their imaginary itself mimics the dominant cult of youth, that the cult of youth reinforces middle-ageism, and that middle-ageism hardens gerontophobia. Surely, age studies can be class-conscious and even in many ways antihierarchical without being a priori hostile to development, seniority, and intergenerational politics.

AGE IS A NICE NEW DEVIL

When critics foreground their chosen age class and ignore or scale down others, it's often for a good reason, such as focusing resistance to gerontophobia, middle-ageism, youth as crisis. But age fragmentation jams us onto tiny separate terrains constructed by dominant culture. My own work on the midlife before *Aged by Culture* proves this: it got rewardingly more interdisciplinary without getting off that particular dime. Even now, I find the current of midlife studies strong. The difference is that as an age critic I have to justify this pull— not, unfortunately for us all, hard to do. We don't have much in the way of age studies yet. On the whole—with exceptions to be noted—we have sophisticated, fascinating, and revelatory slice-of-life studies. And we're likely to have more, because such expertise is hard to win and remains valuable.

To undertake age studies proper, some critics and theorists need to study the concept of the life-course imaginaries, so that those specializing in particular stages may work with a sense of the problematics of the whole. (Some humanistic gerontologists, like Jay Gubrium, work with the concept of "the whole life," which sensitizes them in listening to elderly informants. But the method of going "in search of life as a whole" doesn't seem to require asking elders questions about their exposure to the successive age cultures of the twentieth century, or asking similar questions of younger people—questions that would allow us to historicize the imaginaries.) [36]

Clearly, representations of the crises of old age, the midlife, and youth operate simultaneously, in their curious antagonistic ways, on American culture. There should be speculation about whether and how the "three" crises interrelate. (And, as I observed earlier, there are far more than three.) Do these crises get sequenced in "the popular imagination" so that current young adults believe in and anticipate for themselves, one or another life-course imaginary of their time? Violence and disrespect at the start of adulthood; rigid pathways and rigor mortis at the other end; in the middle, premature superannuation, literal or metaphorical? Or perhaps, for some in a higher class, beauty, flexibility, and promise in youth; lavish consumption, long life, and boughten friends at the end; in the middle, a contest between the "too-late" syndrome and a high age/wage curve, healthy positive middle-aging, retirement by choice. Decline or progress, with all their possible range of genre responses, from heroic endurance to despair.

But let's ask also whether people in different cohorts "read" the same sequence at all. If you're a child now, in or out of the science museum, you're not learning the same narratives a child learned in the 1940s. If you're thirty now, you are probably misreading or skipping the chapters that "Boomers" are supposed to attend to. If you are eighty, "middle age" probably did not have the same meaning then as "the midlife" does for people who are fifty now. It's no good snapping, "This is all unreal," or, for that matter, "Who's hypostasizing age cohorts now?" Age fictions have effects, presumably different ones depending on class, race, sexuality—and also depending on stage. Without reifying all cohort construction, we should be able to investigate this hypothesis. And a final question. Is it possible phenomenologically if not in logic that the social status of all age classes qua age classes is declining? So that even if you are privileged enough to get to read or write the higher-class version of the progress narrative, there's still something sour about being reminded of yourself as having an age? This would follow from the historical metatheory that age is becoming a more totalizing and negative identity.

A political scientist predicted in the 1990s that more public policy debates would be cast in young-versus-old terms. "Age will likely be to the next millennium what race [and, I would add, gender and sexual orientation, have] been to the last half of the twentieth century—a high-profile, highly divisive problem for which it will be extremely difficult to devise solutions that work." [37] Once the wrong terms for a problem are locked in place, solutions often exacerbate the problem. Age ideology will very likely be manipulated as we have seen: to construct standard biographies that exclude our sweet particularity even when they don't end in later-life sorrow, to force groups into combat for allegedly scarce goods, to divide the citizenry and the workforce (and promote slice-of-life studies), to explain history and preclude intergenerational solidarity. How age gets constructed is opportunistic; for many deeply conservative political forces, opportune.

Age theory is getting under way in the nick of time. I hope. It needs to prioritize what it wants to resist. In advance of anticipated debate, I have here singled out fragmentation of the life course as one giant-sized enemy. But slice-of-life studies per se are not the main obstacle to raising our age consciousness. We can all deepen our suspicion of age divisions and stage attributions, those we inherit and those ideology tosses up next. (I believe I got a little extra edge from having been born before the Boomers and not feeling hailed in any personal way by their being falsely characterized.) Many cultural critics and more critical gerontologists can agilely accept the need for analyzing the life-course imaginaries and retheorizing "the whole life." The difficulties for practice are conceptual, psychological, disciplinary. Even age critics, merged and deconstructive, age may turn out to be the category most resistant to erosion, the most biological of all the supposed givens, and even (out of a curious remnant of positivist pride) the one and only remaining *real.* Even a mature age critic writes at any given moment out of only one age location, one generation, one historical experience of aging, calmed by the illusion of generational solidarity that comes from having moved from one age to the next.

The generations must unite against life-course dismemberment. While deconstructing stage and cohort differences, age studies could also emphasize a variety of connections and continuities. Likenesses and reciprocity between familial generations, mutual influences, links between the fictive life slices, and whole-life approaches—representations of these exist in plenty, but seem sentimental (aren't they merely ideal?) unless they are explicitly promoted as resistances to fragmentation and age war. Kathleen Woodward fulfills this requirement and rewrites the oedipal narrative to boot, by writing touchingly about loving bonds between herself and her grandmother. Historian Tamara Hareven shows how "one generation transmits to the next the ripple effects of the historical circumstances that shaped its life history"; psychologists, how adolescent individuation affects midlife parents; memoirist Alix Kates Shulman, in *A Good Enough Daughter,* how much a midlife caretaker can enjoy her frail funny mother suffering from Alzheimer's. Cultural critics Jenny Hockey and Allison James find that tropes of dependency constructed for controlling children are used to marginalize the elderly.[38]

Perhaps age autobiography needs to find more persuasive, valorizing ways of describing forms of personal continuity. Were we able to start our life storytelling from the ground of a seamless life course, it would be easier for the self to lovingly craft its *own* life peaks and markers (as Jo Spence thought so important). Some feminists—Margaret Urban Walker and Judy Long, for example—critique continuous narrative because it can be too smooth, distortingly modeled on the (formerly all-male) careers of the middle-classes.[39] But belief in continuity does not guarantee smoothness or progress. It can promise nothing but an added measure of inner resistance against dismemberment, and a heightened alertness to external threats. If people have names for the vicissitudes of fate and history that they have survived (holocaust, exile, counterrevolution, depression, family tragedy, chronic illness), can we not train ourselves to name speed-up and the slice-and-dice machines that we survive? Surviving decline ideology could become something more than a lifestyle matter or a joke, something more heroic, as we come to take the assaults of all the dehumanizing time machines more seriously. Life-course continuity could be envisioned alternatively, where this makes sense, as based on the metaphor of the *evolution* of identities. To me the "wick" could be merely that the Latest Self remembers. Its useful arrogance about *its* right to tell *its* stories *its* way could exponentially multiply into resistance if more people considered possessiveness about telling their stories—without excessive interference from master narratives—to be a sacred personal and collective right. In any case, stressing psychological continuity in acceptable ways is going to matter more in this century, as age theorists position ourselves to answer the question, "What life-course imaginaries can *we* develop to replace the sequential-crisis model of the ages?" As more subsystems of the decline narrative are identified, our joint creativity will have to seek out shared ideals and political platforms on which to build an antidecline movement. Whatever we call the movement, how can we make "the life course" a meaningful cause?

Heightening age consciousness is a prerequisite. A critical pedagogy can formulate appropriate training at every level from Head Start to Elderhostel. How could teachers prepare children under fifteen to encounter the "Face Aging" booth in all its future avatars? How would they prepare parents and grandparents to engage children who have gone through the booth? Age critics, monitoring the media, can treat "age" as a specialty for which expertise is required and put suspect allegations of age difference on the defensive. Researchers can provide the information that assures others of the subjective value and epistemological soundness of their cause.

What principles underlie an antidecline movement? Objectivity? From the standpoint of what age? Equality? Equalized longevity is a human right. Based as it must be on health and well-being from birth throughout the life course, it could rally more adherents to national health insurance. "Age equality," however, would be a treacherous goal. Theorists of the other body-based binaries and youth-oriented cultural critics, who have fought for equality elsewhere, should not fall for it here. Within the capitalist neoliberal context—probably within any system—we can have no such automatism about blindly letting age hierarchy slide out of historical memory. Were those in the middle years to find themselves "equal" competitors with the young in the workforce, the wage race to the bottom would indeed have hit bottom. We must be willing to maintain the proposition that in current historical circumstances a hierarchy by age is the only fair and universal one, and that a modest, democratized economic age hierarchy throughout working life is one foundation of a decent society. Gerontologists and political scientists, aware of the cultural devaluation that can afflict even the prosperous "young old," and cultural critics concerned about the future of the young, should lend their moral authority to shoring up and expanding legislation and institutions that rebuild seniority, sustain modest midlife age/wage peaks, and restrain the worst inequalities within the age classes. If we lose the midlife as a time of respect, aside from every other loss that entails, we lose all hope of fighting ageism and gerontophobia in the United States. And given the global reach of the multinationals, whatever disempowerment they can accomplish here will become more easily exportable to other countries. In eastern Europe, in the global south (wherever middle classes are expanding, perhaps assisted by governments relying on secure tax revenues and stable high employment), middle-ageism can prevent people aging-into-the-midlife from obtaining a premium for experience, helping their children, saving a little, keeping their dignity through old age. Age is a cause—like race and gender—that rightfully allies itself with principles of narrative freedom, economic justice, and human rights. There are many ways to contribute to a revolution.

←——————→

Studies in Optimistic Philosophy (1903) was the subtitle of a famous early longevity text.[40] At the beginning of the twenty-first century, age studies can begin to be optimistic only as, with strengths joined, we learn to name all the current enemies of the life course, even inside ourselves and within our disciplines—when we can accurately describe the methods they deploy and institute new resistances that have some chance of success.

Acknowledgments

Since 1990, the complex move from calling myself a cultural critic to calling myself an age critic has also involved crossing interdisciplinary lines in various directions. This has been a source of excitement—the kind not unmixed with anxiety—and pleasure. The opportunities often arose serendipitously. I had a question that couldn't be answered without a sideward move; or a journal editor expressed interest in an essay I was already writing (which then needed revision for her audience); or an editor in an adjacent field asked whether I would write something specifically for his readers. Some of these instigators guided me around pitfalls; some simply encouraged me to press on. My work in this book has benefited from the attention of wonderful editors, including Anne Fadiman, Henry Giroux, Laurence Goldstein, George Katsiafikas, Ruth Ray, and Rick Shweder. In retrospect I can see how these new practices formed my particular path into the emerging field I named "age studies."

I was for many years an independent scholar, perching temporarily at various welcoming local institutions. At Brandeis, Shula Reinharz invented the concept of the long-term affiliation and built a center to house the artists, scholars, and writers in the program. The Women's Studies Research Center offered me an interdisciplinary home in 1996, and I have been there since. The scholars have provided me with generous helpings of collegiality, inspiration, and critique.

I have been fortunate to have found excellent interns through the Student-Scholar Partnership at the WSRC. Rene Burrows Rapaporte financed it for years; in the fall of 2002, my undergraduate partner's work was supported by Carol Goldberg and Michele Kessler. Rebecca Smith was invaluable in doing research and preparing the bibliography in 2001–2. Sara Gruen did a splendid job helping me compile the index in the fall of 2002. Keyword indexes are pedagogical tools for readers, and making them can reveal conceptual strengths (or flaws) in a book, as well as unsuspected connections. I am grateful to earlier Brandeis interns for research help, especially Elissa Goodman and Debra Mazer.

At the University of Chicago Press, Carlisle Rex-Waller did a meticulous job of copyediting. David Brent, my editor, guided me through the shoals of the process with the wisdom of long experience. Elizabeth Branch Dyson was indefatigably calm.

Connie Higginson found the catalog for the Feldmann show at the Musée d'Art Moderne de la Ville de Paris.

On chapters 1, 2, and 6, special thanks to Nancer Ballard, Mary Mason, and Roz Barnett, for detailed notes that amounted to a long conversation, and to Andrea Petersen, Frinde Maher, Linda Dittmar, and the other members of my Left Study Group, for an intense conversation on content and structure. Frinde, in particular, suggested how to "unbraid" my themes. Thanks to John Price for warning about dangers in the term "the life course."

A shorter version of chapter 3 was published in the *American Scholar* (spring 2000). Another version was published in the *Review of Education, Pedagogy, and Cultural Studies*.

Chapter 4 was published in a shorter version in the *Michigan Quarterly Review* 31, no. 1 (winter 1992). That version was reprinted in *Twentieth Century Literary Criticism*, vol. 78, ed. Jennifer Gariepy (New York: Gale, 1998).

A number of specialists in sociology and economics helped me on various aspects of chapter 5, including Larry Mishel at the Economic Policy Institute and Bob Ross. Interpreting the data was my responsibility.

An earlier version of chapter 7 was published in *Declining to Decline: Cultural Combat and the Politics of the Midlife* (Charlottesville: University of Virginia Press, 1997). The differences between the two versions indicate how far I have come since then as an age critic, and the similarities suggest the inertia of our culture. That version had benefited enormously from the suggestions and reflections of Charles Altieri, Michael Brown, Penelope Sales Cordish, David Gullette, Nancy K. Miller, Alix Kates Shulman, Sabine Sielke, Werner Sollers, Kathleen

Woodward, an anonymous reviewer, and the members of the Northeastern University Women's Studies Colloquium present on April 28, 1994. Part of the current version was published in the *Brandeis Review* 18, no. 4 (1998): 22–25.

The Obermann Seminar at the University of Iowa in the summer of 1999 critiqued an early version of chapter 8 thoroughly. Thanks especially to Ruth Ray and Teresa Mangum. Part of this chapter appeared, in a slightly different form, in *Profession 2001* (New York: Modern Language Association of America, 2001), 99–108.

My thanks to Pam Gien, Laurence Senelick, Elinor Fuchs, and Herbert Blau for the best kinds of help on chapter 9. Also to members of my audience present on February 12, 2002, at the Women's Studies Research Center at Brandeis, especially Louise Lopman.

Ruth Ray beautifully helped me edit an earlier published version of chapter 10, which appeared in *Handbook of the Humanities and Aging*, 2d ed., edited by Thomas R. Cole, Robert Kastenbaum, and Ruth E. Ray (New York: Springer, 2000), 214–34. Teresa Brennan, as delightful as she was brilliant, commented on the section of this chapter that referred to her work.

Thanks to the librarians at Widener Library and at the Schlesinger Library, Radcliffe Institute for Advanced Studies, and special thanks to Annette Fern in the Harvard Theater Collection.

←——————→

My mother, Betty Eisner Morganroth, has been an inspiration at every stage of my work in age studies. She also edited a number of chapters of this book, with her schoolteacher's highly trained eye for grammar, diction, and tone.

Sean Gullette edited chapter 1 with experienced deftness and gives me hope that age critics will emerge in the future at ever younger ages. David Gullette has been a thoughtful editor, a source of moral, financial, and emotional support, and a co-combatant.

Notes

CHAPTER ONE

1. Sontag, *On Photography*, 38.
2. Bass, "Secrets of Aging," F1.
3. Griffin, "Children Face Up to Aging," 7.
4. Woolf, "The Moment," 3.
5. Spence, *Cultural Sniping*, 72.
6. In the field called sociology of childhoods, "ageism" refers to the ways adults misuse their power over children and adolescents.
7. Ronald and Juliette Goldman "confirm the onset from a very early age of induction to a biologically based decline model . . . not only with Australian children but in all the samples" (*Children's Sexual Thinking*, 103).
8. Sontag, *On Photography*, 87. Harms and Kellner, "Toward a Critical Theory of Advertising," cite Leiss and Klein as confirming Baudrillard's idea that images dominate text in an economy based on privatized commodity consumption.

9. Sontag, *On Photography*, 124.
10. Renaud told me that Nancy Burson had done a show at the Franklin Institute in Philadelphia in 1995 in which she crackled the "skin" of photographed subjects as if they had been Renaissance oil paintings. Burson had worried about the negative effects of this "aging" on children. She was nevertheless showing her exhibit in New York in 2002.
11. Sontag, *On Photography*, 87.
12. Feldman, "Narratives of National Identity," 129.
13. Mary Russo, "Aging and the Scandal of Anachronism," 25.
14. Frank Cordelle, a photographer, is producing a series called "Century," in which about a hundred women are shown naked. They are representative, he says, in ethnic and religious terms, in body types and bodily experiences, including rape victims, anorectics, "cutters," the disabled (http://century.conknet.com). The *Esquire* photographer was Diego Goldberg.
15. Hepworth, *Stories of Ageing*, 39.
16. Spence, *Cultural Sniping*, 192, emphasis added.
17. Giddens, *Modernity and Self-Identity*, 146 ff. Giddens mentions "generations," "kinship," "family," but his conclusions seem unnecessarily abstract because he doesn't use the terms "age" or "aging."
18. Hall, "On Postmodernism and Articulation," 137.
19. I first used the phrase "aged by culture" in "What, Menopause *Again?*"
20. Anthropologist Richard Shweder says it is the American *midlife* that is exported. I think he would agree that other aspects of the postmodern life course are likely to be exported as well. See Shweder, introduction to *Welcome to Middle Age!* x. On the particular American midlife that gets exported, see Gullette "Midlife Discourses in the Twentieth-Century United States."
21. I offered this name for the field in 1993: see "Creativity, Aging, Gender," 45 and 42–46, and Wyatt-Brown, "Aging, Gender, and Creativity," 5. On "age studies" in general, see Gullette, "Age Studies, and Gender," in *Encyclopedia of Feminist Theories*.
22. Berti and Bombi, *The Child's Construction of Economics*, 198.
23. Donald, "The Central Role of Culture in Cognitive Evolution," 35.
24. Berger, *Pig Earth*, 175.
25. Peters, "The Development of Collaborative Story Retelling," 392.
26. Summarized in Chandler et al., "Continuities of Selfhood," 75, also 72. For a mini-bibliography of studies of continuity when confronted by affliction, see Cohler, "The Life Story," 174 n. 5.
27. Goldman and Goldman, *Children's Sexual Thinking*, 115–16. Associations children have with the gendered "stages" of life were cued by stick figures showing a crawling baby, a small kid, a teenager, a young adult, and an old person (nota bene, no midlife figures). Among the eleven-year-olds, more chose an older age than the same age, which suggests that to them being teenaged has more prestige. Only one child out of 240, an eleven-year-old girl, "pointed out that there were good

things about each stage of life depicted" (106). The Goldmans required the children to choose "the best" age, teaching the concept of rivalry between age classes.

28. Chandler et al., "Continuities of Selfhood," 77, 76.

29. "Age identity" was a concept I used in *Declining to Decline* (1997), but this book contains a fuller definition.

30. Geduld, introduction to *The Definitive Time Machine*, 2.

31. In *Safe at Last in the Middle Years* (1988), I warned that decline narrative is often produced by writers who are worrying aloud in dramatic ways about the un-known future of their life course.

32. Spence, *Cultural Sniping*, 50.

33. On Norwegian parents' nonverbal cues and negotiations that teach children the meaning of aging, see also Solberg, "Negotiating Childhood," 126 – 44. There seems to be very little work on socialization into age and aging.

34. Fiese and Marjinsky, "Dinnertime Stories," 67.

35. Broughton, "An Introduction to Critical Development Psychology," 6; see also 10, 19.

36. See Gullette, "Midlife Heroines, 'Older and Freer' " (chapter 5 in *Declining to Decline*); also *Safe at Last in the Middle Years*

37. I first learned about age grading from historian Howard O. Chudacoff—an age studies practitioner *avant la lettre*—in his convincingly documented *How Old Are You?* (1989).

38. *Boston Globe,* April 13, 2001, B4.

39. Carolyn Steedman argues that in the nineteenth century, "the ideas of growth and development came to be more and more articulated around observation of the young of the species, and particularly in terms of human children" (*Strange Dislocations,* 94). She sees this turn as a way to dehistoricize history, remove it from "the time that allowed growth and decay" (95). In relation to current children, "progress" is an ideal model, as the culturists say, to distinguish it from real psychosocial conditions. But as a widespread cultural narrative, it influences institutions and affects real psychosocial conditions.

40. Eleanor E. Maccoby finds that "some children" develop a "pervasive internal locus of control" while others "feel they are at the mercy of fate or luck" (*Social Development,* 285). Beatrice and John Whiting found that children in all cultures increasingly take responsibility for younger children (*Children of Six Cultures*).

41. Giroux, *Stealing Innocence,* 11.

42. Buckingham talks about some functions of this figure of the threatened child in *After the Death of Childhood,* 11–12. Many sociologists of childhood are hostile to the term "needs" because they say, quite rightly, that adults construct them for children. I am constructing needs for adults as well as children, and doing both openly.

43. On the term "age class," see Gullette, *Declining to Decline,* 4 – 5, and "Midlife Discourses in the Twentieth-Century United States."

44. For interesting definitions of "the American Dream," see Hearn, *The American Dream in the Great Depression,* chapter 6. For the difference between feminist and masculinist metaphors of "development" I am indebted to Ellin Kofsky Scholnick, "Engendering Development," especially page 39.
45. Giddens, *Modernity and Self-Identity,* 202.
46. Hareven, *Family Time and Industrial Time,* 359–61.
47. Giddens remarks that "a person's identity" is to be found "in the capacity to *keep a particular narrative going*" (*Modernity and Self-Identity,* 54). On adult resistance, see Davis, "Not Dead Yet," 174.
48. Handel, "Perceived Change of Self among Adults," 327.
49. Bauman, "From Pilgrim to Tourist," 24.
50. The age/wage curve is sometimes called the "age/earnings profile." See Stern, "Poverty and the Life Cycle," 529. "Curve" points to its ideal form in an age hierarchy. "Profile" points to its bumpiness under actual economic conditions.

CHAPTER TWO

1. Hall, "Who Needs Identity?" 6. Hall credits Stephen Heath with the concept of "suturing effects." His own term is often "identification."
2. *Getting over Getting Older* is the title of a 1997 book by Letty Pogrebin.
3. Laws, "Tabloid Bodies, 3–10. In 2002 Proctor and Gamble announced a fifty million dollar campaign to sell its ordinary toothpaste for two dollars more to women aged thirty to forty-four as "youthening" (Pittman, "Crest 'Rejuvenating' Effects").
4. Goffman, *Stigma,* 9.
5. Pierre Bourdieu provides definitions and some exemplifications of the term "symbolic capital": "a legitimate possession grounded in the nature of its possessor" (129), but does not discuss it in relation to youth and age (*The Logic of Practice,* 118–21).
6. On signs that men are aged by culture earlier and more intensively than they used to be, and at midlife begin to look nearly as vulnerable as women, see Gullette, "All Together Now?" in *Declining to Decline.* On identity stripping, see 6, 8, 197, 169–70, 215–16.
7. Menon, "Middle Adulthood in Cultural Perspective," 67. Menon is basing his argument on data and reports from the MacArthur Research Network on Successful Midlife Development. One of my essays, "Midlife Discourses in the Twentieth-Century United States," is taken as the alternative view. I believe I am here making the MacArthur case even more strongly than they do, by adducing evidence from fiction and other representations, social history, and economic history, to explain why this class and gender group is telling a progress story, if indeed they are.

8. See American Board of Family Practice, *The Physicians' View of Middle Age*. This survey literature does not consider a subject's relationship to the master narrative of decline or the interviewer's interest in eliciting progress narratives.

9. Staudinger and Bluck, "A View on Midlife Development from Life-Span Theory," 20. The term "postmaternal" is mine: it refers to women who mother at the period in their lives when their offspring have aged into independent adulthood, if they do. See Gullette, "Postmaternity as a Revolutionary Feminist Concept."

10. Giele, "Innovation in the Typical Life Course."

11. "The future will look like the pre-pension era," said one expert interviewed in Simon-Rusinowitz et al., "Future Work and Retirement Needs," 35.

12. Gisela Labouvie-Vief writes, typically, that "to formulate more positive accounts of the 'second half of life' has become ever more urgent" ("Positive Development in Later Life," 365). I want to emphasize the conditions in which accounts are formulated.

13. Thomas R. Cole and Ruth E. Ray, critical gerontologists from the humanistic wing of the field, pose some of the critical questions with regard to positive aging in old age: "Where did the idea of successful aging come from in the first place? What are its conceptual limitations and ambiguities?" (Cole and Ray, introduction to *The Handbook of the Humanities and Aging*, 2d ed., xix). Cole's earlier *Journey of Life* ends with a persuasive argument against positive aging.

14. Wallis, "Species Questions," 505.

15. Newman, "A Different Shade of Gray," 280 n.2. See also Sorlie, Baklund, and Keller, "U.S. Mortality by Economic, Demographic, and Social Characteristics."

16. Responses to the Great Depression, as historian Glen H. Elder showed in a famous book, varied among siblings quite close in age: see *Children of the Great Depression* (1974).

17. See table 2.22 in Mishel, Bernstein, and Schmitt, *The State of Working America, 2000–2001,*. 158: Wages for entry-level college-educated men went up 14.9 percent in that boom period; for college-educated women, 9.4 percent. Wages for entry-level men and women with a high school education also went up over 6 percent. "Experience" (aging relevant to the workplace) comprehends all the "human capital" developments: e.g., training, firm, or industry-specific knowledge, working acquaintances, personal development.

18. On the experience differentials, see Mishel, Bernstein, and Schmitt, *The State of Working America, 2000–2001*, table 2.17 and page 148. Age studies asks economists to look regularly at longitudinal data as well, in order to follow various cohorts' actual age/wage curves. I do this in chapter 6.

19. This is my analysis based on U.S. Bureau of the Census data, Income Table P8. From Census data I can't match Mishel's sample, which compares people aged twenty-five to thirty-five with people aged thirty-five to fifty.

20. Slesnick, *Consumption and Social Welfare*, 150.

21. Madrick, "Enron, the Media, and the New Economy," 18.

22. Labaton, "You Don't Have to Be Old to Sue for Age Discrimination," 7.

23. The term "middle-ageism" first appeared in Gullette, "The Wonderful Woman on the Pavement." See also Gullette, *Declining to Decline.*

24. Laws, "Understanding Ageism," 115.

25. Pierre Bourdieu argues against an "'economism' that seeks to grasp an 'objective reality' quite inaccessible to ordinary experience by analysing the statistical relationships among distributions of material properties" (*The Logic of Practice,* 135). My personal example shows how changes in their own economic distributions become intelligible to life storytellers.

26. Bourdieu, *The Logic of Practice,* 108.

27. Rose, "Identity, Genealogy, History," 139.

28. Heckhausen, "Adaptation and Resilience in Midlife," 349.

29. For the concept of measuring hidden ideologies I am indebted to my colleague, social psychologist Rhoda Unger. A new term like "age ideology" may work as "'a sign to avoid reduction.' . . . Without having exactly theorized what [the new term] is and how it works, [I use it to speak] of other possibilities, of other ways of theorizing the elements of a social formation and the relations that constitute it" (Slack, "The Theory and Method of Articulation," 117).

30. Goffman, *Stigma,* preface, n.p.

31. My publications on the midlife as it was constructed between 1880 and 1930 include "The Puzzling Case of the Deceased Wife's Sister," "Inventing the 'Postmaternal' Woman," "Midlife Discourses in the Twentieth-Century United States," "Male Midlife Sexuality in a Gerontocratic Economy."

32. Joan Acker was talking about gender, in "Class, Gender, and the Relations of Distribution," 477. I borrow her language.

33. Huyssen, "Present Pasts," 31. I learned the terms "individual time," "family time," and "industrial time" from historian Tamara Hareven, *Family Time and Industrial Time.*

34. The point is made by Kerby, *Narrative and the Self,* 39.

35. Habermas, *The Philosophical Discourse of Modernity,* 6.

36. Data from Nancer Ballard et al. (Employment Issues Committee of the Women's Bar Association), *More Than Part-Time.*

37. Schor, *The Overworked American.*

38. "The long midlife" is a term I created to describe the phenomenology of a differently age-graded sexual system (celibate youth until twenty-five, the long midlife, and then old age) among men in nineteenth-century America and Britain (see Gullette, "Male Midlife Sexuality in a Gerontocratic Economy," 58–89).

39. Feldman, "Narratives of National Identity," 139.

40. See Kohli, *Time for Retirement,* and chapter 5 below.

41. Simon-Rusinowitz et al., "Future Work and Retirement Needs," 35.

42. Aucoin, "Spinning the 'Rugrats' Forward a Decade," D1.

43. I've written about the construction of nostalgia as a way of socializing relatively young people into the ideology of middle age as decline (see "Midlife Discourses in the Twentieth-Century United States," 22).

44. Ackerman, "In the Memory Mines," 13.

45. See Gullette, "The Exile of Adulthood."

46. Menchú, *Me llamo Rigoberta Menchú*, 144.

47. The term "decadism" is my own and describes the artificial division of life time into ten-year intervals. See Gullette, *Declining to Decline*, 4.

48. For a while it offered a new magazine for the self-identified as they turned fifty. Carlson, "AARP Unveils New Magazine: *My Generation* Will Target Boomer Members," 18.

49. One model might be a study by Laurence J. Kotlikoff in which he asked forty-nine Boston University MBA students and undergrads to make imaginary savings decisions. They were told not to leave behind any unspent money at age seventy-five, but they were so cautious that they left an "astounding $250,000" on average ("Can People Compute?" 377, 363). Females saved more than males; Asians, Italians, and blacks more than white Protestants. This experiment appears to have been conducted in 1987.

50. Nagel, "In the Stream of Consciousness," 74.

51. See Kathleen Woodward's essay "The Cultural Politics of Anger and Wisdom," 3.

52. Stan Grossfeld used the phrase "seniors aged 50 and older" in the *Boston Globe* in 2001; the headline was "AIDS: A Threat to Elderly." An Associated Press article discussing workers over forty referred to them repeatedly as "the elderly" (Holland, "High Court Case to Determine Legal Clout of Older Workers," A4). *The Progressive Populist* called protesters aged thirty-seven, fifty-five, and fifty-nine "elderly" (Kozlovsky, "You're as Old as You Feel," 5). Safire's headline said, "Don't Call Me 'Near Elderly,'" but he did, in his regular column, "On Language," 22.

53. Kausler, "Memory and Memory Theory,"; Huyssen, "Present Pasts," 28.

54. *Kimel et al. v. Florida Board of Regents*, 528 U.S. 98–791, 19, 20 (2000).

55. Bach, "Movin' On Up . . . ," 16.

56. Greenhouse, "Supreme Court Hears Arguments on Major Issue in Age Bias Law," A27. The case is *Adams et al. v. Florida Power Corporation*, 535 U.S., 01–584 (2002).

57. My informant here is a Brandeis junior who says, "I know I am smart and beautiful, so then why am I threatened by these younger girls?"

58. Aucoin, "The Beauty Within," B5.

59. Elkind, *The Hurried Child*, 7

60. Harris, "The Rationalization of Infancy," 36–37.

61. Kohli, "Social Organization and Subjective Construction of the Life Course."

62. Hall, "On Postmodernism and Articulation," 148.

63. From Harrison's *Making the Connections*, quoted in Brentlinger, "Thanksgiving in the Year '02," n.p.

CHAPTER THREE

1. Rifkin, *The End of Work,* 190. The largest employer in 2003 is fairness-challenged Walmart.
2. Kalleberg et al., *Nonstandard Work, Substandard Jobs.*
3. Wallis, "'Progress' or Progress?" 58 n. 6.
4. David Lipsky and Alexander Abrams pointed out that before the recession, Xers had been described as exactly the opposite: "determined, career-minded, fiercely self-resilient" (quoted in "Youth Gone Bad," 5).
5. For a similar analysis, see Sidler, "Living in McJobdom."
6. In early 1993 a *New York Times* article, countering negative Xer stereotypes, mentioned among many other articles a cover story in the *New Republic* on "the twenty-something myth" (Israel, "Lost in the Name Game," section 9, 1). Nix, "not yet thirty," provides a list of publications that produced Xer articles in the "late 1991–early 1992" period, in "Hoax! Why the Ex-Generation Never Existed," M10.
7. In August 1996 a survey sponsored by the American Stock Exchange of eight hundred well-educated people aged twenty-five to thirty-four showed that some do invest. The survey was widely reported.
8. Hornblower, "Great Xpectations," 3, 58.
9. See Acland's *Youth, Murder, Spectacle* and chapter 10 below.
10. The first use of "aging Baby Boomers" I've found came in 1982, in Shapiro, "Halfway There at Thirty-five," 16. The first *New York Times* use appeared a few months later in Shannon, "Economy Puts the Brakes on Motorcycle Sales," section 3, 17.
11. Peterson, "Thirty-Somethings, It's Time for XYZzzzz of the Generation Gap," 3.
12. Andersen, "The Culture Industry," 30.
13. Sege, "The Aging of Aquarius," C1. Sege's data—how many "boomer women never had children"—ignored the fact that many women between thirty-four and fifty-two are still of childbearing age.
14. This language—summarizing the attitude of George Carlin, the comedian—sums up the attitudes of many journalists. Interview with Carlin, "Outspoken," 56.
15. For a snapshot of differences between the "first" and "second" waves of Boomers, and between "the haves" and "have nots" in the first wave, see Simon-Rusinowitz et al., "Future Work and Retirement Needs." 34–39.
16. An AARP-sponsored poll, for example, asked "Baby Boomers" from thirty-four to fifty-two how satisfied they are with the amount they are putting aside for retirement, ignoring both class (e.g., differences between incomes) and where they were in the family life course. See Knox, "Boomers See Work Coloring Golden Years," A3.
17. Woodward, "Inventing Generational Models," 154.
18. See Kleyman, "'Geezer' Slur even in *Scientific American*," 19.

19. See Vienne, "Branding."
20. Israel, "Lost in the Name Game."
21. Trueheart, "The Young and the Restless," D7.
22. Sullivan, "Talking Trash about My Generation."
23. Kirn, "Crybaby Boomers," A23.
24. Howe and Strauss, *13th Gen* (1993). This expanded their long article "The New Generation Gap," in the *Atlantic Monthly,* December 1992.
25. Frank Rich also retorted, saying Generation X "has been much too sweatily trying to upstage my boomer generation" ("Reality Bites Again," section 4, 17). But his article was not used as evidence the way the other three were. The *New Republic* article was written by Michael Kinsley ("Back from the Future," 6). The *Newsweek* article was written by David Martin ("The Whiny Generation").

    For the doing-justice campaign, see Smillie, "The Generational Divide Paints Unfair Portraits of the Young," 18.
26. Bartlett, "The Whining Winds Down."
27. Giles, "Generalizations X," 62.
28. Introduction to Phillips, "Baby Boomers Come of Age," 69.
29. Greenberg, "In the Shadow of the Sixties."
30. In *Generations,* Devoney Looser thinks that the stereotyping of third-wave feminists is "an extension of media images" circulated about slackers (38–39), E. Ann Kaplan describes some bad effects of generational language on feminism (22), and Judith Roof's chapter exposes the general dangers to feminism of using generational models (69–87).
31. Coupland, *Generation X,* 21.
32. Simons, "The Youth Movement," 65; Moore, "Xers to Baby Boomers," B6.
33. Hunter, "Work, Work, Work, Work!" 38.
34. Grunwald, "Trial by Media," 31.
35. Dirck, "Baby Boomers under Fire Again," 1B; Ratan, "Why Busters Hate Boomers," 57. Bruce Farriss, in a 1995 article soothingly titled, "All They Wanna Do Is Have Some Fun," mentioned in passing that "Boomer bashing is a favorite activity on the 'alt.society.generation-x' 1995 newsgroup." The first article I found that notices "Boomer-bashing" is Clarence Page's "Lament of the Twentysomethings," from 1991—early in the war.
36. Dunne, "Virtual Patriotism," 99.
37. Williams in Howe and Strauss, *13th Gen,* 43.
38. Menand, "The Seventies Show," 131.
39. Quoted in Glazer, "Overhauling Social Security," 434.
40. Lawrence, "Political Battlegrounds of the Future," 6A. Writing in the *Guardian,* Richard Thomas said that "[i]n the US, the generational fiscal conflict has led to some nasty street clashes," without saying what they were ("The Budget: Analysis," 20).
41. Toner, "Generational Push Has Not Come to Shove," section 4, 1

42. McGrath, "Live Fast, Die Old," 14.
43. Seligman and Strasko, "What's Behind the Twenty Something 'Movement,'" 6–7, and Riemer and Cuomo, "The Generation Gambit," 14–16. Riemer and Cuomo called Xer hostility the property of no more than "a small group of friends" funded by the right wing, but they feared it could become more widespread.
44. See Eisner, *Social Security* and *Three Great Deficit Scares*.
45. Westlund, "Good Jobs at Others' Expense," A14.
46. Scales, "Clinton Vows to Let States Help Parents," A8.
47. Thompson, "Editor's Corner," 8.
48. Temper, "Q & A," 13.
49. Weisner, personal communication. See also Weisner and Bernheimer, "Children of the 1960s at Midlife," 211–57.
50. Dietrich, "Fitting in at Work Isn't a Women's Issue," A10.
51. Bartlett, "The Whining Winds Down."
52. DiManno, "Face Facts, Boomers."
53. Williams, *Modern Tragedy*, 100. On other emotions created by the new material conditions of the workplace, see Sennett, *The Corrosion of Character*.
54. His mother, a nurse practitioner, told me this story. Her husband, also a defense computer analyst, lost his job when all those over fifty in his firm were laid off.
55. Snyder, *The Cliff Walk—a Memoir of a Job Lost and a Life Found*. One of the few memoirs about midlife job loss, it smooths off its political edge, as the subtitle indicates, by welcoming change in a knee-jerk New Age way and accepting the myth that at midlife adaptability is easy.
56. Williams, "Trash That Baby Boom," 177. The first version of "Trash That Baby Boom: It's Time for Forty-Somethings to Release Their Choke Hold on American Culture" appeared in the *Washington Post* in 1994. Then it appeared in Howe and Strauss's book, and then in *Next*.
57. "Generation X-onomics," 27. Louv, however, in "Xers Size Up Futures with Great Optimism," reported a survey in which 59 percent of blacks and 71 percent of Hispanics expected that they would be better off than their parents, versus 49 percent of whites (A3). In "'Slackers' Energetic, Optimistic," Sullivan reported on a survey in the early 1990s that found that Americans in their twenties believed that their generation would be less prosperous than their parents', but that they themselves would be better off.

  In general, statistics about class differences among Xers or downward mobility among midlife workers did not get widely reprinted or, which would be more important for breaking a binary, printed together.
58. Anderson, "Still Cool after All These Years," 1.
59. Monroe, "Getting Rid of the Gray," 29. See also Gullette, *Declining to Decline*, chapter 12.
60. See table 1.30 in Mishel, Bernstein, and Schmitt, *State of Working America, 1996–97*, 96. The data, covering the period 1968–91, come from Peter Gottschalk.

61. Giles, "Generalizations X," 62. See also Hornblower, "Great Xpectations" (this *Time* cover story uses the short Xer season [1965–77] to get a 45 million cohort to weigh against 78 million Boomers).

62. When (occasionally) defined as those born between 1961 and 1981, "Xers" add up to 80 million. See Gratiot, "Generation X."

63. Cohorts in social science research need to be tightly defined, but the subjects need not be strictly the same age: witness, for example, American women who joined the second wave of feminism or Germans who joined the Nazi party in its first years.

For an attack on Strauss and Howe's use of named age stratifications in *Generations,* see Quadagno et al., "Setting the Agenda for Research on Cohorts and Generations."

64. Ryder, "The Cohort as a Concept in the Study of Social Change," 73.

65. Hardy and Waite, "Doing Time," 12.

66. Stirling, "The Search for Database Marketing Talent," 28; Anderson, "Still Cool after All These Years," 1.

67. Pratt, "Scratches on the Face of the Country," 139.

68. Gelman and Taylor, "Gender Essentialism in Cognitive Development," 178.

69. For some criteria, see Alwin, "The Political Impact of the Baby Boom"; also Hardy, *Studying Aging and Social Change.*

70. Mannheim, "The Problem of Generations," 53.

71. Richmond, *A Long View from the Left,* 62.

72. Lorde, *Sister Outsider,* 117.

73. My work in progress, *Midlife Fictions: The Invention of the Middle Years of Life,* examines the period 1900–1935, including the first generation gap constructed during and after the First World War.

74. Torben Grodal sees melodrama as training for "the passive aspects of life" in *Moving Pictures,* 254. The Xer-Boomer war operates in many genres.

75. Said, *Reflections on Exile,* 504, 503.

76. My work in progress, *The Postmaternal Phenomenon,* explores these issues: see my "Valuing 'Postmaternity' as a Revolutionary Feminist Concept" and "Wicked Powerful."

77. Nelson and Cowan, *Revolution X,* xxi.

CHAPTER FOUR

1. Although Ian McEwen is British, *The Child in Time* could be added because it was praised so highly in the United States.

2. I discuss the deaths of adult children in Gullette, "Wicked Powerful."

3. Bumpass and Aquilino, *A Social Map of Midlife,* table 17.

4. Ricoeur, "Narrative Time," 169.

5. Using the scale, psychologist Joann Montepare found that adolescents fear many

of the future life events I list below. She presented her work at a talk given at the Wellesley Center for Research on Women in the early 1990s.

6. Ferrucci, "The Dead Child," 60. See also Stewart, *Death Sentences,* and Kuhn, *Corruption in Paradise.*

7. See Gullette, "The Exile of Adulthood."

8. My essay "Valuing 'Postmaternity' as a Revolutionary Feminist Concept" is about making conscious a "moment" when a woman who has raised a child to independence realizes that her parental responsibility has lessened.

9. There's a chapter about Tyler and another about Drabble in Gullette, *Safe at Last in the Middle Years.*

10. A formula devised by Robert Korasek measures a gap between an employee's level of control over the work situation and the burden of responsibility she or he feels. Research by Peter Schnall and others shows that measurable conditions of high responsibility and low control are highly correlated with the physiological state of hypertension (see Schnall et al. *The Workplace and Cardiovascular Disease*). Presumably parental stress could also be measured on the same scale.

11. Schwartz, *Disturbances in the Field,* 133. After the first citation of a novel, page numbers will appear in the text.

12. Tyler, *The Accidental Tourist,* 258.

13. Morrison, *Beloved,* 132.

14. Irving, *The World According to Garp,* 456.

15. Heller, *Something Happened,* 315.

16. Theorists noted the "waning" of the oedipal complex in the late 1970s: see Benjamin, "Oedipal Riddle" and her bibliography. Kathleen Woodward thinks we need to counter the oedipal story consciously, because it keeps us fixed us within the family triangle. She emphasizes the way it precludes thinking in terms of generational unity or three-generational models (see Woodward, "Inventing Generational Models").

17. Hall, "My Son My Executioner," 19.

18. See Gullette, "Midlife Heroines, Older and Freer," in *Declining to Decline.*

19. Ford, *The Sportswriter,* 374.

20. Updike, "One Big Interview," 519.

21. Updike, *Rabbit Redux,* 329.

22. Updike, *Rabbit Is Rich,* 73.

23. Alther, *Other Women,* 61.

24. Hijuelos, *Mr. Ives' Christmas,* 180.

CHAPTER FIVE

1. The literature is vast and the examples are all around us. Mishel, Bernstein, and Schmitt give a good brief summary in *The State of Working America, 1996–97,* 19.

2. Kohli and Rein, "The Changing Balance of Work and Retirement," 1.
3. Bumpass and Aquilino, "A Social Map of Midlife," table 55. College-educated men were dropping out less. Still, their workforce participation dropped 8 points. For women college graduates—the most privileged women—the drop was from 79 percent to 60 percent: 19 points. Conservatives deny that women want to be full-time in the labor market at these ages. Many authors in Kohli et al., *Time for Retirement*, argue that they do, and I argue that postmaternal women can. Jay Ginn and Sara Arber found similar needs and steep declines among women in Britain (see "Midlife Women's Employment and Pension Entitlement," 813–19).
4. Jacobs, Kohli, and Rein, "Testing the Industry-Mix Hypothesis of Early Exit," 53.
5. Sheppard, "The United States: The Privatization of Exit," 264, 268.
6. Paul Attewell provided me with this data, which he adjusted to rectify Census Bureau procedures that lower the apparent rate of unemployment. Only people who have been employed continuously for three years prior to displacement are counted. Those who had lost jobs earlier in the 1990s recession would thus have gone uncounted.
7. Sheppard, "The United States: The Privatization of Exit," 3.
8. Butler and Weatherly, "Poor Women at Midlife," 510, 514.
9. Nicholson, "Fifty-Plus Workers Hit by Cutbacks," 3.
10. Gregory, *Age Discrimination*, 114, 115, 116.
11. Ibid., quoted page 7.
12. Nicholson, "Fifty-Plus Workers Hit by Cutbacks," 3.
13. Jacobson, LaLonde, and Sullivan, "Long-Term Earnings Losses," 2–20. Tracked five years later, the high seniority workers had lost about 25 percent of their prior earnings.
14. Quoted in Brand, "Global Capitalism," 57.
15. See also Don J. Snyder's memoir, *Cliff Walk* (1997) and Faye Macdonald Smith's novel *Flight of the Blackbird* (1996).
16. Based on the U.S. Bureau of the Census, *Historical Income Tables, 2000*, tables P8, P-8a, P-8b. For African American women the peak has been forty-five to fifty-four (every year but one) since 1994, and for African American men every year since 1990.

    Before 1983 (for all men) and 1991 (for all women), the median peaks came between thirty-five and forty-four. Census data counts by decade, not lustrum. If women were peaking between forty-five and fifty rather than fifty and fifty-four, this data could not show it.
17. Those with the lowest educational attainments also peak late in life because they must continue to work, but of course the peak is very low.
18. Based on Census data, calculations by the New Strategist Editors, in *American Men and Women*, 231.
19. Women's Bureau, Department of Labor, *Mildife Women Speak Out*.

20. U.S. Bureau of the Census, *Money Income of Households 1991*, P60, and *Current Population Reports, 1992*.

21. Hacker, "Paradise Lost," 33, using data from Kevin Phillips.

22. Based on U.S. Bureau of the Census, *Historical Income Tables, 2002*, table P8 (1947–2001).

23. Barnet, "Lords of the Global Economy," 755.

24. Mishel, Bernstein, and Schmitt, *The State of Working America, 1996–97*, 284.

25. Blanton, "Golden Illusions," 28. Blanton's data are from 1998. Women had saved an average of $33,816.

26. Barlett and Steele, *America: What Went Wrong?* xi.

27. Sheppard, "The United States."

28. Scott Adams's mini-history implies that labor market conditions were nearly perfect in the past. His point, of course, is to critique current practices. See Adams, "Dilbert's Creator Thrives on Your Corporate Blues," 2C.

29. Sheak, "U.S. Capitalism," 33–57. See also Aronowitz and DeFazio, *The Jobless Future*. Prisoners and college students are not counted as part of the workforce.

30. Guillemard, "France: Massive Exit through Unemployment Compensation," 127, 128, 165, 166. We need more qualitative research like this.

31. On the way group character can be constructed to influence law, see Gullette, "The Puzzling Case of the Deceased Wife's Sister," 142–66. "Needs interpretation" comes from Fraser, *Unruly Practices*, 113–90.

32. Sheehan, "Ain't No Middle Class," 91–92.

33. Guillemard and van Gunsteren, "Pathways and Their Prospects," 364, 367.

34. Guillemard, "France: Massive Exit through Unemployment Compensation," 178.

35. The size of the cohorts is based on Census data, calculations by the New Strategist Editors, *American Men and Women*.

36. Chomsky, introduction to *Corporations Are Gonna Get Your Mama*, 7

37. Robert Eisner, private communication.

38. Kohli and Rein, "The Changing Balance of Work and Retirement," 6, 15.

39. Eskil Wadensjö, "Sweden: Partial Exit," 287, 284.

40. See the Senate Committee on Labor and Public Welfare, Senate Special Subcommittee on Aging, *Middle-Aged and Older Workers Full Employment Act of 1968*.

41. Miles, *The Department of Health, Education and Welfare*, 154.

42. Reich, *Tales of a New America*, 124. I am making the *aging* of the workers, and their *midlife* position, more explicit than Reich does.

43. Simic, "Aging and the Aged in Cultural Perspective," 2.

44. Kearl and Hoag, "The Social Construction of the Midlife Crisis," 296.

45. Based on a paragraph from Fraser, *Unruly Practices*, using her terms "enclave" and "canalize."

46. One example: an entire issue of *Extra!* entitled "Ageism" (March/April 1997).

47. On a nineteenth-century version of what I call the long midlife, see Gullette, "Male Midlife Sexuality in a Gerontocratic Economy," 58–89.

CHAPTER SIX

1. Wiegman, "Unmaking," 39. In Wiegman's historiography, the "foundational" culturalist essay in feminist theory is Gayle Rubin's "Thinking Sex."
2. "The Secret of Long Life," 13.
3. One such example, of undoing thirty years of "aging" by six months of exercise, comes from physiologist William Haskell (in Morton, "Which Is More Dangerous, Aging or Inactivity?" C1). Morton winds up using the phrase "effects of aging and lifestyle," which maintains a distinction while blurring the differences.

   On the relations between job strain, hypertension, and heart disease, see Schnall et al., "Why the Workplace and Cardiovascular Disease?" 1–6.
4. Gullette, "Midlife Discourses in the Twentieth-Century United States."
5. On my being diagnosed with arthritis, see Gullette, "Ordinary Pain" in *Declining to Decline.*
6. Hacking, *The Social Construction of What?* 12, 32.
7. I am indebted to Kathleen Woodward for raising this question (private communication).
8. Bourdieu said this in 1984, about denial of the work of sociologists, in *Distinction,* 11.
9. I take the phrase "socially informed humanities" from a self-description of the *South Atlantic Quarterly* (1997), edited by Frederic Jameson.
10. In this paragraph, and in a few other places in this chapter, I have been guided by Richard Shweder's lucid and diverting "Cultural Psychology: What Is It?"
11. Gardiner, "Theorizing Age with Gender," 94.
12. Copper, "Voices: On Becoming Old Women," 55.
13. On Sudnow's distinctions, see Gullette, *Declining to Decline,* chapter 10.
14. Rossi and Rossi, *Of Human Bonding,* 11.
15. Boal, "Glossary," 377; Butler, *Bodies that Matter,* 68.
16. James and Prout, preface to *Constructing and Reconstructing Childhood,* 2d ed., x.
17. James, Jenks, and Prout, *Theorizing Childhood,* 184.
18. Director David W. Ellis is quoted in Schorow, "Uncovering the 'Secrets of Aging' at the Museum of Science," 41.
19. Woodward, *Aging and Its Discontents,* 21; Achenbaum, *Crossing Frontiers,* 11.
20. See Katz, "Alarmist Demography."
21. Christine Overall makes the point about totalizing identities in *A Feminist I,* 163, talking about passing, ageism and ableism. Chris Shilling says that consumer culture helps promote among people the experience of "*becoming* their bodies, in the sense of identifying themselves either negatively or positively with the 'exterior' of the body" and fearing that it will "fall apart." This fear is often related to decline discourses. See Shilling, *The Body and Social Theory,* 35.
22. Giroux, "Slacking Off," 73.
23. Squier, *Babies in Bottles;* Hockey and James, *Growing Up and Growing Old.*

24. Troyansky, "Historical Research into Ageing, Old Age, and Older People," 51
25. *Figuring Age* is edited by Kathleen Woodward. It includes art, poetry, and essays by E. Ann Kaplan, Mary Russo, Anne Basting, Vivian Sobchak. *The Handbook of Humanities and Aging,* edited by Cole, Kastenbaum, and Ray, has essays written from within disciplines and from cross-disciplinary perspectives. (Disclosure: I have an essay in each.)
26. Hall, "Cultural Studies and Its Theoretical Legacies," 271.
27. Grosz, "The Problem of Theory," 8, 13.
28. Hareven, *Family Time and Industrial Time,* 185–88.
29. The Age Studies book series, edited by Anne M. Wyatt-Brown, was published by University of Virginia Press between 1993 and 2000. The Rockefeller Fellowships were brought to the Center for Twentieth Century Studies at the University of Milwaukee by then director Kathleen Woodward.
30. Woodward, introduction to *Figuring Age,* x.

CHAPTER SEVEN

1. Nicolaus, quoted by Stuart Hall in "Cultural Studies and the Centre," 26.
2. Altieri, "Temporality and the Necessity of Dialectic"; Fraser, "The Uses and Abuses of French Discourse Theories," 55; Jameson, "*Ulysses* in History," 146.
3. Hall, "Ethnicity," 296; Brockmeier, "Identity," 455.
4. Yet an age is sometimes implied. How old is the implied agent/subject of feminist postmodernist theory, busy "doublecrossing" and defying phallocentrism, causing "trouble," being "unruly," "messing up" margins and center?
5. Just as, in chapter 2, when "temporality" proved an overgeneralized concept with regard to the work span, my age studies habits led me to try to specify some particular biases of ideology that influence the sense of life time: for example, speed-up.
6. We need to make a habit of trying to add age in order to stimulate theory. The lists—"race and class and gender and . . ."—omit age or include it perfunctorily. These lists are not merely gestures of inclusiveness, important as that would be for age studies. They are in themselves theoretical statements. Lists imply assertions of relevance and importance: an omission implies an ideological position. Lists state or imply relationships between and among variables known not to be perfectly "homologous" (Slack and Whitt, "Ethics and Cultural Studies," 579).
7. Williams, "The Writer," 25.
8. Hall, "Ethnicity," 296.
9. Eagleton, *The Gatekeeper,* 51.
10. In Nicaragua, people speak of the Americans as having "dynamic" characters, as if the power to make change were independent of class, gender, race, and national power.

11. Lively, *The Road to Lichfield,* 155.
12. Polkinghorne says of self that its "historic unity" includes "not only what one has been but also anticipation of what one will be." Quoted by C. R. Barclay in "Composing Protoselves through Improvisation," 56.
13. Mukherjee, *The Holder of the World,* 6.
14. Andrew Ross discusses cultural identities in *Real Love* (191 and all of chapter 9) in the context of cultural justice.
15. Jordan, "Report from the Bahamas," 327.
16. In *Beyond Ethnicity,* Werner Sollors's use of "descent and consent" is analogous. See also Appiah, "Identity, Authenticity, Survival," 150–56.
17. Hall, "Ethnicity," 302, 301. Many antiessentialists believe self-identification is primarily oppositional: see Patai, "The View from Elsewhere, 45; Appiah, "Identity, Authenticity, Survival" 153–55 (citing Trilling). Charles Taylor countered with the idea that self-identification seeks "recognition."
18. Marcia, "The Identity Status Approach," 166.
19. Bartky, "Phenomenology of a Hyphenated Consciousness," 113–29; Wilkerson, "Is There Something You Need to Tell Me?"
20. Gusdorf, "Conditions and Limits of Autobiography," 38.
21. This idea developed from my trying to add "age" to a list of how "[s]ources of imposed difference . . . are simultaneously sources of diversity which can inform each other" (Gailey, *The Politics of Culture and Creativity,* 15).
22. Gilmore, *Autobiographics,* 44. I don't think Gilmore was considering temporality, although "shakiness" seems a better metaphor for identities watched over time than those contemplated simultaneously at a given moment.
23. Wilkerson, "Is There Something You Need to Tell Me?" 265.
24. Buchmann, *The Script of Life in Modern Society,* 29.
25. On ideal youth, see Goffman, *Stigma,* 134; Woodward, "Youthfulness as a Masquerade," 120. "Youth" was not always so privileged an age class as it is today.
26. Gullette, "The Exile of Adulthood."
27. In psychology, "identity stripping" refers to behaviors that de-individualize a group of human subjects intentionally, as in a concentration camp (Brim, *Ambition,* 25). In sociology, "status degradation" refers to more invisible forces present in everyday social life. In narrative, it is having your faith in your own habitual storytelling shaken.
28. Shweder, preface to *Welcome to Middle Age!* ix.
29. Karp, "A Decade of Reminders" 727; emphasis in original.
30. On how social science can "freeze" a culture, see Agger, "Marxism, Feminism, Deconstruction."
31. Biggs, *The Mature Imagination,* 65.
32. Silverman, *Male Subjectivity,* 48; Wilkerson, "Is There Something You Need to Tell Me?" 260.
33. Beckett, *Endgame,* 11.

34. Ricoeur, *Oneself as Another,* 132.
35. Gullette, *Safe at Last in the Middle Years,* begins with the words "Tooth decay."
36. Bartky, "Foucault, Feminism, and the Modernization of Patriarchal Power," 76–81.
37. Williams, *Modern Tragedy,* 100.
38. Thanks to David Gullette for this rebuttal.
39. Martin, "Are You Losing Your Mind?"
40. "Source memory" is the recollection of where or from whom we learned something. Most speakers rarely know their sources. Teachers do, and tend to value this form of memory highly.
41. In actually practiced age work, relying on "progress" aspects of one's age identity has been the only available tactic. But setting "progress" against "decline" can constitute a terrible, isolated, oscillating, emotional impasse. The way out starts with deconstructing "decline" so that subjects first understand the construction of that predicament.
42. I'm borrowing language used by Fulford quite differently in his *The Triumph of Narrative,* 20.

CHAPTER EIGHT

1. This is my own translation from Roy's *Enchantment and Sorrow:* "Mais avoir accès à ce que l'on possède, intérieurement, en apparence la chose la plus naturelle du monde, en est la plus difficile" (*La détresse et l'enchantement,* 221).
2. Weisner, "Why Ethnography," 307.
3. Mills, *The Sociological Imagination,* 226.
4. Ruth Ray and Sally Chandler call a telling like this one of my mother's "a set piece": it is "repeated, almost verbatim, for the purpose of maintaining a valued self-image and teaching a lesson" ("A Narrative Approach to Anti-Aging," 45).
5. Lentricchia, "In Place of an Afterword," 321.
6. I learned the term "the history of the present" from Lauren Berlant, in "Collegiality, Crisis, and Cultural Studies," 106.
7. Gilmore, *Autobiographics,* 32. To gauge moving from conformity to resistance, sociologist Doris Ingrisch interviewed Austrian women born early in the twentieth century: their unease with gender conformity came only with later-life growth in resistance. See Ingrisch, "Conformity and Resistance as Women Age."
8. This prescription comes from a description of "guided autobiography" given by Birren and Birren, "Autobiography," 289. Linde, in her fascinating *Life Stories,* says that by her definition, life stories "probably begin to develop in early adolescence" (25). I told my first (a decline story) when I was about eight years old.
9. The term comes from Bloom, "Single-Experience Autobiographies," 36–45.
10. For comparable distinctions, some borrowed by anthropology from literary ty-

pology, between the "naive" or "ordinary" insider and the "self-reflexive field account," see the introduction, by Reed-Danahay, to *Auto/Ethnography*, 6–8. On oral "life story" from a communications standpoint, see Charlotte Linde's *Life Stories*; in particular, on the genre's difference from other forms (psychotherapeutic, ethnographic, written), see 37–50.

11. Kenyon and Randall, *Restorying Our Lives*, 16.

12. Nancy K. Miller uses the phrase "autobiography as cultural criticism" as the subtitle of her first chapter in *Getting Personal*. Her emphasis is on "self-narrative woven into critical argument"; her examples come from Adrienne Rich, Alice Walker, and Cora Kaplan.

13. I am indebted for this topography to Sheila Rossan, "Identity and Its Development in Adulthood," 304–5, although I believe that even "core" elements (Catholic, woman) can change/be changed/be said to change.

14. Wikan, "The Self in a World of Urgency and Necessity," 273–74.

15. Age autobiography is more like "sociolinguistic narrative" or oral history in having a spontaneous origin. "In contrast to the stories that serve in DRP [the developmental research paradigm], the oral narratives . . . were not generated by a sequence of pictures, an assigned topic, or a recall exercise" (Bower, "The Role of Narrative in the Study of Language and Aging," 269).

16. This formulation comes from Buss, "Anna Jameson's *Winter Studies*," 44.

17. Feminist developmental psychologist Robyn Fivush points out that researchers still revolve around the issues of "accuracy and retention" (94), although "accuracy and authority can only be understood in the context of what is allowed to be spoken of and what is prohibited" ("Accuracy, Authority, and Voice," 94, 104).

18. Schultz, review of *How Do We Know Who We Are?* by Arnold Ludwig, 420.

19. Paul Ricoeur, a philosopher of narrative and temporality, has drawn a distinction between two kinds of selfhood, *ipse* and *idem*, in *Oneself as Another*, 128 ff.

20. Gordon, *The Rest of Life*, 213.

21. See Nelson, "Sophie Doesn't," 102.

22. Williams, "The Writer," 25.

23. Berman, "Self-Representation," 286.

24. Ray, *Beyond Nostalgia*, 160.

25. Meyer, "The Self and the Life Course," 215.

26. Runyon, *Life Histories and Psychobiography*, 114.

27. Laura Marcus, *Auto/Biographical Discourse*, 273. I do not, however, want to follow her in thinking that this pattern "breaks down" the "conceptual divide" between autobiography and biography. Solipsism doesn't break down so easily.

28. Nabokov, *Speak, Memory*, 57.

29. See Gullette, *Declining to Decline*, chapter 7: "My Mother at Midlife" has a section called "Fifty Ways to Lose Your Midlife Mother."

30. Eliot, *Middlemarch*, 57.

31. Gullette, "How Not to Be a Tourist," "Nicaragua 1991," "Florcita la Suerte."

32. Sarraute, *Childhood,* 33.

33. Ray, *Beyond Nostalgia,* 160.

CHAPTER NINE

1. Weaver, *The Ten Lights of God,* 22.

2. Before women appeared on the European stage, the gender-cross would have been incomplete. Historian Elizabeth Reitz Mullenix credits Peg Woffington in 1740 with producing the first breeches role acted with verisimilitude (*Wearing the Breeches,* 34).

3. Rosalind was described by Helen Faucit in 1893 in typical Victorian terms as feeling a passionate love "at the core" (Faucit, "Rosalind," 142).

4. Feldenkrais, *Body and Mature Behavior,* 34.

5. Sullivan, *Living Across and Through Skins,* 95. Sullivan and I are both qualifying Judith Butler's emphasis on reiteration in performance, which Elin Diamond has noticed in *Performance and Cultural Politics,* 5.

6. Sullivan, *Living Across and Through Skins,* 95.

7. Robinson, in Diamond, *Performance and Cultural Politics,* 248

8. See Giddens, *Modernity and Self-Identity,* 3, 9, 148. What Giddens calls reflexiveness does not always involve a high degree of consciousness.

9. Richard Schechner gives his own reasons for why mainstream theater is an "incredibly fertile area" for performance studies in "TDR Comments," 4–6.

10. See Elinor Fuchs, *The Death of Character:* After quoting Michael Goldman (70), she examines the undermining of the "presence-effect" in twentieth-century theater.

11. In *The Absent Body,* Leder makes a case for why this ideal of "forgetting the body" is so compelling. Adding American versions of ageism and middle-ageism, as I do here, strengthens this case and shows where the argument for "remembering" the body needs to be joined.

12. Rouse, "Textuality and Authority," 155.

13. I saw *The Syringa Tree* staged in the fall of 2000 at Playhouse 91. *How I Learned to Drive* was put on at the American Repertory Theater in 1998. *The Captain's Tiger* was produced by the Manhattan Theater Club (City Center Stage II) in 1999.

14. In November 2001, Pamela Gien kindly let me interview her to discuss these aspects of her performance.

15. Basting, *The Stages of Age,* 137–39.

16. Mai Zetterling, "Some Notes on Acting," in Cardullo et al., *Playing to the Camera,* 150.

17. Fugard, *The Captain's Tiger,* 4.

18. Barrymore, "The Actor," in Cardullo et al, *Playing to the Camera,* 79.

19. In performance studies, according to Jeanie Forte, "the tension generated by the

conflict between a political need, such as feminism's, and the postmodern refusal of a collective response has yet to be examined" (Forte, "Focus on the Body," 261 n. 22).

20. Dana Ivey, in Sonenberg, *The Actor Speaks,* 289.

21. Basting, *The Stages of Age,* 141, 145 (emphasis in original). Since she says he represents experiences even "from the moment of conception" (145), she includes nonconscious bodily "experience" in her definition.

22. States, "The Phenomenological Attitude," 373.

23. Williams, *Unbending Gender,* 191.

24. Vogel's script calls for a twentyish actress to play the Voice of the eleven-year-old, who is not touched, and who appears only at the end. Vogel "strongly recommended" that this actress be of "legal age." She was afraid that the pedophilia would be too disturbing to the audience and the actress.

25. Anne Basting describes the audience's applause of Channing in 1995, as "a complex gratitude. For the mask *and* for the reveal" (*Stages of Age,* 178.)

26. Kathleen Chalfant, in Sonenberg, *The Actor Speaks,* 101.

27. Marcello Mastroianni, "The Game of Truth," in Cardullo et al., *Playing to the Camera,* 155

28. Kruger, *Remote Control,* 76

29. Goethe, "Women's Parts Played by Men," 49 and 50–51 n. 3.

30. Chalfant, in Sonenberg, *The Actor Speaks,* 112.

31. Eisenberg, "Casting," 6.

32. Blau, "Set Me Where You Stand," 257. Fotheringham points out that "writing on live theatre that links the body to a notion of unique individual presence . . . is surprisingly hard to find" ("Theorizing the Individual Body," 25).

33. Matthew Sussman, in Sonenberg, *The Actor Speaks,* 1, 152–53.

34. Quoted by Auslander, "Comedy about the Failure of Comedy," 203.

35. Lillie, "When Local Actors Get Cast," 32.

36. Huston, *The Actor's Instrument,* 36, 88.

37. See Woods, *On Playing Shakespeare,* 10.

38. Mueller et al., "Trait Distinctiveness," 238.

39. Ivey in Sonenberg, *The Actor Speaks,* 294–95; Basting, *The Stages of Age,* 141.

40. Phelan, "Crisscrossing Cultures," 164.

41. Stephen Spinella, in Sonenberg, *The Actor Speaks,* 286.

42. I saw *The Dance of Death* on November 10, 2001, at the Broadhurst Theatre.

43. The term "psychophysical spectrum" comes from Janet Sonenberg, *The Actor Speaks,* 3.

44. "Age hierarchy" is an anthropological term I found in Dickerson-Putman and Brown's *Women's Age Hierarchies.*

45. Blau is quoted in Huston, *The Actor's Instrument,* 35.

46. Kahn, *Roman Shakespeare,* 150.

47. See Gullette, "Wicked Powerful."

48. Blau, private communications, 2002.
49. See, for example, Fuchs, *The Death of Character*.
50. Lamont, introduction to *Women on the Verge*, xvi.
51. Brecht, *Brecht on Theater*, 98, 109.
52. The metaphor of cultural properties I take from Harris, "Whiteness as Property." In global ideology, "youth" is being given the appearance, and some of the realities, of being a valuable kind of property—like "whiteness," another property that few who have it recognize. To treat "aging" as a source of property seems to me faintly humorous and insidiously countercultural.
53. Leder, *The Absent Body*, 85; also 149.
54. Cromby and Nightingale, "What's Wrong with Social Constructionism?" 11.
55. At the lecture I gave February 12, 2002, at the Women's Studies Research Center at Brandeis, many midlife women in my audience instantly tried and failed to do this with older women they knew (their mothers), and used this "failure" as an argument against the whole imaginary exercise. That is why I ask us to start with ourselves.
56. In 1996, there were 56,308 jobs for members of the Screen Actors Guild. Only one in three went to actors over forty. Of these 18,479 jobs, 73 percent went to men and only 27 percent went to women (Holland, "What's Death Got to Do with It?").

CHAPTER TEN

1. Stein, *Geographical History of America*, 63.
2. Chudacoff, *How Old Are You?*; Cole, *Journey of Life*; Graebner, *A History of Retirement*; Katz, *Disciplining Gerontology*; Spacks, *The Adolescent Idea*. On the "postgraduate mother," see Gullette, "Inventing the 'Postmaternal Woman.'"
3. Cole, introduction to the *Journey of Life*, xix; see also Gruman, "Cultural Origins of Present-Day 'Ageism.'"
4. Brown and Martin, "Left Futures," 63.
5. Even in earlier times in places where average age at death was in the forties or fifties, royalty and the rich—including women who survived childbirth—lived long lives. This is still true.
6. On ageism in biotechnology discourse, see Woodward, "From Virtual Cyborgs to Biological Time Tombs"; on youth in Cold War rhetoric, see Medevoi, "Democracy, Capitalism, and American Literature."
7. Males, "The Myth of the Grade-School Murderer," 3.
8. On adolescence as a "dangerous age" see Spacks, *The Adolescent Idea*, 91; and Hareven, "Changing Images of Aging," 123; on 1950s "bad boys," see Medevoi, "Reading the Blackboard." On excessive scapegoating of teens as criminals, see Templeton, "Superscapegoating," 13–14.

9. Stein, *Geographical History of America,* 63; see Gullette, "Creativity, Aging, and Gender."

10. The question of who could be relatively immune to the concept of midlife decline is of immense potential interest. Gerontologists and age critics, people in subcultures or religions that maintain traditional values, feminists, people with instinctual narcissistic resistance to derogatory forces, the top 10 percent of the income curve—members of these groups might have some immunity.

11. Here I bracket both the many "strands" of critical gerontology and the fact that its theorists are perceived as "peripheral" by the rest of the field (Achenbaum, "Critical Gerontology," 21. 23.

12. Conrad, "Old Age in the Modern and Postmodern Western World," 66.

13. Moody, "Overview: What Is Critical Gerontology and Why Is It Important?" xv; Hall, "Cultural Studies and Its Legacies," 278; also Bennett, "Putting Policy into Cultural Studies"; Bell, "What Setting Limits May Mean," 158. AIDS in Africa would be another example.

14. Achenbaum, Weiland, and Haber, *Keywords in Sociocultural Gerontology.*

15. Curiously, the terms "conjuncture" and "representation" are also missing from *A Dictionary of Cultural and Critical Theory,* edited by Michael Payne.

16. Woodward, *Aging and Its Discontents,* 17. On the difference between ageism and gerontophobia, see Woodward, "Gerontophobia."

17. Woodward, *Aging and Its Discontents,* 26, 35, 82, 38, 51.

18. Brennan, "Social Physics," 134.

19. Ibid., 138, 134, 138, 137 (emphasis added).

20. Ibid., 140.

21. Ibid., 138–39.

22. Woodward, *Aging and Its Discontents,* 19.

23. Sudnow, *Passing On,* 65. See my suggestion that the sick and the elderly write their own memoirs rather than letting their midlife children expropriate their experience for "filial illness-and-dying accounts" (*Declining to Decline,* 208–11). Woodward explains the midlife desire to see the old parent as weakened or humiliated as a "reverse Oedipal complex" in which the children enjoy taking the place of the parent in the power seat (*Aging and Its Discontents,* 34, 37, 43).

24. See Benson, *Prime Time,* and Hepworth, "The Mid Life Phase," on the midlife in Great Britain.

25. Bartky, *Femininity and Domination,* chapters 4–7.

26. Newman, "Midlife Experience in Harlem," 259–93; Weisner and Bernheimer, "Children of the 1960s at Midlife," 211–58.

27. Steedman, *Landscape for a Good Woman,* 21, emphasis added. I am thinking of Ruth Behar and Lila Abu-Lughod, to give only two examples.

28. See Acland, *Youth, Murder, Spectacle,* 28; Grossberg, *We Gotta Get Out of This Place,* 175–77.

29. Acland, *Youth, Murder, Spectacle,* 10, 41, 20.

30. Ibid., 48, 73, 83, 14, 112.
31. Ibid., 4.
32. Ibid., 24.
33. Ibid., 118.
34. Medevoi, "Reading the Blackboard," 165. McRobbie's important book was *Feminism and Youth Culture* (1991).
35. Acland, *Youth, Murder, Spectacle,* 137, emphasis added; 121.
36. Weiland, "Social Science toward the Humanities," has a section called "In Search of Life as a Whole," 238–40.
37. McManus, *Young v. Old,* 252. For a review of factors that might make for more or less conflict between age groups between now and 2020, see Bengston, "Is the 'Contract across Generations' Changing?" 3–23.
38. Woodward, "Inventing Generational Models"; Hareven, introduction to *Aging and Generational Relations,* xiv; Shulman, *A Good Enough Daughter;* Hockey and James, *Growing Up and Growing Old.*
39. Walker, "Getting Out of Line"; Long, "Telling Women's Lives."
40. Elie Metchnikov, *The Nature of Man.*

Bibliography

Achenbaum, W. Andrew. "Afterword: Integrating the Humanities into Gerontologic Research, Training, and Practice." In *The Handbook of the Humanities and Aging,* ed. Thomas R. Cole, David B. Van Tassel, and Robert Kastenbaum, 458–72. New York: Springer, 1992.

———. "Critical Gerontology." In *Critical Approaches to Ageing and Later Life,* ed. Anne Jamieson, Sarah Harper, and Christina Victor, 16–26. Buckingham: Open University Press, 1997.

———. *Crossing Frontiers: Gerontology Emerges as a Science.* Cambridge: Cambridge University Press, 1995.

Achenbaum, W. Andrew, Steven Weiland, and Carole Haber, eds. *Key Words in Sociocultural Gerontology.* New York: Springer, 1996.

Acker, Joan. "Class, Gender, and the Relations of Distribution." *Signs* 13, no. 3 (spring 1988): 473–98.

Ackerman, Diance. "In the Memory Mines." In *The Best American Essays,* ed. Kathleen Norris, 1–13. Boston: Houghton Mifflin, 2001.

Acland, Charles R. *Youth, Murder, Spectacle: The Cultural Politics of "Youth in Crisis."* Boulder: Westview Press, 1995.

Adams, Scott. "Dilbert's Creator Thrives on Your Corporate Blues," Interview in the *Miami Herald,* May 26, 1997.

Agger, Ben. "Marxism, Feminism, Deconstruction." In *The Politics of Culture and Creativity: A Critique of Civilization,* ed. Christine Ward Gailey. Gainesville: University of Florida Press, 1992.

Alcoff, Linda Martin. "Who's Afraid of Identity Politics?" In *Reclaiming Identity: Realist Theory and the Predicament of Postmodernism,* ed. Paula M. L. Moya and Michael R. Hames-Garcia, 312–44. Berkeley and Los Angeles: University of California Press, 2000.

Alther, Lisa. *Other Women.* New York: Knopf, 1984.

Altieri, Charles. "Temporality and the Necessity of Dialectic: The Missing Dimension of Contemporary Theory." Paper delivered at the Humanities Center, University of California, Santa Barbara, fall 1990.

Alwin, Duane F. "The Political Impact of the Baby Boom: Are There Persistent Generational Differences in Political Beliefs and Behavior?" *Generations* 22, no. 1 (spring 1998): 46–54.

American Board of Family Practice. *The Physicians' View of Middle Age.* Report 2, conducted by DYG, Inc. Lexington: American Board of Family Practice, 1990.

American Men and Women: Demographics of the Sexes. Ithaca: New Strategist, 2000.

Andersen, Kurt, "The Culture Industry." *New Yorker,* May 18, 1998, 30.

Anderson, Lisa. "Still Cool after All These Years," *Chicago Tribune,* December 31, 1995, 1.

Appiah, K. Anthony. "Identity, Authenticity, Survival: Multicultural Societies and Social Reproduction." In *Multiculturalism: Examining the Politics of Recognition,* ed. Charles Taylor and Amy Gutmann, 149–63. Princeton: Princeton University Press, 1994.

Ariès, Philippe. *Centuries of Childhood: A Social History of Family Life.* Trans. Robert Baldick. New York: Knopf, 1962.

Aronowitz, Stanley, and William DiFazio. *The Jobless Future: Sci-Tech and the Dogma of Work.* Minneapolis: University of Minnesota Press, 1994.

Aucoin, Don. "The Beauty Within." *Boston Globe,* March 18, 2002, B5.

———. "Spinning the 'Rugrats' Forward a Decade." *Boston Globe,* July 20, 2001.

Auslander, Philip, "Comedy about the Failure of Comedy: Stand-up Comedy and Postmodernism." In *Critical Theory and Performance,* ed. Janelle G. Reinelt and Joseph P. Roach, 196–207. Ann Arbor: University of Michigan Press, 1992.

Bach, Amy. "Movin' on Up with the Federalist Society: How the Right Rears Its Young Lawyers." *Nation,* October 1, 2001.

Barclay, C. R. "Composing Protoselves through Improvisation." In *The Remembering Self: Construction and Accuracy in Self-Narrative,* ed. Ulric Neisser and Robyn Fivush, 55–77. New York: Cambridge University Press, 1994.

Barlett, Donald L., and James B. Steele. *America: What Went Wrong?* Kansas City: An-
drews and McMeel, 1992.

Barnet, Richard J. "Lords of the Global Economy." *Nation,* December 19, 1994, 755.

Bartky, Sandra Lee. *Femininity and Domination: Studies in the Phenomenology of Op-
pression.* New York: Routledge, 1990.

———. "Foucault, Feminism, and the Modernization of Patriarchal Power." In *Feminism and Foucault: Reflections of Resistance,* ed. Irene Diamond and Lee Quinby,
61–86. Boston: Northeastern University Press, 1988.

———. "Phenomenology of a Hyphenated Consciousness." In *"Sympathy and Solidarity" and Other Essays,* 113–29.Lanham: Rowman and Littlefield, 2002.

Bartlett, Beverly. "The Whining Winds Down as Boomers Crest the Hill." *Louisville
Courier-Journal,* August 12, 1996.

Bass, Alison. "Secrets of Aging." *Boston Globe,* April 8, 2000, F1.

Basting, Anne Davis. *The Stages of Age: Performing Age in Contemporary American Culture.* Ann Arbor: University of Michigan Press, 1998.

Bauman, Zygmunt. "From Pilgrim to Tourist—or a Short History of Identity." In
Questions of Cultural Identity, ed. Stuart Hall and Paul Du Gay, 18–26. London:
Sage, 1996.

Beauvoir, Simone de. *La Vieillesse.* Paris: Gallimard, 1970.

Beck, Ulrich. *Risk Society: Towards a New Modernity.* Trans. Mark Ritter. London:
Newbury Park, 1992.

Beckett, Samuel. *Endgame.* New York: Grove Press, 1958.

Bell, Nora. "What Setting Limits May Mean: A Feminist Critique of Daniel Callahan's
Setting Limits." In *The Other within Us: Feminist Explorations of Women and Aging,* ed. Marilyn Pearsall, 151–59. Boulder: Westview Press, 1997.

Bengston, Vern E. "Is the 'Contract across Generations' Changing?" In *The Changing
Contract across Generations,* ed. Vern E. Bengston and W. Andrew Achenbaum.
New York: Aldine de Gruyter, 1993.

Benjamin, Jessica. "The Oedipal Riddle: Authority, Autonomy, and the New Narcissism." In *The Problem of Authority in America,* ed. John P. Diggins and Mark E.
Kann, 195–224. Philadelphia: Temple University Press, 1981.

Bennett, Tony. "Putting Policy into Cultural Studies." In *Cultural Studies,* ed. Lawrence
Grossberg and Paula Cary Nelson, 23–50. New York: Routledge, 1992.

Benson, John. *Prime Time: A History of the Middle Aged in Twentieth Century Britain.*
London: Longman, 1997.

Berger, John. *Pig Earth.* London: Writers and Readers Publishing Cooperative, 1979.

Berlant, Lauren. "Collegiality, Crisis, and Cultural Studies." *Profession 1998.* New York:
MLA, 1998.

Berman, Harry J. "Self-Representation and Aging: Philosophical, Psychological, and
Literary Perspectives." In *The Handbook of the Humanities and Aging,* 2d ed., ed.
Thomas R. Cole, Robert Kastenbaum, and Ruth E. Ray, 272–90. New York:
Springer, 2000.

Berti, Anna Emilia, and Anna Silvia Bombi. *The Child's Construction of Economics.* Trans. Gerard Duveen. Cambridge: Cambridge University Press, 1988.

Biggs, Simon. *The Mature Imagination: Dynamics of Identity in Midlife.* Buckingham: Open University Press, 1999.

Birren, James E., and Betty A. Birren. "Autobiography: Exploring the Self and Encouraging Development." In *Aging and Biography: Explorations in Adult Development,* ed. Betty Birren et al. New York: Springer, 1996.

Blanton, Kimberly. "Golden Illusions." *Boston Globe Magazine,* October 28, 2001, 11.

Blau, Herb. "Set Me Where you Stand": Revising the Abyss." *New Literary History* 29, no. 2 (spring 1998): 247–72.

Bloom, Lynn Z. "Single-Experience Autobiographies." *Auto/Biography Studies* 3, no. 3 (fall 1987): 36–45.

Boal, Iain A. "Glossary." In *The Battle of Seattle: The New Challenge to Capitalist Globalization,* ed. Eddie Yuen, George Katsiaficas, Daniel Burton Rose, 371–85. New York: Soft Skull Press, 2001.

Bourdieu, Pierre. *Distinction: A Social Critique of the Judgement of Taste.* Trans. Richard Nice. Cambridge: Harvard University Press, 1984.

———. *The Logic of Practice.* Trans. Richard Nice. Stanford: Stanford University Press, 1990.

Bower, Anne R. "The Role of Narrative in the Study of Language and Aging." *Journal of Narrative and Life History* 7 (1997): 265–74.

Brand, Horst. "Global Capitalism and the Decay of Employment Policy." *Dissent,* fall 1997, 57.

Brantley, Ben. "How to Call a Play into Being by Smearing a Man with Mud." *New York Times,* October 6, 1994, C17.

Brecht, Bertolt. *Brecht on Theater: The Development of an Esthetic.* Ed. and trans. John Willett. New York: Hill and Wang, 1964.

Brennan, Teresa. "Social Physics: Inertia, Energy, and Aging." In *Figuring Age: Women, Bodies, Generations,* ed. Kathleen Woodward, 131–48. Bloomington: Indiana University Press, 1999.

———. "The Two Forms of Consciousness." *Theory, Culture, and Society* 14, no. 4 (1997): 89–96.

Brentlinger, John. "Thanksgiving in the Year '02: A Sermon for the Unitarian Universalist Society of Northampton and Florence." Manuscript.

Brim, Gilbert. *Ambition: How We Manage Success and Failure.* New York: Basic Books, 1992.

Brockmeier, Jens. "From the End to the Beginning: Retrospective Teleology in Autobiography." In *Narrative and Identity: Studies in Autobiography, Self, and Culture,* ed. Jens Brockmeier and Donal Carbaugh, 247–80. Amsterdam: John Benjamins, 2001.

———. "Identity." In *The Encyclopedia of Life Writing,* ed. Margaretta Jolly, 455–56. London: Fitzroy Dearborn, 2001.

Broughton, John. "An Introduction to Critical Development Psychology." In *Critical Theories of Psychological Development*. New York: Plenum Press, 1987.

Brown, Michael E., and Randy Martin. "Left Futures." *Socialism and Democracy* 9, no. 1 (spring 1995): 59–90.

Brown, Rosellen. *The Autobiography of My Mother*. Garden City: Doubleday, 1976.

Buchmann, Marlis. *The Script of Life in Modern Society: Entry into Adulthood in a Changing World*. Chicago: University of Chicago Press, 1989.

Buckingham, John. *After the Death of Childhood: Growing Up in the Age of Electronic Media*. Malden, Mass.: Blackwell, 2000.

Bumpass, Larry L., and William S. Aquilino. *A Social Map of Midlife: Family and Work over the Middle Life Course*. Vero Beach, Fla.: MacArthur Foundation Research Network on Successful Midlife Development, 1994.

Buss, Helen M. "Anna Jameson's *Winter Studies and Summer Rambles in Canada* as Epistolary Dijournal." In *Essays on Life Writing: From Genre to Critical Practice*, ed. Marlene Kadar. Toronto: University of Toronto Press, 1992.

Butler, Judith. *Bodies That Matter: On the Discursive Limits of "Sex."* New York: Routledge, 1993.

Butler, Sandra S., and Richard A. Weatherly. "Poor Women at Midlife and Categories of Neglect." *Social Work* 37, no. 6 (November 1992).

Cardullo, Bert, et al., eds. *Playing to the Camera: Film Actors Discuss Their Craft*. New Haven: Yale University Press, 1998.

Carlin, George. "Outspoken." Interview in *Mother Jones*, March/April 1997, 56.

Carlson, Elliot, "AARP Unveils New Magazine: *My Generation* Will Target Boomer Members." *AARP Bulletin*, February 2001, 18.

Chandler, Michael J., Christopher E. Lalonde, and Bryan W. Sokol. "Continuities of Selfhood in the Face of Radical Developmental and Cultural Change." In *Culture, Thought, and Development*, ed. Larry P. Nucci, Geoffrey B. Saxe, and Elliot Turiel, 65–84. Mahwah, N.J.: Lawrence Erlbaum, 2000.

Chomsky, Noam. Introduction to *Corporations Are Going to Get Your Mama: Globalization and the Downsizing of the American Dream*, ed. Kevin Danaher. Monroe, Me.: Common Courage Press, 1997.

Chudacoff, Howard. *How Old Are You? Age Consciousness in American Culture*. Princeton: Princeton University Press, 1989.

Cohler, Bertram. "The Life Story and the Study of Resilience and Response to Adversity." *Journal of Narrative and Life History* 1, nos. 2–3 (1991): 169–200.

Cohler, Bertram, and David S. de Boer. "Psychoanalysis and the Study of Adult Lives." In *Psychoanalytic Perspectives on Developmental Psychology*, ed. Joseph Masling and Robert F. Bornstein. Washington: Psychoanalytic Psychology Association, 1996.

Cole, Thomas. "The 'Enlightened' View of Aging: Victorian Morality in a New Key." In *What Does It Mean to Grow Old? Reflections from the Humanities*, ed. Thomas R. Cole and Sally Gadow, 117–30. Durham: Duke University Press, 1986.

———. *Journey of Life: A Cultural History of Aging in America.* Cambridge: Cambridge University Press, 1992.

Cole, Thomas R., Ruth E. Ray, and Robert Kastenbaum, eds. *The Handbook of the Humanities and Aging.* 2d ed. New York: Springer, 2000.

Cole, Thomas R., David B. Van Tassel, and Robert Kastenbaum, eds. *The Handbook of the Humanities and Aging.* New York: Springer, 1992.

Committee on Child Psychiatry. *How Old is Old Enough? The Ages of Rights and Responsibilities.* Report no. 126. New York: Brunner/Mazel, 1989.

Conrad, Christoph. "Old Age in the Modern and Postmodern Western World." In *The Handbook of the Humanities and Aging*, ed. Thomas R. Cole, David B. Van Tassel, and Robert Kastenbaum. New York: Springer, 1992.

Copper, Baba. "Voices: On Becoming Old Women." In *Women and Aging: An Anthology by Women.* Corvallis: Calyx Books, 1986.

Coupland, Doug. *Generation X: Tales for an Accelerated Culture.* New York: St Martin's, 1991.

Cromby, John, and David J. Nightingale. "What's Wrong with Social Constructionism." Introduction to *Social Constructionist Psychology: A Critical Analysis of Theory and Practice.* Buckingham: Open University Press, 1999.

Davis, Joseph E. "Not Dead Yet: Psychotherapy, Morality, and the Question of Identity Dissolution." In *Identity and Social Change*, ed. Joseph E. Davis, 155–78. New Brunswick: Transaction, 2000.

Diamond, Elin. Introduction to *Performance and Cultural Politics.* London: Routledge, 1996.

Dickerson-Putman, Jeanette, and Judith K. Brown, eds. *Women's Age Hierarchies: Journal of Cross-Cultural Gerontology* 9, no. 2 (April 1994).

Dietrich, Mark T. "Fitting In at Work Isn't a Women's Issue." *Boston Globe*, February 9, 1998, A10.

DiManno, Rosie. "Face Facts, Boomers, the Bloom is Off Your Rose." *Toronto Star*, June 22, 1998.

Dirck, Joe. "Baby Boomers under Fire Again." *Plain Dealer*, August 22, 1996, 1B.

Donald, Merlin. "The Central Role of Culture in Cognitive Evolution: A Reflection on the Myth of the 'Isolated Mind.'" In *Culture, Thought, and Development*, ed. Larry P. Nucci, Geoffrey B. Saxe, and Elliot Turiel. Mahwah, N.J.: Lawrence Erlbaum, 2000.

Drabble, Margaret. *The Garrick Year.* London: Weidenfeld and Nicolson, 1964.

———. *The Middle Ground.* New York: Ivy Books, 1980.

———. *Thank You All Very Much* (also known as *The Millstone*). New York: Signet, 1965.

Dunne, John Gregory. "Virtual Patriotism." *New Yorker*, November 16, 1998.

Eagleton, Terry. *The Gatekeeper.* New York: St. Martin's, 2001.

Eisenberg, Anna. "Casting." In *The Thirteenth Annual Boston Jewish Film Festival, November 1–11, 2001* [Program Guide], 6. www.bjff.org.

Eisner, Robert. *Social Security: More, Not Less.* New York: Century Foundation, 1998.

————. *Three Great Deficit Scares.* New York: Century Foundation, 1997.

Elder, Glen H. *Children of the Great Depression: Social Change in Life Experience.* Chicago: University of Chicago Press, 1974.

Eliot, George. *Middlemarch.* Ed. Bert G. Hornback. 1871–72. New York: Norton, 1988.

Elkind, David. *The Hurried Child: Growing Up Too Fast Too Soon.* Reading, Mass.: Addison-Wesley, 1981.

Farriss, Bruce. "All They Wanna Do Is Have Some Fun." *Fresno Bee,* March 9, 1995.

Faucit, Helen. "Rosalind." In *On Playing Shakespeare: Advice and Commentary from Actors and Actresses of the Past,* ed. Leigh Woods.New York: Greenwood Press, 1991.

Featherstone, Mike, and Andrew Wernick, eds. *Images of Ageing: Cultural Representations of Later Life.* London: Routledge, 1995.

Feldenkrais, Moshe. *Body and Mature Behavior: A Study of Anxiety, Sex, Gravitation, and Learning.* New York: International Universities Press, 1949.

Feldman, Carol Fleisher. "Narratives of National Identity as Group Narratives: Patterns of Interpretive Cognition." In *Narrative and Identity: Studies in Autobiography, Self, and Culture,* ed. Jens Brockmeier and Donal Carbaugh, 129–44. Amsterdam: John Benjamins, 2001.

Ferris, Lesley, ed. *Crossing the Stage: Controversies on Cross-Dressing.* London: Routledge, 1993.

Ferrucci, Franco. "The Dead Child: A Romantic Myth." *Modern Language Notes* 104, no. 1 (January 1989): 117–34.

Fielding, Henry. *The History of Tom Jones, a Foundling.* Dublin, 1766.

Fiese, Barbara H., and Kathleen A. T. Marjinsky. "Dinnertime Stories." *The Stories that Families Tell: Narrative Coherence, Narrative Interaction, and Relationship Beliefs.* Malden, Mass.: Blackwell, 1999.

Fivush, Robin. "Accuracy, Authority, and Voice: Feminist Perspectives on Autobiographical Memory." In *Toward a Feminist Developmental Psychology,* ed. Patricia H. Miller and Ellin Kofsky Scholnick, 85–105. New York: Routledge, 2000.

Ford, Richard. *The Sportswriter.* New York: Vintage, 1986.

Forte, Jeanie, "Focus on the Body: Pain, Praxis, and Pleasure in Feminist Performance." In *Critical Theory and Performance,* ed. Janelle G. Reinelt and Joseph P. Roach, 248–62. Ann Arbor: University of Michigan Press, 1992.

Fotheringham, Richard. "Theorizing the Individual Body on Stage and Screen; or, the Jizz of Martin Guerre." *Journal of Dramatic Theory and Criticism* 15, no. 2 (spring 2001): 17–32.

Fraser, Nancy. *Unruly Practices: Power, Discourse, and Gender in Contemporary Social Theory.* Minneapolis: University of Minnesota Press, 1989.

————. "The Uses and Abuses of French Discourse Theories for Feminist Politics." In *Cultural Theory and Cultural Change,* ed. Mike Featherstone, 51–71. London: Sage, 1992.

Fuchs, Elinor. *The Death of Character: Perspectives on Theater after Modernism.* Bloomington: Indiana University Press, 1996.

Fugard, Athol. *The Captain's Tiger.* Johannesburg: Witwatersrand University Press, 1997.

Fulford, Robert. *The Triumph of Narrative: Storytelling in the Age of Mass Culture.* Toronto: Anansi, 1999.

Gailey, Christine Ward, ed. *The Politics of Culture and Creativity: A Critique of Civilization.* Gainesville: University of Florida Press, 1992.

Gardiner, Judith Kegan. "Theorizing Age with Gender: Bly's Boys, Feminism, and Maturity Masculinity." In *Masculinity Studies and Feminist Theory: New Directions,* ed. Judith Kegan Gardiner, 90–118. New York: Columbia University Press, 2002.

Geduld, Harry M. Introduction to *The Definitive Time Machine: A Critical Edition of H. G. Wells' Scientific Romance.* Bloomington: Indiana University Press, 1987.

Gelman, Susan A., and Marianne G. Taylor. "Gender Essentialism in Cognitive Development." In *Toward a Feminist Developmental Psychology,* ed. Patricia Miller and Ellin Kofsky Scholnick, 169–90. New York: Routledge, 2000.

"Generation X-onomics." *Economist,* March 19, 1994, 27.

Giddens, Anthony. *Modernity and Self-Identity.* Stanford: Stanford University Press, 1991.

Giele, Janet. "Innovation in the Typical Life Course." In *Methods of Life Course Research: Qualitative and Quantitative Approaches,* ed. J. Z. Giele and G. H. Elder, 231–63. Thousand Oaks, Calif.: Sage, 1998.

Giles, Jeff. "Generalizations X." *Newsweek,* June 6, 1994, 62.

Gilmore, Leigh. *Autobiographics: A Feminist Theory of Women's Self-Representation.* Ithaca: Cornell University Press, 1994.

Ginn, Jay, and Sara Arber. "Midlife Women's Employment and Pension Entitlement in Relation to Co-Resident Adult Children in Great Britain." *Journal of Marriage and the Family* 56, no. 4 (November 1994): 813–19.

Giroux, Henry. "Slacking Off: Border Youth and Postmodern Education." In *Counternarratives: Cultural Studies and Critical Pedagogies in Postmodern Spaces,* ed. Henry Giroux et al. London: Routledge, 1996.

———. *Stealing Innocence: Youth, Corporate Power, and the Politics of Culture.* New York: St. Martin's, 2000.

Glazer, Sarah. "Overhauling Social Security." *CQ Researcher,* May 12, 1995, 434.

Goethe, Johann Wolfgang. *Elective Affinities.* New York, 1872.

———. "Women's Parts Played by Men in the Roman Theater." In *Crossing the Stage: Controversies on Cross-Dressing,* ed. Lesley Ferris. London: Routledge, 1993.

Goffman, Erving. *Stigma: Notes on the Management of Spoiled Identity.* Englewood Cliffs, N.J.: Prentice-Hall, 1963.

Goldman, Ronald, and Juliette Goldman. *Children's Sexual Thinking: A Comparative Study of Children Aged Five to Fifteen Years in Australia, North America, Britain, and Sweden.* Boston: Routledge and Kegan Paul, 1982.

Gordon, Mary. *The Rest of Life: Three Novellas*. New York: Penguin, 1993.

Graebner, William. *A History of Retirement: The Meaning and Function of an American Institution, 1885–1978*. New Haven: Yale University Press, 1980.

Gratiot, Jim. "Generation X: A Term Used for Trashing." *San Diego Union Tribune*, August 7, 1994.

Greenberg, David. "In the Shadow of the Sixties." In *Next: Young American Writers on the New Generation*, ed. Eric Liu. New York: Norton, 1994.

Greenhouse, Linda. "Supreme Court Hears Arguments on Major Issue in Age Bias Law." *New York Times*, March 21, 2001, A27.

Gregory, Raymond F. *Age Discrimination in the American Workplace: Old at a Young Age*. New Brunswick: Rutgers University Press, 2001.

Griffin, Richard. "Children Face Up to Aging." *Cambridge Chronicle*, August 9, 2002, 7.

Grodal, Torben. *Moving Pictures: A New Theory of Film Genres, Feelings, and Cognitions*. Oxford: Oxford University Press, 1997.

Grossberg, Lawrence. *We Gotta Get Out of This Place: Popular Conservatism and Postmodern Culture*. New York: Routledge, 1992.

Grossberg, Lawrence, Cary Nelson, and Paula Treichler, eds. *Cultural Studies*. New York: Routledge, 1992.

Grossfeld, Stan. "AIDS: A Threat to the Elderly." *Boston Globe*, June 4, 2002.

Grosz, Elizabeth. "The Problem of Theory." *theory@buffalo* 5 (1999): 2-16.

Group for the Advancement of Psychiatry. *How Old is Old Enough? The Ages of Rights and Responsibilities*. Report 126. New York: Brunner and Mazel, 1989.

Gruman, Gerald J. "Cultural Origins of Present-Day 'Ageism': The Modernization of the Life Cycle." In *Aging and the Elderly: Humanistic Perspectives in Gerontology*, ed. Stuart F. Spicker, Kathleen Woodward, and David D. Van Tassel. Atlantic Highlands, N.J.: Humanities Press, 1978.

Grunwald, Michael. "Trial by Media." *Boston Globe*, October 10, 1994, 31.

Guillemard, Anne-Marie. "France: Massive Exit through Unemployment Compensation." In *Time for Retirement: Comparative Studies of Early Exit from the Labor Force*, ed. Martin Kohli et al., 127– 80. Cambridge: Cambridge University Press, 1991.

Guillemard, Anne-Marie, and Herman van Gunsteren. "Pathways and Their Prospects: A Comparative Interpretation of the Meaning of Early Exit." In *Time for Retirement: Comparative Studies of Early Exit from the Labor Force*, ed. Martin Kohli et al., 362– 88. Cambridge: Cambridge University Press, 1991.

Gullette, Margaret Morganroth. "Age" and "Aging." In *Feminist Theory: A Dictionary*, ed. Elizabeth Kowaleski-Wallace. New York: Garland, 1996.

———. "Age Studies as Cultural Studies." In *The Handbook of the Humanities and Aging*, 2d ed., ed. Thomas R. Cole, Ruth E. Ray, and Robert Kastenbaum, 214–34. New York: Springer, 2000.

———. "Age Studies, and Gender." In *Encyclopedia of Feminist Theories*, ed. Lorraine Code, 12–14. London: Routledge, 1999.

———. "The Contrived War between 'the Xers' and 'the Boomers.'" *Review of Education, Pedagogy, and Cultural Studies* 23, no. 2 (2001): 137–65.

———. "Creativity, Aging, Gender: A Case Study of Their Intersections, 1910–1935." In *Aging and Gender in Literature: Studies in Creativity,* ed. Anne M. Wyatt-Brown and Janice Rossen, 19–48. Charlottesville: University of Virginia Press, 1993.

———. *Declining to Decline: Cultural Combat and the Politics of the Midlife.* Age Studies series. Charlottesville: University of Virginia Press, 1997.

———. "The Exile of Adulthood: Pedophilia and the Decline Novel." *Novel* 17, no.3 (spring 1984): 215–32.

———. "Florcita la Suerte." *Indiana Review,* summer 2000.

———. "The High Costs of Middle Ageism." *Brandeis Review* 18, no. 4 (1998): 22–25.

———. "Inventing the 'Postmaternal' Woman, 1898–1927: Idle, Unwanted, and Out of a Job." *Feminist Studies* 21, no. 2 (summer 1995): 221–54.

———. "Letter from Nicaragua: How Not to Be a Tourist." *Yale Review* 79, no. 1: 93–116.

———. "Male Midlife Sexuality in a Gerontocratic Economy: The Privileged Stage of the Long Midlife in Nineteenth-Century Age Ideology." *Journal of the History of Sexuality* 5, no.1 (1994): 58–89.

———. "Midlife Discourses in the Twentieth-Century United States: An Essay on the Sexuality, Ideology, and Politics of 'Middle Ageism.'" In *Welcome to Middle Age! (And Other Cultural Fictions),* ed. Richard A. Shweder, 3–44. Chicago: University of Chicago Press, 1998.

———. "Nicaragua 1991: Going On." *North American Review,* fall 1991.

———. "Politics of Middle Ageism." *New Political Science* 20, no. 3 (1998): 263–82.

———. "The Puzzling Case of the Deceased Wife's Sister: Nineteenth-Century England Deals with a Second-Chance Plot." *Representations* 31 (summer 1990): 42–166.

———. *Safe at Last in the Middle Years: The Invention of the Midlife Progress Novel.* Berkeley: University of California Press, 1988.

———. "Valuing 'Postmaternity' as a Revolutionary Feminist Concept." *Feminist Studies,* 28, no. 3 (December 2002): 553–72.

———. "What, Menopause *Again?*" *Ms.,* summer 1993.

———. "Wicked Powerful: The Postmaternal in Contemporary Film and Psychoanalytic Theory," and "Response." *Gender and Psychoanalysis,* no. 5 (spring 2000): 107–39 and 149–54.

———. "The Wonderful Woman on the Pavement. Middle-Ageism in the Postmodern Economy." *Dissent,* fall 1995, 508–14.

Gusdorf, Georges. "Conditions and Limits of Autobiography." In *Autobiography: Essays Theoretical and Critical,* ed. James Olney, 28–48. Princeton University Press, 1980.

Habermas, Jürgen. *The Philosophical Discourse of Modernity: Twelve Lectures.* Trans. Frederick Lawrence. Cambridge: MIT Press, 1987.

Hacker, Andrew. "Paradise Lost." *New York Review of Books,* May 13, 1993, 33.

Hacking, Ian. *The Social Construction of What?* Cambridge: Harvard University Press, 1999.

Hall, Donald. *Old and New Poems.* Boston: Houghton Mifflin, 1990.

Hall, Stuart. "Cultural Studies and the Centre: Some Problematics and Problems." In *Culture, Media, Language,* ed. Stuart Hall et al. London: Hutchinson, 1980.

———. "Cultural Studies and Its Legacies." In *We Gotta Get Out of This Place: Popular Conservatism and Postmodern Culture,* ed. Lawrence Grossberg et al., 277–94. New York: Routledge, 1992.

———. "Ethnicity: Identity and Difference." In *Border Texts: Cultural Readings for Contemporary Writers,* ed. Randall Bass, 295–305. Boston: Houghton Mifflin, 1999.

———. "On Postmodernism and Articulation." In *Stuart Hall: Critical Dialogues in Cultural Studies,* ed. David Morley and Kuan-Hsing Chen, 131–50. London: Routledge, 1996.

———. "Who Needs Identity?" Introduction to *Questions of Cultural Identity,* ed. Stuart Hall and Paul Du Gay. London: Sage, 1996.

Handel, Amos. "Perceived Change of Self among Adults: A Conspectus." In *Self and Identity: Perspectives across the Lifespan,* ed. Terry Honess and Krysia Yardley-Matwiejczuk, 320–37. London: Routledge, 1987.

Hardy, Melissa A., ed. *Studying Aging and Social Change: Conceptual and Methodological Issues.* Thousand Oaks, Calif.: Sage, 1997.

Hardy, Melissa A., and Linda Waite. "Doing Time: Reconciling Biography with History in the Study of Social Change." In *Studying Aging and Social Change: Conceptual and Methodological Issues,* ed. Melissa A. Hardy. Thousands Oaks, Calif.: Sage, 1997.

Hareven, Tamara K. "Changing Images of Ageing and the Social Construction of the Life Course." In *Images of Ageing: Cultural Representations of Later Life,* ed. Mike Featherstone and Andrew Wernick, 119–34. London: Routledge, 1995.

———. *Family Time and Industrial Time: The Relationship between the Family and Work in a New England Industrial Community.* Lanham, Md.: University Press of America, 1993.

———, ed. *Aging and Generational Relations: Life-Course and Cross-Cultural Perspectives.* New York: Aldine de Gruyter, 1996.

Harms, John, and Douglas Kellner. "Toward a Critical Theory of Advertising." In *Illuminations: The Critical Theory Website,* Dec. 5, 2000. www.uta.edu/english/dab/illuminations/kell6.

Harris, Adrienne E. "The Rationalization of Infancy." In *Critical Theories of Psychological Development,* ed. John M. Broughton. New York: Plenum Press, 1987.

Harris, Cheryl I. "Whiteness as Property." In *Critical Race Theory: The Key Writings That Formed the Movement,* ed. Kimberlé Crenshaw et al., 276–91. New York: New Press, 1995.

Hearn, Charles R. *The American Dream in the Great Depression.* Westport: Greenwood Press, 1977.

Heckhausen, Jutta. "Adaptation and Resilience in Midlife." In *Handbook of Midlife Development,* ed. Margie E.Lachman, 345–94. New York: Wiley, 2001.

Heller, Joseph. *Something Happened.* London: Cape Press, 1974.

Hepworth, Mike. "The Mid Life Phase." In *Social Change and the Life Course,* ed. Gaynor Cohen, 134–55. London: Tavistock, 1987.

———. *Stories of Aging.* Philadelphia: Open University Press, 2000.

Hijuelos, Oscar. *Mr. Ives' Christmas.* New York: HarperCollins, 1995.

Hockey, Jennifer, and Allison James. *Growing Up and Growing Old: Ageing and Dependency in the Life Course.* London: Sage, 1993.

Holland, Dorothy, "What's Death Got to do with It?" Paper delivered at the Obermann Seminar on Later Life, University of Iowa, 1999.

Holland, Gina, "High Court Case to Determine Legal Clout of Older Workers," *Boston Globe,* March 21, 2002, A4.

Hollie, Pamela G. "Mass-Marketing of Eye Care." *New York Times,* May 3, 1984, D1.

Hornblower, Margot. "Great Xpectations," *Time,* June 9, 1997, 3.

Howard, Maureen. *Expensive Habits: A Novel.* New York: Summit, 1986.

Howe, Neil, and William Strauss. "The New Generation Gap." *Atlantic Monthly,* December 1992, 79.

———. *13th Gen.* New York: Vintage, 1993.

Hunter, Mark. "Work, Work, Work, Work!" *Modern Maturity,* May/June 1999, 38.

Huston, Hollis. *The Actor's Instrument: Body, Theory, Stage.* Ann Arbor: University of Michigan Press, 1992.

Huyssen, Andreas. "Present Pasts: Medica, Politics, Amnesia." *Public Culture* 12, no. 1 (2000): 21–38.

Ingrisch, Doris. "Conformity and Resistance as Women Age." In *Connecting Gender and Ageing: A Sociological Approach,* ed. Sara Arber and Jay Ginn. Buckingham: Open University Press, 1995.

Irving, John. *The World According to Garp.* New York: Dutton, 1978.

Israel, Betsy. "Lost in the Name Game." *New York Times,* February 14, 1993, section 9.

Jacobs, Klaus, Martin Kohli, and Martin Rein. "Testing the Industry-Mix Hypothesis of Early Exit." In *Time for Retirement: Comparative Studies of Early Exit from the Labor Force,* ed. Martin Kohli et al., 67–96. Cambridge: Cambridge University Press, 1991.

Jacobson, Louis S., Robert J. LaLonde, and Daniel G. Sullivan. "Long-Term Earnings Losses of High Seniority Displaced Workers." *Economic Perspectives* 17, no.6 (1993): 2–20.

James, Allison, Chris Jenks, and Alan Prout, *Theorizing Childhood.* Cambridge: Polity, 1998.

James, Allison, and Alan Prout, eds. *Constructing and Reconstructing Childhood: Contemporary Issues in the Sociological Study of Childhood.* 2d ed. London: Falmer, 1997.

Jameson, Fredric. "*Ulysses* in History." In *James Joyce: A Collection of Critical Essays,* ed. Mary T. Reynolds, 145–58. Englewood Cliffs, N.J.: Prentice-Hall, 1993.

Jarrell, Randall. *No Other Book: Selected Essays.* Ed. Brad Leithauser. New York: Perennial, 1999.

Jones, Joyce E., and Claudia J. Peck. "Human Capital, Socioeconomic, and Labor Market Effects on the Wage Differential: A Case for Using Age Cohorts." *Home Economics Research Journal* 22, no. 1 (September 1993): 1–38.

Jordan, June. "Report from the Bahamas." In *A Stranger in the Village,* ed. Farah J. Griffin and Cheryl J. Fish, 319–29. Boston: Beacon, 1998.

Kahn, Coppélia. *Roman Shakespeare: Warriors, Wounds, and Women.* London: Routledge, 1997.

Kalleberg, Arne L., et al. *Nonstandard Work, Substandard Jobs.* Washington, D.C.: Economic Policy Institute, 1998.

Karp, David. "A Decade of Reminders: Changing Age Consciousness between Fifty and Sixty Years Old." *Gerontologist* 28, no. 6 (1988): 727–38.

Katz, Stephen. "Alarmist Demography: Power, Knowledge, and the Elderly Population." *Journal of Aging Studies* 6, no. 3 (1992).

———. *Disciplining Gerontology.* Charlottesville: University of Virginia Press, 1996.

Kausler, Donald H. "Memory and Memory Theory." In *The Encyclopedia of Aging,* ed. George L. Maddox, 429–32. New York: Springer, 1987.

Kavanagh, James H. "Ideology." In *Critical Terms for Literary Study,* ed. Frank Lentricchia and Thomas McLaughlin. Chicago: University of Chicago Press, 1990.

Kearl, Michael C., and Lisbeth J. Hoag. "The Social Construction of the Midlife Crisis." *Sociological Inquiry* 54, no.3 (summer 1984): 296.

Kennedy, William. *Ironweed: A Novel.* New York: Viking, 1983.

Kenyon, Gary M., and William L. Randall. *Restorying Our Lives: Personal Growth through Autobiographical Reflection.* Westport, Conn.: Praeger, 1997.

Kerby, Anthony Paul. *Narrative and the Self.* Bloomington: Indiana University Press, 1991.

Barbara Kingsolver, *Poisonwood Bible.* New York: HaperCollins 1998.

Kinsley, Michael. "Back from the Future." *New Republic,* March 21, 1994, 6.

Kirn, Walter. "Crybaby Boomers." *New York Times,* July 2, 1997, A23.

Kleyman, Paul, "'Geezer' Slur Even in *Scientific American.*" *Aging Today,* November/December 2000, 19.

Knox, Richard A. "Boomers See Work Coloring Golden Years." *Boston Globe,* June 3, 1998, A3.

Kohli, Martin. "Social Organization and Subjective Construction of the Life Course." In *Human Development and the Life Course: Multidisciplinary Perspectives,* ed. Aage Sorensen, Franz E. Weinert, and Lonnie R. Sherrod. Hillsdale, N.J.: Lawrence Erlbaum, 1986.

Kohli, Martin, and Martin Rein. "The Changing Balance of Work and Retirement." In

Time for Retirement: Comparative Studies of Early Exit from the Labor Force, ed. Martin Kohli et al., 1–35. Cambridge: Cambridge University Press, 1991.

Kohli, Martin, et al., eds. *Time for Retirement: Comparative Studies of Early Exit from the Labor Force.* Cambridge: Cambridge University Press, 1991.

Kotlikoff, Laurence J., with Stephen Johnson and William Samuelson. "Can People Compute? An Experimental Test of the Life-Cycle Consumption Model." In *Essays on Savings, Bequests, Altruism, and Life-Cycle Planning,* ed. Laurence Kotlikoff. Cambridge: MIT Press, 2001.

Kozlovsky, Mary Ann. "You're as Old as You Feel." Letter to the Editor, *Progressive Populist,* August 15, 2001, 5.

Kruger, Barbara. *Remote Control: Power, Culture, and the World of Appearances.* Cambridge: MIT Press, 1994.

Kuhn, Reinhard Clifford. *Corruption in Paradise: The Child in Western Literature.* Hanover, N.H.: University Press of New England, for Brown University Press, 1982.

Labaton, Stephen. "You Don't Have to Be Old to Sue for Age Discrimination." *New York Times,* February 16, 2000, 7.

Labouvie-Vief, Gisela. "Positive Development in Later Life." In *The Handbook of the Humanities and Aging,* 2d ed., ed. Thomas R. Cole, Ruth E. Ray, and Robert Kastenbaum. New York: Springer, 2000.

Lamont, Rosette C., ed. *Women on the Verge: Seven Avant-Garde American Plays.* New York: Applesauce, 1993.

Lawrence, Jill. "Political Battlegrounds of the Future." *USA Today,* August 8, 1997, 6A.

Laws, Glenda, "Tabloid Bodies: Aging, Health, and Beauty in Popular Discourses." Manuscript, n.d.

———. "Understanding Ageism: Lessons from Postmodernism and Feminism." *Gerontologist* 35, no. 1 (1995): 112–18.

Leder, Drew. *The Absent Body.* Chicago: University of Chicago Press, 1990.

Lentricchia, Frank. "In Place of an Afterword—Someone Reading." In *Critical Terms for Literary Study,* ed. Frank Lentricchia and Thomas McLaughlin. Chicago: University of Chicago Press, 1990.

Lillie, Jim. "When Local Actors Get Cast—and When They Don't." *American Theatre,* October 1999, 30ff.

Linde, Charlotte. *Life Stories: The Creation of Coherence.* New York: Oxford University Press, 1993.

Lively, Penelope. *The Road to Lichfield.* London: Heinemann, 1977.

Long, Judy. "Telling Women's Lives: 'Slant,' 'Straight,' and 'Messy.'" In *Current Perspectives on Aging and the Life Cycle,* vol. 3: *Personal History through the Life Course,* ed. David Unruh and Gail S. Livings,: 191–223. Greenwich, Conn.: JAI, 1989.

Looser, Devoney, and E. Ann Kaplan, eds. *Generations: Academic Feminists in Dialogue.* Minneapolis: University of Minnesota Press, 1997.

Lorde, Audre. *Sister Outsider: Essays and Speeches.* Trumansberg, N.Y.: Crossing Press, 1984.

Louv, Richard. "Xers Size Up Futures with Great Optimism." *San Diego Union-Tribune,* June 12 1996, A3.

Maccoby, Eleanor E. *Social Development: Psychological Growth and the Parent-Child Relationship.* San Diego: Harcourt Brace Jovanovich, 1980.

MacIntosh, Peggy. "How White-Skin Privilege Commonly Frames U.S. Academic Writing: Examples to Consider from Five Disciplines." Wellesley Center Luncheon Seminar, Wellesley College, September 18, 1989.

MacManus, Susan A., with Patricia A. Turner. *Young v. Old: Generational Combat in the Twenty-First Century.* Boulder: Westview Press, 1996.

Madrick, Jeff. "Enron, the Media, and the New Economy." *Nation,* April 1, 2002, 17–20.

Males, Mike. "The Myth of the Grade-School Murderers," *Extra!* May/June 2001, 3.

Mannheim, Karl. "The Problem of Generations." In *Studying Aging and Social Change: Conceptual and Methodological Issues,* ed. Melissa A. Hardy. Thousands Oaks, Calif.: Sage, 1997.

Marcia, James E. "The Identity Status Approach to the Study of Ego Identity Development." In *Self and Identity: Perspectives across the Lifespan,* ed. Terry Honess and Krysia Yardley-Matwiejczuk, 161–71. London: Routledge, 1987.

Marcus, Laura. *Auto/Biographical Discourse: Theory, Criticism, Practice.* New York: St. Martin's, 1994.

Martin, David. "The Whiny Generation." *Newsweek,* November 1, 1993.

Martin, Steve. "Changes in the Memory After Fifty." *New Yorker,* January 19, 1998, 88.

McGrath, Charles. "Live Fast, Die Old." *New York Times Magazine,* February 21, 1999, 14.

McMurtry, Larry. *Terms of Endearment: A Novel.* New York: Simon and Schuster, 1975.

McRobbie, Angela. *Feminism and Youth Culture: From "Jackie" to "Just Seventeen."* Boston: Unwin Hyman, 1991.

Medevoi, Leerom. "Democracy, Capitalism, and American Literature: The Cold War Construction of J. D. Salinger's Paperback Hero." In *The Other Fifties: Interrogating Mid-Century American Icons,* ed. Joel Foreman. Urbana: University of Illinois Press, 1997.

Medevoi, Leerom. "Reading the Blackboard: Youth, Masculinity, and Racial Cross-Identification." In *Race and the Subject of Masculinities,* ed. Harry Stecopoulos and Michael Uebel, 138–69. Durham: Duke University Press, 1997.

Menand, Louis. "The Seventies Show." *New Yorker,* May 28, 2001, 128–33.

Menchú, Rigoberta. *Me llamo Rigoberta Menchú y así me nació la conciencia.* Mexico City: Siglo XXI, 1992.

Menon, Usha. "Middle Adulthood in Cultural Perspective: The Imagined and the Experienced in Three Cultures." In *Handbook of Midlife Development,* ed. Margie E. Lachman, 40–74. New York: Wiley, 2001.

Metchnikov, Elie. *The Nature of Man: Studies in Optimistic Philosophy.* New York: Putnam, 1903.

Meyer, John W. "The Self and the Life Course: Institutionalization and Its Effects." In *Human Development and the Life Course: Multidisciplinary Perspectives*, ed. A. B. Sorensen. Hillsdale, N.J.: Lawrence Erlbaum, 1985.

Miles, Rufus E. Jr. *The Department of Health, Education and Welfare.* New York: Praeger, 1974.

Miller, Arthur. *Death of a Salesman.* New York: Viking, 1949.

Miller, Nancy K. *Getting Personal: Feminist Occasions and Other Autobiographical Acts.* New York: Routledge, 1991.

Mills, C. Wright. *The Sociological Imagination.* New York: Oxford University Press, 1959.

Mishel, Lawrence R., Jared Bernstein, and John Schmitt. *The State of Working America, 1996–97.* Washington, D.C.: Economic Policy Institute, 1997.

———. *The State of Working America, 2000–2001.* Ithaca: ILR Press, 2001.

Monroe, Ann. "Getting Rid of the Gray." *Mother Jones,* July/August 1996, 29.

Moody, Harry R. "Overview: What Is Critical Gerontology and Why Is It Important?" In *Voices and Visions of Aging: Toward a Critical Gerontology,* ed. Thomas R. Cole et al. New York: Springer, 1993.

Moore, Michelle, "Xers to Baby Boomers: Thanks for Nothing." *Orange County Register,* June 10, 1998, B6.

Morrison, Toni. *Beloved: A Novel.* New York: Knopf, 1987.

Morton, Carol Cruzan. "Which Is More Dangerous, Aging or Inactivity?" *Boston Globe,* October 2, 2001, C1.

Mukherjee, Bharati. *The Holder of the World.* New York: Knopf, 1993.

Mueller, John H., et al. "Trait Distinctiveness and Age Specificity in the Self-Concept." In *Self-Perspectives across the Life Span,* ed. Richard P. Lipka and Thomas M. Brinthaupt, 223–55. Albany: SUNY Press, 1992.

Mullenix, Elizabeth Reitz. *Wearing the Breeches: Gender on the Antebellum Stage.* New York: St. Martin's, 2000.

Nabokov, Vladimir. *Speak, Memory: A Memoir.* New York: Grosset and Dunlap, 1947.

Nagel, Thomas, "In the Stream of Consciousness." *New York Review of Books,* April 11, 2002, 74–76.

Nelson, Rob, and Jon Cowan. *Revolution X: A Survival Guide for Our Generation.* New York: Penguin, 1994.

Newman, Katherine. *A Different Shade of Gray: Midlife and Beyond in the Inner City.* New York: New Press, 2003.

———. "Midlife Experience in Harlem." In *Welcome to Middle Age! (And Other Cultural Fictions),* ed. Richard A. Shweder, 259–93. Chicago: University of Chicago Press, 1998.

Nicholson, Trish, "Fifty-Plus Workers Hit by Cutbacks." *AARP Bulletin,* 1.

Nix, Shann. "Hoax! Why the Ex-Generation Never Existed." *San Francisco Examiner,* June 12, 1994, M10.

Nuessel, Frank. "Literature." In *The Image of Older Adults in the Media: An Annotated Bibliography.* Westport, Conn.: Greenwood Press, 1993.

Overall, Christine. *A Feminist I: Reflections from Academia.* Orchard Park, N.Y.: Broadview, 1998.

Page, Clarence. "Lament of the Twentysomethings." *Chicago Tribune,* August 11, 1991.

Patai, Daphne. "The View from Elsewhere: Utopian Constructions of 'Difference.'" In *"Turning the Century": Feminist Theory in the 1990s,* ed. Glynis Carr, 132–50. Lewisburg: Bucknell University Press, 1992.

Patterson, Orlando. *The Ordeal of Integration: Progress and Resentment in America's "Racial" Crisis.* Washington, D.C.: Civitas/Counterpoint, 1997.

Payne, Michael. *A Dictionary of Cultural and Critical Theory.* Oxford: Blackwell, 1996.

Peters, Ann M. "The Development of Collaborative Story Retelling by a Two-Year-Old Blind Child and His Father." In *Social Interaction, Social Context, and Language: Essays in Honor of Susan Ervin-Tripp,* ed. Dan I. Slobin and Susan Ervin-Tripp, 391–416. Mahwah, N.J.: Lawrence Erlbaum, 1996.

Peterson, Karla. "Thirty-Somethings, It's Time for XYZzzzz of the Generation Gap." *San Diego Union-Tribune,* June 9, 1994, "Night and Day," 3.

Phelan, Peggy. "Crisscrossing Cultures." In *Crossing the Stage: Controversies on Cross-Dressing,* ed. Lesley Ferris, 155–70. London: Routledge, 1993.

Phillips, Julie. "Baby Boomers Come of Age and Generation X Sounds Off." *Utne Reader,* March/April 1994, 69.

Pittman, Elana. "Crest 'Rejuvenating' Effects." Manuscript, Communications Department, Simmons College, 2002.

Prager, Jeffrey. *Representing the Past: Psychoanalysis and the Sociology of Misremembering.* Cambridge: Harvard University Press, 1998.

Pratt, Mary Louise. "Scratches on the Face of the Country." In *"Race," Writing, and Difference,* ed. Henry Louis Gates, Jr. Chicago: University of Chicago Press, 1985.

Quadagno, Jill, et al. "Setting the Agenda for Research on Cohorts and Generations: Theoretical, Political, and Policy Implications." *The Changing Contract across Generations,* ed. Vern L. Bengston and W. Andrew Achenbaum. New York: Aldine de Gruyter, 1993.

Ratan, Suneel. "Why Busters Hate Boomers." *Fortune,* October 4, 1993, 57.

Ray, Ruth E. *Beyond Nostalgia: Aging and Life-Story Writing.* Age Studies series. Charlottesville: University of Virginia Press, 2000.

Ray, Ruth E., and Sally Chandler, "A Narrative Approach to Anti-Aging." *Generations,* no. 25 (winter 2001/2002): 44–48.

Reed-Danahay, Deborah E. Introduction to *Auto/Ethnography: Rewriting the Self and the Social,* ed. Deborah Reed-Danahay. Oxford: Berg, 1997.

Reich, Robert B. *Tales of a New America: The Anxious Liberal's Guide to the Future.* New York: Times Books, 1987.

Reinelt, Janelle G., and Joseph R. Roach, eds., *Critical Theory and Performance.* Ann Arbor: University of Michigan Press, 1992.

Rich, Frank. "Reality Bites Again." *New York Times,* March 20, 1994, section 4, 17.

Richmond, Al. *A Long View from the Left: Memoirs of an American Revolutionary.* New York: Delta, 1972.

Ricoeur, Paul. "Narrative Time." *Critical Inquiry* 7, no. 1 (1980): 169–90.

———. *Oneself as Another.* Trans. Kathleen Blamey. Chicago: University of Chicago Press, 1992.

Riemer, Hans, and Christopher Cuomo. "The Generation Gambit: The Right's Imaginary Rift between Young and Old," *Extra!* March/April 1997, 14–16.

Rifkin, Jeremy. *The End of Work: The Decline of the Global Labor Force and the Dawn of the Post-Market Era.* New York: Tarcher/Putnam, 1995.

Robinson, Amy. "Forms of Appearance of Value: Homer Plessy and the Politics of Privacy." In *Performance and Cultural Politics,* ed. Elin Diamond, 239–65. London: Routledge, 1996.

Roof, Judith. "Generational Difficulties; or, The Fear of a Barren History." In *Generations: Academic Feminists in Dialogue,* ed. Devony Looser and E. Ann Kaplan, 69–87. Minneapolis: University of Minnesota Press, 1997.

Rose, Nikolas. "Identity, Genealogy, History." In *Questions of Cultural Identity,* ed. Stuart Hall and Paul Du Gay, 128–50. London: Sage, 1996.

Ross, Andrew. *Real Love: In Pursuit of Cultural Justice.* New York: New York University Press, 1998.

Rossan, Sheila. "Identity and Its Development in Adulthood." In *Self and Identity: Perspectives across the Lifespan,* ed. Terry Honess and Krysia Yardley-Matwiejczuk, 304–19. London: Routledge, 1987.

Rossi, Alice, and Peter Henry Rossi. *Of Human Bonding: Parent-Child Relations across the Life Course.* New York: Aldine de Gruyter, 1990.

Rouse, John. "Textuality and Authority in Theater and Drama: Some Contemporary Possibilities." In *Critical Theory and Performance,* ed. Janelle G. Reinelt and Joseph P. Roach, 146–57. Ann Arbor: University of Michigan Press, 1992.

Rousseau, Jean Jacques. *Julie, or the New Heloise.* Paris, 1763.

Roy, Gabrielle. *La détresse et l'enchantement.* Montreal: Les Editions du Boréal, 1988.

Runyon, William McKinley. *Life Histories and Psychobiography: Explorations in Theory and Method.* New York: Oxford University Press, 1984.

Russo, Mary. "Aging and the Scandal of Anachronism." In *Figuring Age: Women, Bodies, Generations,* ed. Kathleen Woodward, 20–33. Bloomington: Indiana University Press, 1999.

Ryder, Norman B. "The Cohort as a Concept in the Study of Social Change." In *Studying Aging and Social Change: Conceptual and Methodological Issues,* ed. Melissa A. Hardy. Thousand Oaks, Calif.: Sage, 1997.

Safire, William. "On Language: Don't Call me 'Near Elderly.'" *New York Times Magazine,* February 8, 1998, 22.

Said, Edward. *Reflections on Exile and Other Essays.* Cambridge: Harvard University Press, 2000.

Sarraute, Nathalie. *Childhood.* Trans. Barbara Wright. New York: Braziller, 1984.

Scales, Ann. "Clinton Vows to Let States Help Parents." *Boston Globe,* May 24, 1999, A8.

Schechner, Richard. "TDR Comments: Mainstream Theatre and Performance Studies." *TDR* 44, no. 2 (summer 2000): 4–6.

Schnall, Peter, et al. *The Workplace and Cardiovascular Disease.* Occupational Medicine: State of the Art Reviews, vol. 15, no. 1. Philadelphia: Hanley and Belfus, 2000.

Schneider, Barbara, and David Stevenson. *The Ambitious Generation: America's Teenagers, Motivated but Directionless.* New Haven: Yale University Press, 1999.

Scholnick, Ellin Kofsky. "Engendering Development: Metaphors of Change." In *Toward a Feminist Developmental Psychology,* ed. Patricia H. Miller, and E. K. Scholnick. New York: Routledge, 2000.

Schor, Juliet. *The Overworked American: The Unexpected Decline of Leisure.* New York: Basic Books, 1991.

Schorow, Stephanie. "Uncovering the 'Secrets of Aging' at the Museum of Science." *Boston Herald,* April 5, 2000, 41.

Schultz, William Todd. Review of *How Do We Know Who We Are?* By Arnold Ludwig. *Biography* 22, no. 3 (summer 1999): 416–20.

Schwartz, Lynne Sharon. *Disturbances in the Field.* New York: Harper and Row, 1983.

"The Secret of Long Life." *Modern Maturity,* November/December 2001, 13.

See, Carolyn. *Golden Days.* New York: Ballantine, 1987.

Sege, Irene, "The Aging of Aquarius," *Boston Globe,* May 12, 1998, C1.

Seligman, Miles, and Aimee Strasko. "What's Behind the Twenty Something 'Movement'?" *Extra!* March/April 1994, 6–7.

Senate Committee on Labor and Public Welfare, Senate Special Subcommittee on Aging. *Middle-Aged and Older Workers Full Employment Act of 1968.* Washington, D.C.: GPO, November 1968.

Senelick, Laurence. "Boys and Girls Together: Subcultural Origins of Glamour Drag and Male Impersonation on the Nineteenth-Century Stage." In *Crossing the Stage: Controversies on Cross-Dressing,* ed. Lesley Ferris, 80–95. London: Routledge, 1993.

Sennett, Richard. *The Corrosion of Character.* New York: Norton, 1998.

Shannon, Dan. "Economy Puts the Brakes on Motorcycle Sales." *New York Times,* April 11, 1982, section 3, 17.

Shapiro, Walter. "Halfway There at Thirty-Five." *Washington Post Magazine,* January 24, 1982, 16.

Sheak, Robert J. "U.S. Capitalism, 1972–1992: The Jobs Problem." *Critical Sociology* 21, no.1 (1995): 33–57.

Sheehan, Susan. "Ain't No Middle Class: Profile of Des Moines, Iowa Residents Kenny Merten and Family." *New Yorker,* December 11, 1995, 91–92.

Sheppard, Harold L. "The United States: The Privatization of Exit." In *Time for Retirement: Comparative Studies of Early Exit from the Labor Force,* ed. Martin Kohli et al., 252–83. Cambridge: Cambridge University Press, 1991.

Shilling, Chris. *The Body and Social Theory.* London: Sage, 1993.

Shoemaker, Sydney, and Richard Swinburne. *Personal Identity.* Oxford: Blackwell, 1985.

Shulman, Alix Kates. *A Good Enough Daughter: A Memoir.* New York: Schocken, 1999.

Shweder, Richard A. "Cultural Psychology: What Is It?" Introduction to *Cultural Psychology: Essays on Comparative Human Development,* ed. James W. Stigler, 1–43. New York: Cambridge University Press, 1990.

———, ed. *Welcome to Middle Age! (And Other Cultural Fictions).* Chicago: University of Chicago Press, 1998.

Sidler, Michelle. "Living in McJobdom: Third Wave Feminism and Class Inequality." In *Third Wave Agenda: Being Feminist, Doing Feminism,* ed. Leslie Heywood and Jennifer Drake. Minneapolis: University of Minnesota Press, 1997.

Silverman, Kaja. *Male Subjectivity at the Margins.* New York: Routledge, 1992.

Simic, Andrei. "Aging and the Aged in Cultural Perspective." In *Life's Career—Aging: Cultural Variations on Growing Old,* ed. Barbara Myerhoff and Andrei Simic. Beverly Hills: Sage, 1978.

Simon-Rusinowitz, Lori, et al. "Future Work and Retirement Needs: Policy Experts and Baby Boomers Express Their Views." *Generations* 22, no. 1 (spring 1998): 34–39.

Simons, John. "The Youth Movement." *U.S. News and World Report,* September 23, 1996, 65.

Slack, Jennifer Daryl. "The Theory and Method of Articulation in Cultural Studies." In *Stuart Hall: Critical Dialogues in Cultural Studies,* ed. David Morley and Kuan Hsing Chen, 112–27. London: Routledge, 1996.

Slack, Jennifer Daryl, and Laurie Anne Whitt. "Ethics and Cultural Studies." In *Cultural Studies,* ed. Lawrence Grossberg, Cary Nelson, and Paula Treichler. New York: Routledge, 1992.

Slesnick, Daniel T. *Consumption and Social Welfare: Living Standards and Their Distribution.* Cambridge: Cambridge University Press, 2001.

Smillie, Dirck. "The Generational Divide Paints Unfair Portraits of the Young." *Christian Science Monitor,* June 23, 1994, 18.

Smith, Faye McDonald. *Flight of the Blackbird.* New York: Scribner, 1996.

Smith, Sidonie, and Julia Watson, eds. *Women, Autobiography, Theory: A Reader.* Madison: University of Wisconsin Press, 1998.

Snyder, Don J. *The Cliff Walk—a Memoir of a Job Lost and a Life Found.* Boston: Little, Brown, 1997.

Sobchak, Vivian. "Scary Women: Cinema, Surgery, and Special Effects." *Figuring Age: Women, Bodies, Generations,* ed. Kathleen Woodward, 200–211. Indianapolis: University of Indiana Press, 1998.

Solberg, Anne. "Negotiating Childhood: Changing Conceptions of Age for Norwegian Children." In *Constructing and Deconstructing Childhood: Contemporary Issues in the Sociological Study of Childhood,* ed. Allison James and Alan Prout, 126–44. London: Falmer, 1997.

Sollors, Werner. *Beyond Ethnicity: Consent and Descent in American Culture.* New York: Oxford University Press, 1986.

Sonenberg, Janet, ed. *The Actor Speaks: Twenty-four Actors Talk about Process and Technique.* New York: Three Rivers, 1996.

Sontag, Susan. *On Photography.* New York: Dell, 1977.

Sorlie, P. D., E. Backlund, and J. B. Keller. "U.S. Mortality by Economic, Demographic, and Social Characteristics." *American Journal of Public Health* 85 (1995): 949–56.

Spacks, Patricia Ann Meyer. *The Adolescent Idea: Myths of Youth and the Adult Imagination.* New York: Basic Books, 1981.

Spence, Jo. *Cultural Sniping: The Art of Transgression.* London: Routledge, 1995.

Squier, Susan Merrill. *Babies in Bottles: Twentieth-Century Visions of Reproductive Technology.* New Brunswick: Rutgers University Press, 1994.

States, Bert O. "The Phenomenological Attitude," In *Critical Theory and Performance,* ed. Janelle G. Reinelt and Joseph P. Roach, 369–79. Ann Arbor: University of Michigan Press, 1992.

Staudinger, Ursula M. and Susan Bluck. "A View on Midlife Development from Life-Span Theory." In *Handbook of Midlife Development,* ed. Margie E.Lachman, 3–39. New York: Wiley, 2001.

Steedman, Carolyn. *Landscape for a Good Woman: A Story of Two Lives.* New Brunswick: Rutgers University Press, 1987.

———. *Strange Dislocations: Childhood and the Idea of Human Interiority, 1780–1930.* Cambridge: Harvard University Press, 1995.

Stein, Gertrude. *Geographical History of America.* New York, Vintage, 1973.

Stern, Mark F. "Poverty and the Life Cycle, 1940–1960." *Journal of Social History* 24, no.3 (1991): 529.

Stewart, Garrett. *Death Sentences: Styles of Dying in British Fiction.* Cambridge: Harvard University Press, 1984.

Stirling, David, "The Search for Database Marketing Talent." *Direct Marketing,* August 1997, 28.

Sudnow, David. *Passing On: The Social Organization of Dying in the County Hospital.* Englewood Cliffs, N.J.: Prentice-Hall, 1967.

Sullivan, Richard, "'Slackers' Energetic, Optimistic." *Indianapolis Star,* June 14, 1996.

———. "Talking Trash about My Generation." *Dallas Morning News,* April 13, 1994.

Sullivan, Shannon. *Living Across and Through Skins: Transactional Bodies, Pragmatism, and Feminism.* Bloomington: Indiana University Press, 2001.

Temper, Susan E. "Q & A." *Senior Times,* June 1998, 13.

Templeton, Robin. "Superscapegoating: Teen 'Superpredators' Hype Sets Stage for Draconian Legislation." *Extra!* January/February 1998, 13–14.

Thomas, Richard. "The Budget: Analysis." *Guardian,* July 3, 1997, 20.

Thompson, Laura. "Editor's Corner." *Simmons News,* September 26, 1996, 8.

Toner, Robin. "Generational Push Has Not Come to Shove." *New York Times Magazine,* December 31 1995, section 4, 1.

Trueheart, Charles. "The Young and the Restless." *Washington Post,* June 30, 1992, D7.

Tyler, Anne. *The Accidental Tourist.* New York: Knopf, 1985.

———. Breathing Lessons. New York: Knopf, 1988.

———. *Celestial Navigation.* New York: Ballantine, 1974.

———. *Earthly Possessions.* New York: Ballantine, 1977.

———. *The Tin Can Tree.* New York: Knopf, 1965.

———. *Searching for Caleb.* New York: Ballantine, 1975.

U.S. Bureau of the Census. *Current Population Reports, 1992.* Prepared by the Geography Division in cooperation with the Housing Division. Washington, D.C., 2000.

———. *Historical Income Tables, 2000.* Prepared by the Geography Division in cooperation with the Housing Division. Washington, D.C.

———. *Historical Income Tables, 2002.* www.census.gov/hhes/income.

———. *Money Income of Households, 1991.* Prepared by the Geography Division in cooperation with the Housing Division. Washington, D.C.

Updike, John. "One Big Interview." In *Picked Up Pieces.* New York: Knopf, 1975.

———. *Rabbit Is Rich.* New York: Knopf, 1981.

———. *Rabbit Redux.* New York: Knopf, 1971.

———. *Rabbit, Run.* New York: Knopf, 1960.

Vienne, Veronique. "Branding: A Uniquely American Phenomenon." In *Design Issues,* ed. D. K. Holland. New York: Allworth Press, 2001.

Vogel, Paula. *How I Learned to Drive.* New York: Dramatists Play Service, 1997.

Wadensjö, Eskil. "Sweden: Partial Exit." In *Time for Retirement: Comparative Studies of Early Exit from the Labor Force,* ed. Martin Kohli et al., 284–323. Cambridge: Cambridge University Press, 1991.

Walker, Margaret Urban. "Getting Out of Line: Alternatives to Life as a Career." In *Mother Time: Women, Aging, and Ethics,* ed. Margaret Urban Walker. New York: Rowman and Littlefield, 1999.

———, ed. *Mother Time: Women, Aging, and Ethics.* New York: Rowman and Littlefield, 1999.

Wallis, Victor. "'Progress' or Progress? Defining a Socialist Technology." *Socialism and Democracy* 14, no. 1 (spring/summer 2000): 45–61.

———. "Species Questions *(Gattungsfragen):* Humanity and Nature from Marx to Shiva." *Organization and Environment* 14, no. 1 (spring/summer 2000): 500–507.

Weaver, Afaa Michael. *The Ten Lights of God: Poems.* Lewisburg: Bucknell University Press, 2000.

Weiland, Steve. "Social Science toward the Humanities." In *The Handbook of the Humanities and Aging,* 2d ed., ed. Thomas R. Cole, Robert Kastenbaum, and Ruth E. Ray. New York: Springer, 2000.

Weisner, Thomas S. "Why Ethnography Should Be the Most Important Method in the Study of Human Development." In *Ethnography and Human Development,* ed. Richard Jessor, Anne Colby, and Richard A. Shweder, 305–24. Chicago: University of Chicago Press, 1996.

Weisner, Thomas S., and Lucinda P. Bernheimer. "Children of the 1960s at Midlife: Generational Identity and the Family Adaptive Project." In *Welcome to Middle Age! (And Other Cultural Fictions)*, ed. Richard A. Shweder, 211–58. Chicago: University of Chicago Press, 1998.

Westlake, Donald. *The Ax*. New York: Warner Vision, 1997.

Westlund, Michael, "Good Jobs at Others' Expense Are No Good at All." *Orange County Register*, August 10, 1996, A14.

Whiting, Beatrice B., and John W. M. *Children of Six Cultures: A Psycho-Cultural Analysis*. Cambridge: Harvard University Press, 1975.

Wiegman, Robyn. "Unmaking: Men and Masculinity in Feminist Theory." In *Masculinity Studies and Feminist Theory: New Directions*, ed. Judith Kegan Gardiner, 31–59. New York: Columbia University Press, 2002.

Wikan, Unni. "The Self in a World of Urgency and Necessity." *Ethos* 23, no. 3 (September 1995): 259–85.

Wilkerson, William S. "Is There Something You Need to Tell Me? Coming Out and the Ambiguity of Experience." In *Reclaiming Identity: Realist Theory and the Predicament of Postmodernism*, ed. Paula M. L. Moya and Michael R. Hames-Garcia, 251–78. Berkeley and Los Angeles: University of California Press, 2000.

Williams, Joan. *Unbending Gender*. Oxford: Oxford University Press, 2001.

Williams, Ian. "Trash That Baby Boom: It's Time for Forty-Somethings to Release Their Choke Hold on American Culture." *Washington Post*, January 2, 1994, W10.

Williams, Raymond. *Keywords: Vocabulary of Culture and Society*. New York: Oxford University Press, 1976.

———. *Modern Tragedy*. Stanford: Stanford University Press, 1966.

———. "The Writer: Commitment and Alignment." *Marxism Today* 24 (June 1980): 22–25.

Women's Bar Association of Massachusetts (Nancer Ballard et al.), Employment Issues Committee. *More Than Part-Time: The Effect of Reduced-Hours Arrangements on the Retention, Recruitment, and Success of Women Attorneys in Law Firms*. Boston, 2000.

Women's Bureau, Department of Labor. *Mildife Women Speak Out: Assessing Job Training and the Status of Working Women, A Statistical Profile of Midlife Women Aged Thirty-five to Fifty-four*. Washington, D.C.: GPO, October 1993.

Woods, Leigh, ed. *On Playing Shakespeare: Advice and Commentary from Actors and Actresses of the Past*. New York: Greenwood Press, 1991.

Woodward, Katherine. *Aging and Its Discontents: Freud and Other Fictions*. Bloomington: Indiana University Press, 1991.

———. "The Cultural Politics of Anger and Wisdom: Envisioning the Future of Aging." In *Fashioning Age: Cultural Narratives of Later Life*, ed. Teresa Mangum. Special issue of the *Journal of Aging Studies* 17, no. 1 (spring 2003).

———. "From Virtual Cyborgs to Biological Time Bombs." In *Culture on the Brink:*

Ideologies of Technology, ed. Gretchen Bender and Timothy Druckrey, 47–64. Seattle: Bay Press, 1994.

———. "Gerontophobia." In *Feminism and Psychoanalysis: A Critical Dictionary,* ed. Elizabeth Wright. Cambridge: Blackwell, 1992.

———. "Inventing Generational Models: Psychoanalysis, Feminism, Literature." In *Figuring Age: Women, Bodies, Generations,* ed. Kathleen Woodward. Bloomington: Indiana University Press, 1999.

———. "Late Theory, Late Style: Loss and Renewal in Freud and Barthes." In *Aging and Gender in Literature: Studies in Creativity,* ed. Anne M. Wyatt-Brown and Janice Rossen. Charlottesville: University Press of Virginia, 1993.

———. "Simone de Beauvoir, Aging and Its Discontents." In *The Private Self: Theory and Practice of Women's Autobiographical Writings,* ed. Shari Benstock, 90–113. Chapel Hill: University of North Carolina Press, 1988.

———. "Youthfulness as a Masquerade." *Discourse* 11 (fall/winter 1988): 119–42.

———, ed. *Figuring Age: Women, Bodies, Generations.* Bloomington: Indiana University Press, 1999.

Woolf, Virginia. "The Moment: Summer's Night." *The Moment, and Other Essays.* London: Hogarth Press, 1947.

Wyatt-Brown, Anne M. and Janice Rossen, eds. *Aging and Gender in Literature: Studies in Creativity.* Charlottesville: University of Virginia Press, 1993.

Yeats, William Butler. *Collected Poems.* New York: Macmillan, 1959.

"You Called Us Slackers. You Dismissed Us as Generation X. Well, Move Over. We're Not What You Thought." *Time,* June 9, 1997.

"Youth Gone Bad." *Extra!* September/October 1994, 5.

Index of Keywords

adulthood
  as exile, 31, 65
  markers of, in fiction, 65
African Americans, 190
  "blackness" as a changing identity, 78
  and deaths of children, 62
  health problems of, 24
  income inequality of, 84
  in middle-class, 22–23, 84–85
age, 111, 173, 195–96
  and age studies, 27, 105–119
  as automatic agent of change, 17
  as biological given, 102, 104
  as concept: parallels to gender or race,
    27, 32, 60, 104–5, 107, 118, 130, 138,
    139; problem of definition, 106, 116
  as cultural construct, category, system,
    11, 13, 17, 28, 35–36, 102–5; aversion
    to subject of, 38, 111; lack of critical
    attention to, 36, 60, 105, 121, 118, 163,
    164
  and gender, 44, 105, 161
  increasing salience of, 23, 31–32, 58, 112,
    179–82, 193
  made to appear natural, 27, 35, 94,
    104–5, 137
  as marker of difference between
    groups, 23, 27, 32, 179–82
  as performance, 159–63
  political uses of, 60, 193; to manage
    crises, 45, 50, 53, 58, 95; to trump
    other differences, 43–44, 58, 149, 180
  as a property of the embodied psyche,
    139, 162, 169–70, 172–74, 181
  as a totalizing identity, 115, 122, 180, 182,
    193; wrongly separated from other
    identities, 27, 162, 171, 180
  and value of being older, 166, 175–77,
    181
  See also age class(es); age cohorts; age
    lore; age studies; aging; aging as a
    narrative

age anxiety, 21, 29, 35, 61, 186, 188. See also
    emotions; fear of aging
Age Autobiographer, 147–53. See also age
    auto/biography, of author; age
    auto/biography, critical
age auto/biography, of author, 25, 28
  as age critic, 28, 154, 188–89, 197
  age identity as "woman," 126, 128–29,
    151–52
  age socialization in, 16
  changing own default body, 160–63
  economic history told by parents, 26,
    143–47, 151, 206n.25
  feminism in, 144, 151–52
age auto/biography, critical, 39, 115,
    142
  analyzing metaphors, 157
  analyzing two-point plots of life story-
    telling, 150, 153, 166
  described, 10, 152, 154
  examining implicit theories of life
    course, 155–56
  finding sources of one's narratives of
    aging, 26, 143–44, 146, 151–57
  improves life storytelling, 137, 147–58,
    194–95
  incorporating psychoanalytic material,
    185–86
  making Oldest Self explicitly present,
    150–54
  writing it creatively, 150, 154, 194
  See also age identity; life storytelling
age binaries, 43, 46, 50, 56
  change versus continuity in, 107, 123,
    127–28
  construction of, 45, 55
  young versus old, 105
  See also age warfare; binary systems;
    progress versus decline; "Xers"
    versus "Boomers," contrived war
    between
age chauvinism, 46; and hate speech, 51

age class(es), 24, 27, 32, 90, 203n.43
  adding gender to, 191
  crises, 180–81, 190, 193
  "middle years" as, 28, 94–95, 101–2
  naturalized, 94, 180
  new ones added to the language, 57
  salience of, 23, 31–32, 58, 112, 179–82
  sequential-crisis model of, 182, 192, 195
  and slice-of-life studies, 28, 112–14, 182,
    192
  versus private age selves, 10
  See also age cohort(s). See under life
    course, dismemberment of into ages
age cohort(s), 31, 32, 43–45, 47, 60
  as basis for age warfare, 43, 49–51, 58
  birth cohorts, problems using, 55–57
  and cultural construction of collective
    identity, 50, 89; generic noun
    phrases in, 56; role of media in natu-
    ralizing, 35, 180; role of pollsters, 36,
    44, 208n.16
  strengthening age as category, 58
  See also "Baby Boomer(s)"; "Genera-
    tion Y"; "Xers"; "Xers" versus
    "Boomers," contrived war between;
    Yuppies
age consciousness, 13, 20, 33, 193
  age-related memories and, 16, 137, 151–
    55
  age studies critique of culture and, 59–
    60, 154
  naive foregrounding of age in, 154–55,
    180
  overcoming obstacles to raising, 32–33,
    156–57
  raised by writers and artists, 7–11, 14,
    78, 104, 129
  raised by writing of age autobiography,
    143–58
  See also age auto/biography; age iden-
    tity; age studies; resistance, to age
    ideology

age critic(s), 5, 20, 104–5, 113, 165, 192;
  weaknesses of, 116, 130, 135, 193–
  94. See also age studies; cultural
  criticism
age culture(s) (United States), 12, 20, 64,
  69, 118
  age divisions in dominant culture, 12,
    31–32, 36, 58, 94, 113, 182
  contest over meanings of age in, 106,
    143
  crimes against the life course, 27–29,
    36, 90, 111
  in crisis, 89–90, 122
  effects on subjectivity, 29, 108
  subcultures, 7, 110
  See also age ideology; culture; internal-
    ization; middle-ageism
age discrimination. See midlife discrimination
age effects, 5
  normal diversity in, 161, 162, 166–72,
    176, 177
  in relation to age gaze, 161, 171, 172, 177
age equality, 23, 92, 195. See also age hierarchy
age gaze, 10, 161–62
  as a decline gaze, 162–63
  looking into "the mirror," 4, 7
  patriarchal, of adults upon youth, 191
  and nonbeing, 178
  See also specular body
age grading, 17, 110. See also age hierarchy; seniority
age hierarchy, 37, 47, 131, 173–75, 204n.50
  age studies and, 192
  fairness of, 45, 188
  learned in childhood, 16, 17
  and patriarchy, 37, 188
  and seniority, 34, 135, 137
  threats to, from capitalism, 34, 37
  See also age equality; age grading;
  seniority

relations with disciplines, 117, 143, 148, 187; critical gerontology, 110, 149, 182; development studies, 110, 112, 113, 142; economics, 79, 116; performance studies, 164

revisioning bodies, 139, 162–77 passim

role of midlife studies in, 101–2, 28, 94–95, 187–89

slice-of-life approaches to, 28, 45, 112–14, 117, 182, 192–94

age theory, 27, 105, 109, 117, 122, 164; and feminist cultural theory, 102

age-wage curve, 31, 87, 90, 154

downsizing and, 54

and family needs, 82, 92

and life storytelling, 143–44

role of, in democracy, 94

and social justice, 85, 94

varies by class, gender, race, 83–85

of women, 84

See also age-wage peaks; premium for experience; working conditions; working conditions, for people at midlife

age-wage peaks, 34, 84–85, 87, 175

groups with low peaks, 91–92

lowering of peaks for men, 25, 86

and progress narrative, 82–87

and Social Security surplus, 49

of women, 23, 25, 47

See also age-wage curve; premium for experience; seniority

age warfare, 49, 95

dependent on age cohorts or classes, 45, 49, 58

between fathers and sons, 47–48, 58, 103

over jobs, 49–50, 52, 54

political functions of, 42, 48–49; 52–54, 58, 191

resistance to, 58–60

between young adults and midlife people, 180

See also age binaries; age cohort(s); progress versus decline; "Xers" versus "Boomers," contrived war between

aging, as aspect of age, 10

aging-into-adulthood, 12, 14, 17, 191

aging-into-retirement, 23

aging-into-the-middle-years, 30, 85, 88

aging-past-preschool, 31

aging-past-youth, 26, 33, 37, 54, 181

as biological experience, naturalized, 102, 104, 133

as biosocial phenomenon, 24, 102–3, 136

as chronology, 9, 130

as culturally constructed, temporal component of age, 13, 27, 105

and distrust of body, 35

experience of, by class, 37, 84, 88

external bodily signs of, 9, 128, 130, 161

history of in United States, 33

as history of selfhood, 10

as synonym for old age and decline, 34, 36, 44, 149

See also age; age ideology; aging, as a decline; aging, as a narrative

aging, as choice of narratives, 10–12, 13, 15–18, 39, 64, 78, 125–26, 129

and biological determinism, 103

about co-identities, 124, 128–29, 132, 143

contest over meanings of aging, 11, 14–18, 37, 137, 143

See also aging, as a decline; aging, as a progress; narrative(s) of aging; progress versus decline

aging, as a decline, 7, 9, 27, 31–32, 38, 48

bodily, 44, 129

early start of, 19, 33–35, 69, 73, 93, 149, 181

experience of, in relation to class, race, 37, 84, 88

aging, as a decline (*continued*)
one of the great cultural oppressions,
122, 137
onset of, as increasingly early, 19, 33–
35, 69, 73, 93, 135, 149
simulated by computer, 3–5, 7–8, 12–
14, 18, 21, 23
as subject of jokes, 33, 34, 36, 131, 133
truth claims for, 134
See also age ideology; decline; decline
narrative(s) of aging; middle-ageism
aging, as a progress, 10
age-wage rise and, 82–85, 87, 143–44
in childhood and after, 15–17
as a property of the embodied psyche,
139, 162, 169–70, 172–74, 176–78, 181
seniority and, 83–86
in the worklife, 82–87
See also age hierarchy; premium for
experience; progress; progress nar-
rative(s) of aging
aging workers. *See* people at midlife;
working conditions, for people at
midlife
American Dream
downsizing of, 51, 85
as an economic life-course narrative,
18, 25, 96, 143, 154–55
as model national biography, 37
as told by author's mother, 143–47
as way to measure injustice, 39
See also positive aging; progress narra-
tive(s) of aging
anger
as age-linked emotion, 32, 33, 51
as force for social change, 38, 89
anti-ageism, 184–87. *See also* anti-
middle-ageism
anti-aging products and practices, 22, 88,
134, 186
antidecline movement, 17
genres of liberation, 39, 117, 138

goals of, 37–39, 85, 91–94
requisites of, 28, 38, 91
role of age studies in, 94–95, 102
anti-middle-ageism, 89, 91–94
feminism and, 23
and full employment plus, 93
goals of, 91–94; government role in,
38, 85
keywords of, 94
recharacterizing the victims, 91
See also antidecline movement; full
employment plus; middle-ageism;
resistance, to age ideology; seniority;
social justice
artists and writers, power of to counter
decline ideology, 7–11, 14, 78, 104, 129
auto/biography(ies), 16, 124, 130
critiques of, 149, 152, 154
as cultural criticism, 150, 155
importance of autobiography, 142–43
on the stage, 164–67
See also age auto/biography, of author;
age auto/biography, critical; age
identity; life storytelling

"Baby Boomer(s)"
as age-cohort identity, 43–44, 47
as aging, 44, 48, 180, 208n.10
alleged attacks on "Xers" by, 44–
47, 53
alleged power of cohort, 22, 44, 47, 51,
54, 93
and "boomer-bashing," 44, 46–47, 51–
52, 54, 93
and economic stagnation, 86
history of term, 43–44
media misrepresentation of, 42–48,
51–53, 89
middle-ageist pseudo-biography of,
43–48, 50, 54, 56, 86, 89, 93, 148
politics of resentment toward, 42, 44,
45, 47–50, 52–54

emotions
  social and historical constructions of, 29–33
  "structure(s) of feeling," 52, 134, 188
  See also age anxiety; anger; "empty-nest" syndrome; energy; fear of aging; life course, life-course pessimism; nostalgia; "parricide"; regret; respect; revenge; speed-up; wisdom
employment
  at midlife, 19, 30
  decline in full-time, 30, 80–82
  dropping participation rates, 80–81
  of young adults, 82–83
  See also full employment plus; middle-ageism; premature supernannuation; unemployment
"empty-nest" syndrome, 103, 174, 179. *See also* postmaternal women
energy, 184–186; restored by recovery novels, 74
envy, as age-linked emotion, 46, 89
experience
  economic premium for, 25–26, 34, 83–84
  subjective, 131–33, 147, 151
  in workforce, 57

face(s), 9–10, 130; aged by computer simulation, 3–5, 7–8, 12–14, 18, 21, 23. *See also* body; body-mind
families with two generations in workforce, 44
  competition for work, 43, 47, 48, 51
  creating multigenerational unity in, 58–60
  danger of age war to, 42, 45, 50–52, 54, 57–58
  family of author, 41–42, 45
  job-swap myth, 49–50, 52, 54

See also children; fathers; intergenerational solidarity; mothers; parents; young-adult offspring
families with young children, 144
  and age socialization, 16, 18
  and identity formation, 125
  prospective age narrative, 7, 11, 15–18, 20, 154
family-values agenda, 91–94
fathers, 188
  as "Boomers," 47–48, 51
  competition between sons and, 47–48, 58, 103
  father of author, 144–47, 156
  in fiction, 63
fear of aging (as a decline), 4, 21, 26, 65
  aging-past-youth, 19, 26, 33, 65
  aversion to concept of age, 38, 111
  as displacement, 38, 58, 70, 74, 78, 133
  "fear of fifty," 52, 80–87
  in novels, 64–66, 68–71, 74
feminism, 16, 95, 133, 189
  and age/aging, 105–6, 132, 182, 183
  in author's life, 144, 151–52, 189
  and cultural theory, 102
  and ideology critique, 138
  as life process, 23, 160–61
  and life writing, 149, 155
  "waves" as age divisions in, 46, 209n.30
films, 188; age of audience, 191
freedom
  and collective experience, 152, 154, 157
  after retirement, 186
full employment, 92–93
full employment plus, 93
future, 14, 16, 19
  constructed by fiction, 76,
  constructed by prospective narrative, 7, 11, 15–18, 20, 53

middle years (new age class added to life course), 28, 95, 96, 102, 179, 187
   addition of men to, 188
   formerly an unmarked category, 95–96, 101
   See also midlife
midlife
   aging-as-decline at, 34, 54, 91, 132
   devaluation of, as national crisis, 54, 90, 122
   final individuation during, 148
   inimitable in performance, 171
   poverty at, 84
   as prime of life, 22, 30, 44, 54, 80, 188
   as relatively privileged stage, 79, 86
   shortened and trivialized, 30, 95, 206n.38
   socially constructed nature of, 80, 94, 101, 131, 188
   war over value of, 37, 52, 89, 94–96, 101, 106
   See also "Baby Boomer(s)"; men, at midlife; middle-ageism; people at midlife; respect; seniority; women, at midlife
"midlife crisis," 25, 37, 189
midlife discrimination, 54, 105
   addressing, 93
   age of claimants dropping, 26
   disparate impact theory, 34, 93
   by gender, 82
   Kimel vs. Florida Board of Regents, 34, 89
   See also middle-ageism
"midlifers," 96. *See also* people at midlife
midlife studies, 28, 131, 192
mind-body, 9, 128. *See also* body-mind
minorities, 23, 32, 47, 81
mother(s)
   in fiction, 63, 67–68
   in relation to children, 4, 13, 16, 188

represented, 173–74, 188
working, 47

narrative(s) of aging, 10–11, 33, 64, 103, 123–24
   progress versus decline posed in, 15, 19, 24, 69–70, 76–77, 86, 128, 134, 143, 152
   prospective, 7, 11, 15–18, 20, 53, 145, 147
   versions of (by class, race, gender), 18, 24, 188
   See also age auto/biography, critical; decline narrative(s); life storytelling; master narrative(s); photographs, as life-course narratives; progress narrative(s)
"near-elderly," use of term, 34
New Economy, 35, 37, 42. *See also* working conditions
nostalgia, as age-linked emotion
   construction of, 31–33, 134, 149, 152–53
   for young adults, 36
   See also emotions
novel(s), 23, 64, 132
   about deaths of children, 61–78; fear of aging in, 65–66, 68–74; not about the children, 63–64; of recovery, 71, 74–77; sexual anxiety in, 65–66
   as form that constructs the life course, 65–66

oedipal narrative, 194; shift to Laius complex, 69
"old," use of term, 26, 88, 180
   "old old," 181
   as problematizing simile, 176, 181
   "too old," 30, 52, 89, 175
   "young old," 195
   See also "midlife crisis"
old age, 26, 181
   and ageism, 7, 176, 179, 181, 185

constrained by conditions of worklife, 126

as metaphor of loss or decline, 176

rigidity unlinked from, 185–87

Old Economy, 42, 46. *See also* working conditions

overwork, 29–30, 33, 47; and overtime for professionals, 92

parenting, 191

in fiction, 63–68

gender differences in, 69

viewed as perilous responsibility, 66–70

parents

of adult offspring, 50, 82–83, 89, 93, 173, 194

as egalitarian child-rearers, 59

oedipal struggle with offspring, 44

solidarity with offspring, 18, 23, 42, 52, 58–60

as teachers of aging narratives, 4, 13, 16–18, 20, 137–38, 144, 154

and unemployment, 47–49

See also, families with young children; fathers; mothers; postmaternal women

"parricide," as constructed emotion, 51–52

passing, 125, 134, 167, 168

patriarchy, 34, 188

and progress narrative, 83

and seniority, 37, 87

pensions, 42, 87; of women, 81

people at midlife, 91, 94

age-wage peaks of, 80–87

class differences among, 44, 81, 83–84

invisibility versus demonization, 89

middle-class, 22–23, 81

as potential political collective, 96, 194

and poverty, 81, 84

taking care of parents, 92, 194

See also age-wage curves, age-wage peaks; "Baby Boomer(s)"; men, at midlife; midlife; midlife discrimination; parents; women, at midlife

people in old age, 7, 18, 33, 180

possessed of wide range of traits, 170

as retirees, 30, 94–95

subject to master narrative of decline, 21, 118

See also women in old age

permatemps, 42

pharmaceutical industry, 37, 88

photographs

in antidecline projects, 6, 8

as life course narratives, 3–8, 10

See also computer simulation of aging

phototherapy, 10–11, 14, 129

physiomental effects, 160–61, 174, 176

polling, of age cohorts, 36, 44, 208n.16

positive aging, 28, 107, 176, 188

inadvertently silences age critique, 22–24, 44, 95, 102, 107, 182

as proof of power of decline, 22

strengthens intrapsychic resistance, 188

See also progress

posthuman, lure of, 163

postindustrial capitalism. *See* capitalism

postmaternal women, 41, 152, 174, 179

in fiction, 67, 76

working mothers as, 47

premature superannuation, 30, 80–81, 92

in Europe, 37, 88

remedies for, in France, 88, 90, 92

victims of characterized, 89

premium for experience, 34, 83–84

anticipation of, by young people, 37

drops in, over midlife, 25–26, 85–86

threats to, 45–50 passim, 85–86

"preretired," 88

"preseniors," 88

productivity, 83

progress
history as, 24, 123
as a life-course value, 15–19
as a psychocultural need, 19, 26, 37, 123;
transformable into activism, 39
See also seniority, as countersystem to
decline
progress narrative(s) of aging, 15–17, 32, 86
and age-wage curve, 83–85, 144
American dream as, 18, 25, 37, 39, 96
as a cover story, 22–24, 39, 130
democracy and, 37
economic supports of, 19, 26, 55, 83–
85, 143–47, 155
as a genre of life storytelling, 26, 123
improved by techniques of age autobiography, 147, 155
stories of recovery in fiction as, 71,
74–77
taught to children, 16, 17
progress versus decline
breaking the binary of, 39, 157
in the life course, 15, 19, 24, 32, 33, 37,
155
in life storytelling, 86, 128, 134, 143,
146–47, 152
See also age ideology; binary systems,
identity-based
psychoanalysis, ageism and anti-ageism
in, 185–87

race (cultural construct and category),
107; age in relation to, 27, 32, 60,
104–5. *See also* African Americans; body-based categories;
minorities
race studies, critical, 36, 105, 11, 117, 138
regret, as age-linked emotion, 19
resistance, to age ideology, 37–39, 122,
128, 133, 135–38, 176
through age autobiography, 137, 147–
58, 194–95

"denial," as current definition of, 134
through transfer of ideology critique,
138
See also age identity; antidecline movement; anti-middle-ageism; family
values agenda; full employment
plus; seniority
resocialization. *See* age socialization, of
adults
respect, as age-linked emotion, 19
retirement, 30, 146, 179, 186; premature
superannuation, 30, 80–81, 89,
91–92
revenge, as age-linked emotion, 43, 48
rigidity, age-related or not, 185–87

scarcity of work, 82–83; and job-swap
myth, 49–50, 52, 54
science
hormones, and HRT debacle, 132, 182,
185
newer biosocial hypotheses, 68, 102–3,
136
normative social science, 115, 131,
180
and promises of longevity, 24, 103
selfhood
changing the concept of, 138–39
continuity of, 12, 14, 19, 127, 129, 138
manifested sequentially through narratives, 122, 124–26
relationship to past selves, 127–28
See also age auto/biography, critical;
age identity; change(s) in selfhood;
identities, sequential; identities,
simultaneous
self-writing. *See* age auto/biography,
of author; age auto/biography,
critical; auto/biograph(ies); life
storytelling
seniority (legal/institutional and customary), 34, 83–84

welfare, 92

wisdom, as age-linked emotion, 33

women

working conditions

working conditions, for people at midlife,

writers and artists

"Xers," 42–43, 46

"Xers" versus "Boomers," contrived war

young people, 24, 42, 63, 93